GOOD HOUSEKEEPING
Slimmers' Cook Book

GOOD HOUSEKEEPING
Slimmers' Cook Book

Compiled by GOOD HOUSEKEEPING INSTITUTE

Ebury Press
LONDON

First published 1970
by Ebury Press
Chestergate House, Vauxhall Bridge Road
London SW1V 1HF
Reprinted 1971
New edition 1975
Revised edition 1977

ISBN 0 85223 127 X

Edited by Gill Edden

Photographs by Gina Harris

Metric measures in this book are not direct conversions of the
imperial measures, but reasonable equivalents on which to base recipes.
To measure small amounts in millilitres, use standard 15 ml, 10 ml,
5 ml and 2.5 ml spoons, levelling with a knife if measuring dry
ingredients.

Filmset and printed by BAS Printers Limited, Over Wallop, Hampshire
and bound by Webb Son & Co Ltd, London and Glamorgan

Contents

Contents

PART FOUR: RECIPE FILE

PART FIVE: SLIMMING WITH THE FREEZER

PART SIX: WHAT ELSE WILL HELP?

APPENDIX

Colour Plates

Introduction

Slimming or keeping slim certainly doesn't mean boring meals or near starvation. On the contrary, you can enjoy good food and interesting cooking both while you are losing weight and when you are merely aiming to stay slim.

I would particularly like to draw your attention to two chapters of ideas in this book which will make life easier for the slimmer. Plan Your Diet tells you how to select nutritionally balanced menus by using a simple tabular guide. You can choose the kind of foods you like and you can adapt the menu plan for family meals as well. The chapter Slimming with the Freezer is full of ideas for planning menus to cook and freeze ahead. There are also the tried and proved menus and recipes for family slimming, the housewife faced with the daily problem of thinking up a mid-day snack, the man of the family and the overweight child.

A Brief Guide to Food answers many questions about diet and will help you and your family to eat well and stay slim and healthy.

Metric and imperial measures are given for all the recipes, which have of course been tested in the Good Housekeeping Institute.

We would like to remind you of the Good Housekeeping Institute's unique after service: if you have any cookery enquiry, just write to the address below and we shall be pleased to do all we can to help.

Carol Macarthey

Director
Good Housekeeping Institute
Chestergate House
Vauxhall Bridge Road
London SW1V 1HF

A brief guide to food and how it affects us

We are what we eat; every bone, tissue, muscle and hair is built up from materials extracted from the food we swallow. There is no other source for these materials. If we eat the wrong foods, some of the building processes will fail; if we eat too much, some of the materials are put into store in the body, as fat. And if we eat the right food it will go far towards keeping us healthy, fit and active.

So it is essential to know what each sort of food does and how much of it is needed, so that we can be certain of eating the right things. Once we have this information we can go on to work out the best sort of diet for ourselves, to suit our own individual circumstances. Some unfortunate people, of course, have special needs or special problems and they must keep to the diet suggested by their doctor. But all of us should pay reasonable attention to what we eat.

In the following pages we have set out in question and answer form the basic information about nutrition, diets and sensible eating. This is a summary of the whole topic. The particular questions that affect family eating habits most closely are then dealt with at greater length later.

What is meant by diet?
Diet is what we eat and drink; it also covers the special regimens used in treating disorders such as diabetes, and the methods advocated by dietitians (and others less well informed) for controlling obesity. This last usage has become so much a part of commonplace conversation that many people are inclined to equate 'diet' with 'slimming'.

Our ordinary daily diet is made up of the three main constituents of food; carbohydrates, fats and proteins, with small but essential amounts of mineral substances, and vitamins and water.

Carbohydrates are present in many foods, but particularly in jams and preserves, breads, rice and other cereals, potatoes, raisins, pasta and pastries, and sugar itself. When they are eaten, all carbohydrates are converted into simple sugar, glucose, fructose and galactose, which are absorbed into the bloodstream and travel to the body's cells.

The fats in our diet come largely from butter, margarine, cooking fats and vegetable oils, meat (especially bacon), fish and dairy produce. They are emulsified like milk before being absorbed into the bloodstream in the form of glycerides and substances which are known as fatty acids.

Proteins form the basis of life. On being digested, they are ultimately reduced to amino acids. Meats, poultry, fish, eggs, milk and cheese are the commonest animal sources of protein; it is also derived from peas and beans, nuts, cereals and, to a lesser extent, green vegetables and potatoes.

When the end-products of all three components combine with oxygen they produce energy, which is expressed as heat or activity. Carbohydrates and most fats supply only energy. The amino acids of protein, with some fats in addition, go to build up tissues and replace those lost through wear and tear. The energy derived from all three foodstuffs is expressed in terms of Kilocalories (kcal) or kilojoules (kJ). A kcal is a unit of energy, the amount of heat required to raise 1000 grams of water 1°C. One gram of fat produces about nine kcal (37 kJ), one gram of carbohydrate or one gram of protein produces about four kcal (16 kJ). These units are known in everyday speech as 'calories' and 'joules'.

Among the complicated chemical processes essential to life (which is all that is meant by the word metabolism), we need a certain basic amount of energy (calories) merely to breathe and live. That is our *basal metabolism*. On top of that, further calories are needed to perform work. If, however, the amount of calories taken into the body is more than required, the surplus may be converted into fat.

Minerals, obtained from a variety of different foods and water, play essential parts in the processes of metabolism but they do not contribute any energy. Minerals such as calcium, phosphorus and fluorine are needed for teeth and bone; sulphur, zinc, copper and iron go into the formation of tissues, organs and blood cells. Sodium and potassium are needed to keep the water and salts in the cells, tissues and body fluids properly balanced.

Vitamins too fill vital rôles in the chemistry of life, and in effect protect us from 'deficiency diseases' like scurvy, rickets, and beri-beri. Most of them are obtained from animal and vegetable sources outside the body, but some can be formed, e.g. cholesterol and related substances are converted into vitamin D in the skin by the action of ultra-violet light, so exposure to plenty of sunshine reduces the need for dietary vitamin D.

What, then, is a good diet?
A satisfactory diet is a palatable and balanced mixture of foodstuffs which enables metabolism to proceed normally, while supplying enough energy to make possible one's routine way of life. Desirable proportions for the three main components, energy requirements for different occupations, and advisable daily allowance of vitamins have all been calculated, but it is not necessary to take these charts and your weighing-scales to

table. All that is required to feed well and wisely is to get some rough idea of where carbohydrates, proteins and fats are to be found, and to know the main sources of the vitamins, after which the minerals will largely look after themselves.

Energy-producing carbohydrates appear at breakfast in the form of cereals, marmalade, bread and sugar; the need for protein is met by bacon, eggs, bread and milk; and for fats by bacon, milk, butter or margarine. At lunch and dinner such foods as beef, lamb, fish, poultry and the cheeses offer a wide choice of body-building protein, and the fruits and vegetables that traditionally go with good eating provide most of the vitamins we need. For the chief aim in eating well should be to enjoy yourself while having just enough but not one scrap more.

Do we require more or less of the various foods at different ages?
Yes. Our nutritional needs are determined by growth and development, body-size and physical activity, and in women by the special demands of childbirth.
1. Pregnancy and Lactation Women need more food to meet the requirements of the foetus and to provide extra energy to move their heavier bodies about. But if, as often happens, a young woman leaves an active job to sit down at home, her calorie requirements may be actually less. To provide for growing bones, she should drink more milk, while iron and folic acid are commonly prescribed during the months of pregnancy to avert anaemia. In cases of breast-feeding, an extra 600 calories (2510 joules) a day are needed to give milk of 480 calories (2008 joules) value.
2. Childhood Young children's tissues are growing apace, so they need a relatively higher proportion of protein and other nutrients as compared with calories. Milk is therefore an ideal food, supplying necessary calcium. Parents should make sure children drink the school milk they are entitled to. Children also need proportionately more vitamins, so it is usual to give them extra vitamin C in fruit juice, and vitamins A and D in fish-liver oil or concentrates. It is difficult to provide all the iron small children need and so it is best to see that their diet is as mixed as possible.
3. Adolescence Normally, both boys and girls develop greater appetites at this stage of their lives because they are both physically active and subject to a spurt in growth (especially boys). To meet these demands they should be given more of their normal food and extra milk, and avoid the temptation of sweets, which are liable to lead to bad teeth and obesity.
4. Old Age Old people's diet should be no different from that of other adults unless their way of life becomes so inactive that the calorie intake should be reduced. Where they live alone they may find the task of shopping and cooking so irksome that they fail to provide themselves with

a fully nutritious diet. It is often a good idea to add a supplement of vitamin C; many old people go short of this because the acid in things such as oranges doesn't agree with them, and they cut down on vegetables because of the difficulty of preparing them. In such cases, vitamin C should be added in tablet form.

Social isolates, depressed people and bereaved husbands or wives often become so careless of their own welfare that they become undernourished. There is growing circumstantial evidence that quite apart from these unhappy people, there are also mentally normal old folk who are not as well nourished as they might be. The remedy is to ensure that they have at least one square meal a day and that they take to eating fresh fruit and vegetables.

Persons suspected of lacking specific vitamins can top up by taking them in tablet form. Vitamin D can be acquired by exposing the skin to whatever sun may be available. As we age, our bones grow more porous, so that old people, especially women, are particularly liable to break the thigh-bone (or even a rib through laughing). Extra dietary calcium alone does not seem to make any difference, but if you add capsules of vitamin D it may reduce the risk—but seek medical advice.

When ordinary people enjoy good health, does it mean they are already on a balanced diet, even though they may know nothing about nutrition?
Most people in this country are properly nourished—unless they are overeating. Our feeding habits are a combination of habit, availability and education. Neither instinct nor appetite is much help in directing us towards what are the best foods or away from those likely to do us harm. People can starve in the midst of plenty if the food available is unfamiliar, or if they don't know how to cook or prepare it. There was a case of the manager of a large department store who lunched every day at his club, yet turned up in hospital with well-advanced scurvy. He simply had no taste for vitamin C—never ate fruit or green vegetables, and the potatoes he was having at that time of the year were lacking in vitamin C. Similarly, primitive societies often put a taboo on the foods they need most, so that their children are liable to suffer from protein deficiency. On the other hand, people whose intestines are sensitive to gluten (which is the protein in wheat or rye flour) go on eating it so that they remain invalids all their lives. They have no instinctive aversion to the food that does them harm. Most of us are well nourished because, by good chance, most foods are a mixture of things. As long as we eat a good variety of foods we are likely to be well nourished. The best guide is that the more mixed the diet is, the better chance it has of being satisfactory.

What amount of calories do we need? And can they be obtained equally well from carbohydrates, fats and proteins?

The energy requirements of adults depend on the sex, size and composition of the body, physical activity, and the surrounding environment and climate. Within reasonable limits the big three are interchangeable as a source of calories. In a Danish experiment, a man lived on nothing but potatoes for a year and remained fit and healthy. Other people keep well on meat alone, although meat contains fat as well as protein. In the U.K. we eat something like 48 per cent carbohydrate, 40 per cent fat and only 12 per cent protein. Generally speaking, the make-up of national diets throughout the world is pretty much the same, except where they are short of protein. In the U.S.A., and to a lesser extent here, there has been a reduction in the calorie needs during the past 25 years or so, because of increased mechanisation (including the use of lifts, labour-saving machines and private cars), and central heating, which means that you need fewer calories to keep warm.

Does the body need substantially different diets in hot and cold weather?

The answer is no. There is no evidence that the average British diet varies at all seasonally with regard to total calories, or the ratio of carbohydrate to fat to protein. It's true that we are inclined to eat rather different things during the winter, but only because they are then in season, or they appeal to us, not as a matter of nutritional need. In cold weather we keep warm not by eating more but by wearing warmer clothing. Although we tend to eat hot food during cold weather to keep warm, in fact the temperature of the food makes little difference. Half a pint of soup, with a calorie value of 100 calories, would provide 106 calories if served hot. The additional six calories are negligible as a source of energy for heating the body. A large proportion of people's calorie needs in this country is to give them energy for their recreations, but there is a tendency to cut down on these pastimes during very cold—and very hot—weather.

How far do nutrition and inheritance affect physique? For instance, what accounts for the differing build of a pigmy, a bloated European businessman, a stringy Chinese peasant and a pot-bellied New Guinea jungle-dweller?

There is a tendency to attribute fatness largely to diet, and height to our genetic inheritance, but the parts played by nature and nurture are not yet sorted out and often overlap. Japanese whose families emigrated to the U.S. are now growing as tall as Europeans, and even their compatriots in Japan are increasing in height, thanks to better food. In the same way, improved nutrition is accepted as one of the reasons why London school children are taller than they used to be.

In the mixed bag quoted here, pigmies are pigmies for purely genetic reasons. That businessman could well be overweight simply because he is eating or drinking too much. The Chinese peasant is probably lean because of hard work and insufficient rice, and the pot-belly of the New Guinea native is most likely due to enlargement of the liver caused by one of the tropical diseases.

Why are so many people overweight?

Some are above the average weight for their height because they are athletic, and their muscles are particularly well developed. There is nothing wrong with that, nor is there any foundation for the old belief that athletes are likely to die earlier than other people because their muscles undergo fatty degeneration in later life. Other people become overweight because their tissues are retaining too much water. This may be due to disease of the heart, kidneys or liver, and the fluid can be dispelled by taking diuretic tablets, which stimulate the kidneys to excrete more urine. The third and nutritionally most important cause is obesity, which results from the laying down of too much fat tissue within the body and under the skin. Obesity calls for treatment when it raises the body weight by 10 per cent or more above the desirable level.

What are the reasons for obesity?

The fundamental causes of obesity are complex and by no means fully understood but they all result in the intake of energy-providing foods exceeding what is required for everyday living. Disease (such as a disorder of the appestat in the brain) is rarely to blame, though it is quite likely that disturbance of the body's hormone balance accounts for some cases. Heredity is usually quoted as contributing to the picture, but how far our genes are responsible is uncertain, since family feeding habits can cancel out the inherited tendency. Obesity is more prevalent during pregnancy and at the menopause, and more likely to affect middle-aged women than men. Administering female hormones to men gives them a female distribution of fat.

It is an over-simplification to say that fat people eat too much, for one could equally say that they are not taking sufficient exercise for the amount they consume. Whereas overeating is commonly the cause of mild obesity, under-activity is more often the reason for pronounced cases. One may sometimes observe a vicious circle at work—overweight encouraging reduction in activity, so leading to more overweight and then further loss of activity. In fact, markedly obese people need a big calorie intake to move their body about, and quite often they are not excessive feeders, though they *do* tend to be physically inactive. Most likely mechanisation, sedentary work and even the coming of television are all adding to our inertia. Boredom, frustration, anxiety and new social pressures, such as obligatory drinking, the executive's lunch or eating tea with the children, are other aspects of modern life that conspire to make us fat.

Are the foundations of obesity laid down in infancy or childhood by the eating habits started at that time?
It is hard to say whether the so-called appestat in the brain, that regulates the intake of food, is set as early as in infancy. Certainly, a fat baby is less active and by taking less exercise than necessary, it is therefore more inclined to grow into a podgy-looking toddler. This could be the result of environment—the fat baby is often a spoilt baby, who goes on to become a spoilt child and ultimately an undisciplined adult. You may unwittingly be setting an emotional pattern: if you reward the child with food or give it food to keep it quiet when you are busy, you may be setting the pattern for obesity. There is also a strong impression that where parents eat heartily and perhaps excessively the children are encouraged to do the same.

Is anything definite known about the influence of the emotions on appetite?
The effects of emotions on appetite are complex and often unpredictable. Fear, worry, and preoccupation with troublesome problems all tend to inhibit appetite, as does excitement—whether pleasurable or otherwise. Anxiety, which robs some people of appetite, causes others to eat inordinately; the same is true of depression and frustration. Boredom explains why passengers on board ship, patients in hospital wards, and many middle-aged housewives stuff themselves, while rejection and a feeling of insecurity are the reasons some unhappy children overeat. They sometimes turn to food as a substitute for love.

What is the ideal weight and what is 'too fat'?
Putting on a certain amount of weight is so common as to be regarded as almost normal, but the ideal weight is what you were as an active person in your twenties—unless, of course, you were obese then. The insurance companies use this ideal weight as their standard, though it is not based on scientific criteria but on their records. If they think you are 10 lb. (4.5 kg) overweight it might mean you have to pay a higher premium, but you may otherwise feel all right. Life assurance companies are after all bookmakers—and some 100–1 outsiders do last the course and some 3–1 favourites collapse at the first fence.

How reliable are the charts showing the desirable weights for different heights and age, which you see on public weighing machines?
In general, weighing machine charts are reliable if they're not too old. The figures on some of the old machines—and in out-of-date medical text-books—are no longer valid because they were based on measurements of people during the 19th century. Modern data come from a survey of 5 million people insured in the U.S. and Canada during our own time, and probably apply to us here.

Can slimming do any harm?
Not to people in normal health. Your doctor can tell you if there is any condition present that would make slimming inadvisable.

How effective is fasting compared with a balanced, low-calorie diet for shedding weight?
Fasting tends to produce a big loss of weight in a short time, compared with the gradual reduction which the more usual low-calorie diets aim at. In one Scottish study of obesity, patients lost an average of 16.3 lb. (7.4 kg) after ten days fasting. This and other studies also showed that *in-patient* treatment on these lines gives a rather more lasting loss of weight than attendance at obesity clinics. An odd fact is that men make more successful slimmers than women, presumably because they slim for health rather than cosmetic reasons.

Some doctors seem to think it better to admit obese people to hospital in order to get their weight down. Do the methods used in various hospitals differ?
There is a good deal to be said in favour of reducing weight in hospital, especially if a severe calorie reduction is enforced. It is easier to control the patient, and untoward effects, such as weakness, dizziness or swollen ankles, can be appropriately dealt with.

The diets used to treat resistant obesity in different hospitals may vary, but the fundamental principle is always the same: the patient is given a smaller allowance of calories than is required to meet his metabolic needs or perhaps none at all; he is obliged, therefore, to draw on his reserves of fat. In extreme cases, or where weight reduction is necessary to make surgery safer, some Scottish hospitals make the patient fast by giving him only water, unsweetened tea or coffee without milk, and other non-calorie drinks, with or without vitamins, then follow this up with a low-calorie diet.

Is there any drug which genuinely and harmlessly speeds up metabolism?
No-one has yet discovered one that works safely and certainly in a normal

16

person. The thyroid produces a hormone called thyroxine, which stimulates metabolism, and this substance has been tried extensively as an aid to slimming. It has no effect on people whose thyroid glands are functioning properly, unless given in doses toxic enough to cause palpitations and a rapidly beating heart, and this could be dangerous in the elderly and those with weakness of the heart muscle.

More promisingly, workers at the Middlesex Hospital, London, have isolated from the urine of fasting animals a fat-mobilising substance which, when injected into human beings, enables them to utilise readily the body's fat store. But the yield of fat-mobilising substance is small, even from big animals, and it still remains to be purified and identified more precisely.

Do frequent bowel movements, either naturally or with the aid of laxatives, help you to lose weight?
Not at all. Some proprietary slimming products do contain a laxative, and moderate purgation can cause a small loss of fluid from the tissues, but this is made up when you replace the lost fluid with drinks, as in the case of Turkish baths. Though not in themselves effective, these remedies could possibly have a sort of substitution effect by giving you something else to engage your attention, so that you have less time for eating. Some smoking cures also contain a mild laxative, on the same principle. However, taking purgatives regularly is an undesirable practice which should be avoided because, among other things, it can upset the balance of water and salt in the body, making you muddled and dull.

Is there any diet that doesn't make the face look haggard?
There is no effective reducing diet that will selectively spare the face: this will revert towards the original shape and size that was determined by heredity. If, however, you have been overweight for several years, you should not forget, before you decide to slim, the effects of ageing that may have occurred in the meantime. The prudent thing—as with reducing schemes in general—is to lose fat slowly.

Is it possible to spot-reduce by dieting or other means?
Spot-reducing is impossible. Cutting down on food leads to an overall loss of fat but cannot affect specific areas because the mobilisation of stored fat is a general phenomenon. Even plastic surgery is no remedy, for though the surgeon can remove surplus fat, this can grow again between the scars, and may look an awful mess.

You sometimes hear of would-be slimmers wearing plastic pants or brassières in the hope of losing fat from the buttocks or breasts. But even

17

Baked Mackerel (see page 116)

if this encouraged local sweating any loss of water would, again, be only temporary. Similarly, stimulating muscles in the abdomen, buttocks and calves with an electric current can make muscles bigger by causing them to work. But there is no scientific reason to expect—as is sometimes claimed—that this could possibly dispel the subcutaneous fat on top of them. Nor could the muscular work done in this way lower the total body weight unless you kept a large muscle, like that in the calf, working for hours.

Some doctors give injections to 'redistribute fat'. How do they work?
This question presumably refers to a suggestion made about 20 years ago by a doctor practising in Rome that chorionic gonadotrophin (C.G.), one of the hormones acting on sex glands, and obtainable from the urine of pregnant women, might in some unexplained way mobilise body fat from the storage sites, and make it readily available for burning up. On the basis of that notion some doctors have used the hormone to help in the treatment of obesity, taken with a low-fat daily diet of 500 calories (2092 joules). The theory was that if patients were given daily injections of this substance for six weeks they might not feel too miserable while trying to adhere to the diet.

Obviously many people can lose a lot of weight on such a Spartan régime, but has the hormone anything to do with it? To find out, a doctor asked obese patients to take part in a controlled trial, which entailed sticking strictly to this stringent diet. He gave some of them daily injections of C.G., and to others, similar-looking injections which, unknown to both himself and the patients, contained only salt solution. Another group got no injections at all but were weighed twice a week. Those who stayed the course lost about 20 lb. (10 kg) in six weeks. Patients who got injections lost substantially more weight than those who had none—but injections of C.G. had scarcely more effect than those of salty water. The explanation is probably that injections of *anything* may have a psychological or some other effect in helping the slimmer to stick to a diet while the injections are being given.

How good and safe are saccharin products for helping slimmers?
This group of chemicals provides sweetening agents that produce no calories and which, as far as is known, are safe in use. Saccharin is discussed more fully in the section on Sweeteners later in the book.

Is it true that taking a lot of salt or a lot of water can make one fat? And is it unwise to drink with meals?
Quite a few family doctors recommend obese patients to cut down on

18

both salt and water when prescribing reducing diets, but though a big salt intake might possibly add to weight by increasing water-retention, there is no reason for thinking that excess salt *or* water would increase the total body fat. The idea that you shouldn't drink with meals if you want to lose weight is widespread, but entirely a myth, with no scientific basis.

All sorts of things, such as pickles, and fruits like apples, pears and grapes, have the name of being very fattening; is this just nonsense?
Pickles, meaning vegetables in vinegar, do not contain much in the way of carbohydrate, and they are not usually eaten in large amounts. There is, therefore, no reason to regard them as fattening. Similarly, the amount of sugar in most fruit is not enough to add weight in the amount they are consumed, although even this can be a problem for diabetics. Bananas have about twice the calorie content of apples, but are not fattening in the way that bread or sugar is. On a strict reducing diet, however, fruit should be restricted, especially bananas and grapes, which have a high carbohydrate content.

Are Turkish or sauna baths of any value in losing weight permanently?
No, not permanently. In a Turkish bath, where the room temperature may go up to 200°F (92°C), a thermostat in the brain attempts to cool the body by stimulating the sweat glands to do extra work. The fluid lost in this way from the tissues, which is largely water and *not* fat, can amount to 2 lb. (about 1 kg) an hour, so sweating is a popular method with jockeys for temporarily shedding their weight before weigh-in. However, as soon as the resulting thirst is quenched, the weight is put back again, usually within hours, and the same is true of sauna baths.

What part does exercise play in proper reducing schemes?
This is discussed in Part Six, What Else Would Help?

PART ONE

Taking off weight

Who needs to slim? According to the Life Assurance companies, the answer is anybody who is more than 20 per cent above the average for someone of his height and build. According to most doctors, the answer is anybody more than 10 lb. (5 kg) over the average. A simpler answer would be anybody who looks at himself naked in the mirror and realises that he is overweight. And this is probably the most common way of reaching a decision. Most people don't need a pair of scales to tell them that they are too fat. They can simply take a pinch of flesh between their fingers and *feel* the answer.

For some, the moment of truth comes slowly and is long delayed. A woman may go for months telling herself that they don't make size 14 dresses as they used to, until one day she admits that the dresses are just as they've always been, but she has grown larger. Many fat people start almost unknowingly to avoid looking in mirrors, so it's not until they catch a glimpse of themselves unexpectedly that they are forced to acknowledge how large they have become. For one tubby husband the moment of truth came when his wife remarked acidly that there was no room for four breasts in the bed, adding the reminder that fat men are not so attractive to thin girls as fat women are to thin men.

But however delayed the decision, there are certainly a lot of people in Britain who would like to be slimmer. A study in 1967 indicated that about a quarter of the population makes some attempt to lose weight every year. And one in ten patients visiting the doctor about some other problem is advised to slim for health reasons.

What are those health reasons? The overweight child is exposed to the hazards of flat feet, knock knees and back troubles. By the time he grows up, he faces a greatly increased risk of contracting a wide variety of digestive and metabolic disorders—gallstones, cancer of the gall bladder, diabetes, hernia, intestinal obstruction, a stroke, a thrombosis, a coronary. Obesity also predisposes to backache, arthritis and varicose veins, and makes abdominal surgery and childbirth far more difficult. The death rate for overweight people is from one and a half to three times the rate for normal people.

Luckily, eating too much is like smoking—no matter when you stop, it always helps. It doesn't matter how old you are, or how bad your condition, the sooner you get your weight down to a reasonable level and learn to eat sensibly, the better your chances of living a longer and more comfortable life.

So the motives for slimming are simple enough. Being overweight is not only a considerable health risk, it also makes normal living difficult and uncomfortable. Yet though the incentives are obvious, the results are strangely disappointing. Even when slimmers are closely supervised by a hospital, only about a quarter of those who start succeed. For those attempting to reduce without supervision, the failure rate is even higher. It is far easier for the doctor to prescribe a slimming régime than for the patient to stick to it.

Why overweight ?

Before asking why so many people fail to lose weight, it might be better to begin by asking why they put it on in the first place. There is no simple answer. Some obesity is due to medical reasons and can respond only, if at all, to medical treatment. Heredity also appears to play some part. It is known that people with broad frames are more likely to be overweight than people with small frames, and as the bone structure is inherited, it is likely that the tendency to obesity is inherited also. The way that the fat is distributed may also be affected by parentage. If a mother tends to lay down fat particularly on her hips and thighs, her daughter will also tend to put on weight in these areas.

But heredity gives no more than a *tendency* to fat. It means that one person has to guard against putting on weight more carefully than another. It doesn't mean that he will inevitably and necessarily *become* fat. All over-weight people must at some time or another have eaten more than they needed in order to have put on extra weight. This does not mean that they have been greedy. It is simply that they do not need to eat as much food to obtain sufficient energy for their daily bodily needs as do other people. Usually, after a period of gaining weight, the obese person remains stationary for a time. In this period of 'passive' obesity they may actually eat less than normal people and yet remain overweight.

Yet knowing that people become fat through eating more than they need only leads on to the next problem. Why do people overeat? The more doctors investigate the causes of obesity, the more it seems that the major reasons for overeating are emotional ones. Almost nobody thinks of food simply as a fuel to keep the body going—and if people did, we would find their attitude very disturbing.

For most of us food offers security, comfort, satisfaction and pleasure, qualities we seldom get enough of. It frequently begins in childhood; children lacking love from one or both parents turn to food for consolation. Single people or childless married couples are also liable to develop an inordinate love of food to fill the void in their lives—and they usually fail to diet successfully. The food fills a deep psychological need in their lives and they cannot give it up. This sort of eating—compensation eating—is an escape for many lonely or unhappy people, giving them at least some warmth, some pleasure.

There is a further group of people who simply crave food, as a smoker craves a cigarette. It may begin in childhood with a chubby toddler showing a preference for sweet foods. By the time he is adult, he will have a craving for food that defies reason, sometimes going on food binges that may put on as much as 6 lb (3 kg) in one day. Like any addict, these food addicts are likely to lie to themselves and their doctors about how much they eat. This is especially true of night eaters, who in one American study only calculated the food they ate during the day, feeling somehow that the food they ate in their nightly raids on the fridge didn't count.

Among the people whose normal attitude to food is more controlled are some who put on weight under certain specific pressures. Although the majority of people lose weight when they are worried because they are too tense to eat, there is a sizeable minority of men and women who put on weight under stress because they turn to food as a distraction from their anxieties. Others may put on weight when they are depressed. One study of 500 slightly overweight patients found that 370 ate more when they were nervous or worried, and a further 95 of them ate more when they were idle or bored.

Starting right

Because our attitude to food is so bound up with our emotional outlooks, the ability to slim is more a problem for the mind than for the body. There is no mystery about losing weight; any normal person can do so if he eats the right amount of food for a long enough period. But the mind must be prepared first.

Most people rush into a diet with no preparation, lose a few pounds, get bored, go back to eating normally again and so put back all the weight they have lost. Dr. Jean Mayer, a Harvard physiologist, calls this 'The rhythm method of girth control', and it is certainly widespread. It shows in the seasonal fluctuations of dieting. Sales of diet products soar in January and February when dieters suffer from a post-Christmas feeling of guilt, and climb again in May and June as they struggle to get into their swimsuits ready for their holidays. If the first diet had been successful, the second wouldn't be necessary.

One of the reasons for this failure is that dieting is undoubtedly an unnatural act. Most people are only just getting used to the idea that affluence is here to stay and that there will be enough food to go round tomorrow, and next year. After so many centuries of shortage and uncertainty, and after the deprivations of the war years and the years of rationing, it seems hard to expect that we should stint ourselves now.

People don't like having things taken from them. They especially dislike giving up something as pleasurable as food and drink. And it isn't an easy process. Unlike the alcoholic who simply throws away his bottle for good, or the smoker who never opens another packet, you have to go on eating some food, day after day. You can't avoid temptation, you have to learn how to handle it. No wonder so many people find it difficult.

On the whole, men make much more successful dieters than women, probably because their motivation is stronger. The majority of men diet because they are worried about the health risks attached to obesity, often after being refused a policy by a life assurance company or being asked for a higher premium. Women on the other hand usually slim in order to look prettier. And the cosmetic reason doesn't seem to be as forceful. A man choosing between overeating and an early death will probably decide to eat less; a woman choosing between overeating and looking a little more attractive to her husband might well reach out for the food. But women face the same health risks as men. So if vanity isn't a powerful enough incentive, the desire for a better life might be.

The attitude of the society people move in also shapes their attitude towards weight control. A survey in London in 1968 revealed that one in two working and lower-middle-class women was overweight, but only one in five of upper-middle and upper-class women. Besides the fact that the richer women would find slimming easier because they could better afford a variety of non-fattening foods, there is also an aesthetic pressure. In our present society, the slim figure is thought to be beautiful and the fat figure ugly. In the upper levels of society, where the wife's appearance may be important to her husband both by impressing business clients and when joining in his social life, there will be a lot of pressure on her to slim. In the lower levels of society the woman does not have this social rôle and her appearance is less important. Also, since half the women she knows are likely to be overweight, she will not feel conspicuous or abnormal. And in these environments, where the memory of hard times is still vivid, a plump wife may be subconsciously regarded as a sign of prosperity and well-being.

Meeting the obstacles

Once decided upon, for whatever reasons, a slimming diet will demand all your virtues and your vices, your intelligence and your cunning and, above all, your self-control. The virtues are very important, especially those of determination, perseverence and steadfastness. Dieting is slow, hard work, with periods when there seems to be little result to show for all the effort. It is no good going into a diet casually, if you really want it to work. It's better to do it properly once than to spend all your life in a series of half-hearted and ineffectual attempts.

You must use your mind. If you are vain, you can encourage yourself by looking in the mirror and thinking how much slimmer you are. Even if no one else notices at first, you will. If you are mean, think how much less your cheese salad is costing than the three-course meal the man opposite is having. Don't depend on your friends for help. For some reason they are likely to be your worst enemies at this time. They'll tell you that you're getting too thin, that you're looking haggard, that it will make you ill, that you've done enough now. Ignore them—they are only envious of your superior will power. People just can't resist trying to persuade a dieter to eat something fattening. If he succumbs, they get a lovely warm glow of power. He gets nothing, of course. And remember, when you drop dead of a heart attack, they won't say, 'Oh poor thing, if only I'd talked to him and persuaded him to diet and encouraged him and seen him through'. They'll say, 'What did you expect? He was always so fat'. You must be prepared to go it alone.

New eating pattern wanted

Having decided to diet, and knowing that most doctors agree you should try to regain the weight you were at 25, the next step is to decide which diet to follow. The great temptation is to try a drastic diet, to get the whole unpleasant business over within 21 or 28 days and see immediate results. This is understandable, but unlikely to lead to success.

In the first place, losing weight is only a small part of the problem—keeping the weight off once it has been lost is even more important. And to do this means learning a whole new pattern of eating. A crash diet may make you lose weight, but it will teach you nothing about food habits, so you are likely to put back all the weight you have lost as soon as you return to eating normally. The further disadvantage of the crash diet is that it is terribly boring, tedious and unpleasant, and thus the temptation to break it usually proves overwhelming.

There is little point in losing weight if you are not going to remain slim. It is better therefore to set a new pattern for your appetite. How much you eat will depend very much on your own particular needs. But if you eat a regulated amount of food and still fail to lose, you will just have to eat even less. You must find out what your individual system needs.

Probably the most successful method of slimming is to adopt the low-carbohydrate diet. You *can* lose weight by counting the calories of everything you eat and seeing that they never exceed a certain number, but

24

this involves a great deal of tedious calculation. And a process that is tedious and troublesome will soon be abandoned. With the low carbohydrate diet you simply cut out all sugars (honey, syrup, jam and all sweets, in addition to sugar itself) and reduce starches (bread, potatoes, etc.). Cut out also canned fruit, cakes, biscuits and pastry.

Whichever foods you cut down on will lead to some weight loss, but cutting down carbohydrates gives the fastest results. It is also less dangerous than cutting down on proteins, as these not only give you energy but also build up and renew the body tissue. You could cut down on fats, omitting any taken in the form of chips, crisps and fried foods, but eating daily a small portion of butter or oil to add variety and flavour to your diet. Even when sticking to the non-sugar diet you can still eat a wide range of alternative foods. This will whet your appetite and eliminate the boredom of slimming, and also ensure that you get all the vitamins you need.

Speed is not a very important factor when you are slimming. If you try to lose too quickly and eat little more than starvation rations, you may suffer from depression and listlessness and find life hardly worth living. Unless you eat enough to remain energetic and optimistic you will soon start to feel that dieting is not worthwhile. You must not allow the period of your diet to become one of gloom and boredom. It is better to think of your diet as six months of controlled but pleasant eating than as four weeks of misery.

A comfortable and reasonable weight loss is an average of 2 lb (1 kg) a week. You should try to weigh yourself regularly while you are dieting, but don't expect the weight loss to be steady. It varies from person to person. Some lose a lot at once and then find that the rate falls off, others lose fairly consistently, say 1 lb (0.5 kg) a week with little variation. It is important to use the same weighing machine each time, as they do tend to differ slightly, and it is best to weigh yourself at the same time in the same clothes, perhaps once a week. Remember your weight will vary at different times of the day. After a big meal you will naturally weigh more, after a night's sleep perhaps less. Women also tend to weigh a few pounds more during their periods, because their bodies retain more fluid at this time. This will disappear immediately after the period, so women should not worry too much about their rate of weight loss at these times.

One of the most important factors to remember when you are dieting is to eat as many different kinds of food as you can of those that are allowed. This will stop you thinking of your diet as a time of deprivation, for you will discover a wide range of dishes available. It is also important to face the fact that in some respects your diet is for life. This doesn't mean that you will always have to limit your intake. Once you have lost all your fat you can start to eat bigger meals again. But the *sort* of food you eat on your slimming diet will have to remain the basis of your diet all your life, if you are not to put back your fat.

People who have been fat once are more likely to put on fat in the future than people who have always been thin. It seems as if the fat cells remain, waiting to be filled up once more, whereas the thin person would have to make the fat cells from scratch. For this reason, though a slimming diet can be abandoned once it has been successful, a sensible diet must persist. Although you may be able to go back to eating some potatoes and bread in the future, you must basically retrain your appetite so that you never again want *large* quantities of these starchy foods.

Goodbye to nibbles

Another habit you must learn to give up for ever is that of nibbling little bits of food all day long. Some people are genuinely baffled as to why they put on weight, because they just have no idea how much food they are eating. These people tend to nibble all day long, almost without noticing. And all these bits of food add up. It may be only a couple of chocolate biscuits with the morning coffee, one cake with the afternoon tea, a few chocolates or crisps in the evening with the television. But it comes to rather a lot, day after day. Even half a lump of sugar a day more than you need will put on 1 st. (6.4 kg) in 20 years. This nibbling has to stop. If you find it very difficult at first, at least try nibbling a tomato, a bit of carrot or an apple. Some people keep a supply of hard-boiled eggs in the fridge and eat one when they get hungry. For some reason, although a hard-boiled egg contains the same number of calories as a soft one, it makes a much more satisfying snack. Usually, if you can just avoid eating between meals for two whole weeks you will be surprised to think that you ever wanted all those scraps of food.

Once you have decided to cut out all fattening foods and all titbits, how should you eat the food you are allowed? It has recently been found that it probably helps to eat five or six small meals a day instead of two or three larger ones. The reason seems to be that once you start your digestive system working, it continues for longer than is needed. In other words, it uses up extra energy. If you set it to work five or six times a day instead of only two or three times, you will use up quite a lot of extra energy and so burn up some of your fat.

Having a number of smaller meals also has the advantage of staving off the pangs of hunger so that you are not tempted to eat too much at the next meal. You may eat a slice of ham and a few grapes, or a 5 oz (141 g) carton of natural yoghurt (plain yoghurt contains 75 calories a carton, fat-free yoghurt 68 calories but fruit-flavoured yoghurt 160), or a piece of cheese and an apple. And if one light meal leaves you feeling a little unsatisfied, you can always comfort yourself with the thought that it is only two or three hours to the next one. But having more meals must not mean that you eat more food. The total consumed during the day must not exceed the limit you have set for yourself, or you will cease to lose weight. It is not easy to follow this system, however, if you are out at work, as you will probably not be able to break off to eat every three hours. It is more suited to the housewife at home.

Traps to avoid

There are one or two simple mistakes that people make through mis-understanding the way their body functions. For instance, you don't need to eat an extra large meal just because you know you won't get the chance to eat again for some time. Your body doesn't work on this minute to minute basis, and will come to no harm if it is has to wait a while for the next consignment of fuel. Nor should you panic about feeling hungry and try to avoid it at all costs. Your stomach has got to learn to be satisfied with less, and putting food into it at the first sign of protest will simply slow up the learning process. Anyway, some slimmers find there is a feeling of smugness or even perverse pleasure about being slightly hungry.

Although you must avoid starchy foods if you are going to lose weight successfully, you must also face the fact that you will not succeed with your diet if you are too miserable. You will be tempted to discard it. If you are torn between your strict diet and your inclinations, it might be sensible to make an occasional exception rather than to abandon the idea of slimming altogether.

Many diets, for example, forbid all alcohol because it has a high calorie content (see chart on page 232). But a man who is used to having a regular drink at lunchtime or after work may after a few days find this an intolerable sacrifice or too embarrassing to explain, and so abandon the whole idea of the diet. It is better to have the odd drink, counting it as food, and try to cut down on something else that can be relinquished with less regret. You might even find support from some nutritionists; an experiment in America in 1962 showed that patients who drank a glass of wine with their evening meal lost more weight than patients who did not. You might do less harm to your diet, however, by changing your drink— see the chart on page 232.

Support and sympathy

Slimming by yourself isn't much fun. Although your attempt to diet is important to you, the details are not really interesting to anyone else. If your friends and family are eating normal meals and feeling full and satisfied, they will find it hard to appreciate why you find it such a struggle to avoid eating a slice of bread or a biscuit. Since they do not understand your suffering, they are unfortunately not likely to sympathise with it.

Yet you need a great deal of sympathy and encouragement at this time. If you can persuade someone to take an interest in your endeavour, you will find it much less of a burden. The ideal person is your doctor. The Food Standards Committee recommend that anyone intending to lose more than 1 st. (6.4 kg), especially if the condition is of long standing, should seek advice from a doctor or dietitian. Anyone with a medical handicap such as blood pressure or heart trouble should also consult a doctor. He will convince you that the diet is worthwhile and important. This is one reason why the miracle cures work. No injections or pills can really make you slimmer. But if they are combined with regular visits to a sympathetic doctor (and the expensive cures usually do include just this), his encouragement will ensure that the accompanying diet is followed.

But many doctors in general practice simply do not have enough time to give this sort of attention to their patients. They will certainly agree to see them in advance to advise on whether to diet, and how best to do so, but it is unlikely that they can manage to see the patient at very frequent intervals after that. Again, although the British Medical Association believes that dieting to lose weight should be done under a doctor's supervision, so far few doctors have had any formal training in weight control.

If your doctor can't give you regular attention, it is worth trying to find someone else who can. Some of the most successful slimmers are husbands and wives, who can spur each other on day by day and share their troubles and praise their achievements. A married couple, who know each other's weakness and strength, are the ideal dieting companions.

Sometimes a doctor will arrange for a small group of his overweight patients to meet and compare their experiences. The best results seem to come with groups of no more than ten, as this allows the members to take a really personal interest in each other. This is especially true for anyone who has been overweight for a long time. These people often feel ashamed of their bodies and are afraid of being laughed at and rejected and hurt. To find a sympathetic friend or a club that shares the same problem, can be a great help.

Are you vulnerable?
Besides taking these major steps, there are lots of smaller ways in which you can help yourself to stick to your diet. Boredom is one great threat. The housewife at home, surrounded by temptation, having to cook frequent meals for her family, often worried by the countless small irritations

and problems of running her home and attending to her children, may turn to food as a refuge. Some company from a friendly neighbour would cheer her up better than food, and if no one drops in she should go out and seek it. Idleness is another problem; people often nibble a snack just to kill time, especially if they are hanging around the house at the weekend. If you see an empty day coming up, try to think of a positive way of filling it. And if you feel you must have a snack this evening while you watch television, go out to the cinema instead, away from temptation.

Another vulnerable dieter is the man who has just given up smoking. Lots of people complain that they put on weight as soon as they give up smoking and use this as an excuse to return to their addiction, preferring apparently the risk of cancer to the risk of a stroke. This is probably a re-flection on our social values. Most people can't really imagine what it means to die a few years earlier than might be expected. But they have a very clear picture of what it would be like to be overweight meanwhile, and shun the prospect.

Doctors have failed to uncover any metabolic reason why smokers should put on weight when they stop and though many do, about half of them lose the weight again within two months. The others should just try to find a substitute to keep their fingers and mouths occupied. Nibbling sweets and nuts is a poor solution. Some men try worry beads; women are luckier, they can always knit. But to say that giving up smoking has made you fat is untrue. It is food, and food alone that makes you fat. Those rolls of flesh can't be made out of fresh air.

The housewife going on a slimming diet should try to start with a storecupboard empty of fattening foods. You *could* try sitting in the kitchen with a loaf and will-power, but it's easier if you don't buy the loaf in the first place. A girl going out to work will find a cooked breakfast will prevent her getting pangs of hunger at mid-morning and so save her from the temptation of elevenses. The businessman will find it helps to start off his lunch with a little mixed salad or clear soup. This will take the edge off his appetite and help him resist the lure of potatoes. You can achieve the same effect by taking a slimming pill—but soup is so much pleasanter.

Another thing that needs a little ingenuity when you are dieting is your social life. There are slimmers who maintain that it is simply impossible, and that it is better to give up a social life, or join friends only if no food or drink is involved, at a cinema or theatre or sports match. But this may seem too harsh a restriction, and there are people whose job or social position demands that they attend a certain number of business or official lunches or dinners.

The best thing to do is to prepare for the meal in advance. If you know you are going to eat three or four courses in the evening, you should cut down on all the rest of your food that day, keeping going on tomato juice if possible. You won't faint just from one day's abstention. You could limit the damage of the actual meal by refusing a bread roll, and taking just a small helping of potato. But it is rude to insist on following your diet absolutely if your hostess has gone to a lot of trouble, and an embarrassing personal intrusion if it is a public occasion. It is better to enjoy your dinner at the time, and make allowances for it when you are on your own.

What about fasting?

As an alternative to dieting, some people favour a complete fast. It would be foolish for anyone to attempt this for more than two or three days without medical advice and it is best done under supervision, since the person fasting needs to rest. It is usually advised only for people who are grossly overweight, or for anyone due for an urgent operation who must get rid of some of his fat before the surgeon can perform. But even in hospital a fast has its dangers. Early in 1969 a 20-year-old girl died after spending 30 weeks in hospital on a starvation diet. She had had nothing but vitamin tablets and calorie-free drinks. She had reduced successfully from 18–10 st. (114–63 kg) and had started eating under supervision when she died. The cause seems to have been a type of heart failure—the heart muscle had wasted away. Post-mortems of people dying of starvation in concentration camps also revealed that during a long fast the body consumes not only its fat store, but also its muscles, internal organs and bone marrow.

It might seem unlikely that anyone would voluntarily fast to this extent. But there is a long-recognised, though still baffling, mental disorder named *anorexia nervosa*, which should perhaps be mentioned. With this neurosis the patient, usually a female, and often at puberty, deliberately refuses food for a variety of abnormal reasons, though she may explain her odd behaviour by saying she is only 'slimming'. As such patients may persist until they die from starvation, they are usually treated in hospital, where they may have to be forcibly fed and given injections of insulin to create an appetite, or to receive psychotherapy. There is no evidence that this disorder is more prevalent today than it was hundreds of years ago, and it must be emphasised that the condition is the *cause* of excessive and dangerous 'slimming'—not the result.

The too-chubby child

A child who is overweight presents a completely different problem to the adult. The chief difficulty is that he may not understand why you want him to eat less. But fat children must lose weight. The child who grows up overweight faces genuine and serious problems. He may develop flat feet, knock knees or back complaints through the strain put on his delicate growing bones by excess weight, and as an adult he will be exposed to all the ills of obesity.

There is another side-effect of obesity in childhood, more important perhaps for boys than for girls, and that is its effect on height. In his early years, the fat child is almost always taller than other children in his age group. But this advantage is only temporary. The fat child reaches maturity earlier than his thin contemporary, often by one or two years. As growth normally stops within two or three years of puberty, the fat child, through maturing sooner also stops growing sooner. The final result is that although some overweight children reach normal height, the majority fall short. It is hard that a man should be condemned to being smaller than his fellows, simply because he was too heavy as a child.

But even worse, from the child's point of view, is the attitude of his friends. Children, either through ignorance or wilfulness, can be very cruel, and fat children are always tormented at some time or another by their friends. It isn't always meant unkindly. Tubby children are naturally rather poor at games and sports because they are slow and awkward. The fat boy is always the last to be picked for the team, because his condition makes him a liability and this is bound to make him feel unwanted and rejected. The apparent cheerfulness of the overweight child is all too often just a desperate attempt to make friends and draw a protective shield over the loneliness and misery he really feels.

The cause of his obesity may be physical or emotional. Some children inherit a tendency to put on weight, and the stronger this tendency is, the earlier it will show. These children are generally slow in movement and have a strong liking for food. They are a mother's ideal, as they have fewer food fads than other children. They also tend to show a preference for sweet and starchy foods from an early age.

Food makes such an emotional impact on children that they often use it as an outlet for their emotional problems. In the early months it is associated very directly with the mother, and the baby may cling to food as a way of maintaining contact with the mother, especially if she only bothers with him while he is eating. The baby will prolong the process in order to extend his association with his mother. It is also a source of power, as children quickly realise that by refusing food they can punish their parents, but most often it is a source of comfort. Many overweight children eat too much out of a neurotic desire to please their parents, instinctively sensing a rejection.

Often a mother will protest that her plump toddler doesn't eat a lot of food. To some extent she is probably mistaken, because the child is usu-

31

ally eating sweets and odd slices of bread and butter and she may not be aware of how these mount up. But it is certainly not true to say that fat children are necessarily greedy. Their problem is not that they are eating a lot, but that they are eating more than they need. The child's nutritional needs are a completely individual affair. Some just do not use up as much food for growth and energy as others and so will always need less.

Gaining his co-operation

Treatment isn't easy. In the first place, the child must want to lose weight himself. If he is simply put on a diet by his parents with no explanation, it will almost certainly fail. The child will probably interpret the sudden reduction in food as a punishment for something or other and refuse to co-operate. And if the child doesn't understand the point of the diet, he will only go away and eat sweets when the parents aren't looking.

The diet must be as discreet as possible. Children can be hideously embarrassed if they feel they are being singled out in any way, and it is best if the diet can be unobtrusively managed. The mother should try as far as she can to avoid making the child feel deprived. One of the easiest and fairest things is to see that if one child in the family has to be denied sweets, the other children share the ban. It is asking too much of any small child to expect him to do without chocolates while his brothers and sisters gorge. And giving up sweets will save the other children's teeth anyway. The same principle applies to the diet meals. Since they are varied and appetising, there is no reason why the other offspring should not share them, and this will help to make the overweight child feel less conspicuous. The parents must use tact to avoid hurting his feelings, as a fat child is terribly vulnerable.

There are other steps the mother can take, in addition to restricting his intake. If the school is not too far away and the roads are quiet, it is better to encourage him to walk every day than to drive him there. Daily exercise is an indispensable part of a child's slimming programme. And doctors who have taken a special interest in obese children find that group therapy works particularly well with them.

At this age, children depend a great deal on the approval of their peers. This has been demonstrated at the summer camps in America run especially for fat girls. At some the parents pay no fees if the girl fails to lose weight, but in the community atmosphere weight loss is usually rather impressive. The girls enjoy sharing their troubles and taking part in the games and sports hitherto dominated by their thinner contemporaries.

Whatever support she finds, the mother must persevere until the child's weight is down to normal—her local Health Clinic will be able to tell her what the average weight for a child of that height should be. And she

32

must keep on reminding herself that giving food to a child is not always the best way of showing love.

When the pace slows down

The most disheartening phase in any diet comes when all weight loss seems to have come to an end. Most people find that the initial results are quite encouraging. They may lose 4–5 lb (about 2 kg) in the first week, almost as much in the second. But the rate of loss usually falls off slowly and surely. There will be weeks in which no weight comes off at all. This is when real determination is called for. Fat is not lost evenly. At first it goes from the superficial stores just under the skin—this is one reason why slimmers often complain that their faces look haggard. The fat slips away from all over the body; you cannot choose which bits should go first. The last to go is the deep-store fat which in women is found mainly on the hips and thighs, in men on the abdomen. Women find this extremely irritating, as they are usually keen to lose weight off their hips, and find that this is the last place to show results. But if they persevere long enough, it will come off the hips as well. You just need patience in the final weeks.

And when you have finally and triumphantly lost all the pounds you set out to lose, what is the next step? Well you should try to come off your diet slowly and gradually. Tempting as it will be to celebrate by going out to a five-course dinner, this could too easily be the first step on the slippery slope back to obesity. It is better to come off cautiously, taking a little more at a time and watching your weight so that you can discover just how much you can eat and still keep your weight constant. Keep repeating to yourself the slimmer's watchword: 'A moment on the lips, a lifetime on the hips' and see if you can keep that weight off.

This is where the 'maintenance menus' in Part Two will come into their own. But meantime, you need the menus and the recipe suggestions that follow here, and as you study them, you will see how to juggle with the permitted foods. The recipes are in Part Four—make full use of them, to avoid monotony; don't just learn a meagre half-dozen dishes and stick to them regardless, or you will bore yourself and the family into rebellion.

Slimming as a family enterprise

We all seem to find slimming easier if we have company. Someone to sympathise with our problems, somebody to compete and compare with, someone to encourage us when we grow despondent. If the whole family decides to slim, it will make each member's task a little easier. And it will lighten the mother's burden considerably, as it means she has only one type of menu to cater for.

A few basic rules apply to everyone on a slimming diet. In the first place, *all* sugar must be eliminated; anyone who can't manage without the taste of sweetness should substitute a saccharin preparation in drinks and food. Butter consumption should be cut down to half an ounce per person daily, and low-fat milk should replace ordinary milk.

Starchy foods should be avoided. Starch-reduced bread, crispbread and rolls can be substituted instead. And the habit of nibbling snacks between meals must be broken. Scones, biscuits, cakes, jams, sweets and chocolates all add to your weight problem and must be renounced. If you find yourself desperate for something to nibble, try a stick of celery or a carrot instead. Better still, talk about your urge to someone else in the family and so enlist help in fighting the temptation.

These are the general guide lines to follow for family slimming. Remember that protein provides the same number of calories per gram as carbohydrate, but builds the body as well as providing energy. Because it has this extra work to do, there is no chance of it piling up in the body as surplus fat.

Breakfast	A serving of raw fruit or unsweetened fruit juice or stewed fruit. An egg or serving of fish or bacon with tomato 1 slice of bread (starch-reduced) Tea or coffee with milk but no sugar
Mid-morning	Cup of tea or coffee (no sugar), or yeast or meat extract drink Raw fruit or vegetable if hungry
Lunch/Supper	Small serving of fish, meat, egg or cheese dish and salad vegetables 1 slice of bread (starch-reduced) or 1 starch-reduced crispbread or roll Piece of fresh fruit Tea or coffee (no sugar)

Mid-afternoon	Cup of tea or coffee or glass of PLJ lemon juice
Dinner	Clear soup
	Large serving of meat
	Large serving of green vegetables or tomatoes
	Average serving of a root vegetable—onions, carrots, leeks, turnips
	1 medium-sized potato *or* 1 oz. (25 g) rice
	Fresh fruit or yoghurt

The menus which follow will eliminate the necessity of preparing separate meals for those who require slimming and those who don't; for the latter, you simply supplement the main meal by potatoes; where crispbreads or starch-reduced (S.R.) rolls are mentioned, ordinary bread or bread rolls can be eaten; sauces may be made to go with meat and vegetables.

The slimmer must of course forget about the starchy foods and eat as much as desired of any fresh greens available. Use a minimum of butter on toast, crispbreads and starch-reduced rolls, so that some of the daily $\frac{1}{2}$ oz. (15 g) is kept for use in cooking—a great flavour-booster. Don't skip a meal—three regular, balanced meals are essential to satisfy both physiological and psychological requirements.

Slimming family menus for a month

Breakfast This meal is a very important start to the day and must never be skipped. You should, however, omit fried foods; replace ordinary bread, etc., by starch-reduced bread, rolls or crispbreads; use unsweetened fruit juices and fruits, or else sweeten them with an artificial sweetener. Make full use of yeast extracts as a spread, instead of marmalade, honey and so on.

Here are some sample breakfast menus, showing the general pattern to follow: ring the changes on bacon, eggs, meats, fish and so on, as well as varying the fruit course.

Breakfast	Boiled Egg	Grapefruit Halves
	2 Energen Rolls	Grilled Sausage and Egg
	Tea/Coffee/Milk	1 slice of Starch-reduced Bread
		Tea/Coffee/Milk
	Iced Fruit Juice	
	Grilled Bacon and Tomato	
	1 Starch-reduced Crispbread	
	Tea/Coffee/Milk	

Day	Lunch/Supper	Dinner
1	Haddock Roly-poly	Roast Shoulder of Lamb Broccoli Carrots Fruit Salad
2	Mexicalli Soup Open Sandwich (cold lamb)	Veal Marengo Baked Potatoes Apple Soufflé
3	Cheese Soufflé Green Salad	Beef Olives with gravy Cabbage Raspberry Delight
4	Courgettes Créole Crispbread Fruit	Mushroom Bouillon Lamb Chops and Gooseberry Sauce Baked Tomatoes Cheese and Biscuits
5	Stuffed Tomatoes–2 Green Salad	French Rabbit Casserole Courgettes Créole Spanish Cream
6	Scotch Haddock Cucumber Salad	Bengal Chicken Curry Rice Fresh Fruit
7	Stuffed Peppers with Tomato Sauce	Grilled Steak with Onion Rings Vegetable Salad
8	Cheese Omelette Crispbread Fresh Fruit	Sole with Mushrooms Brussels Sprouts Tomatoes Apricot Cream
9	Shrimp Mint Salad Fresh Fruit	Tipsy Chops Peas and Carrots Cheese and Biscuits
10	Spanish Omelette Crispbread Fresh Fruit	Beef and Pineapple Casserole Baked Potato Cabbage
11	Salmon Salad	Pollo alla Cacciatore Spinach Blackberry Whip

Day	Lunch/Supper	Dinner
12	Stuffed Onions Fresh Fruit	Veal Goulash Broccoli and Baked Tomatoes Steamed or Baked Egg Custard
13	Vegetable Cocktail Soup Open sandwiches	Bacon and Beef Loaf Mustard Sauce Pickled Beet French Beans Spiced Pear Grill
14	Fish Chowder Crispbread Fresh Fruit	Liver and Bacon Kebabs Rice Green Salad Cheese and Biscuits
15	Leek and Bacon Savoury Crispbread Fresh Fruit	Grilled Steak Endive and Tomato Salad Crispy Top
16	Hot Slaw Salad Fresh Fruit	Grilled Gammon Rasher Brussels Sprouts Carrots
17	Soused Herrings Orange Salad	Poulet Chasseur Cabbage Carrots Fresh Fruit
18	Mushroom Casserole	Tomato Bouillon Monks' Mackerel Broccoli and Creamed Potatoes
19	Dutch Hussar's Salad Fresh Fruit	Parcha Seek Kabob Green Beans
20	Aubergines Provençales Fresh Fruit	Roast Beef Peas and Carrots
21	Tuna Salad Starch-reduced Rolls	Leek and Liver Casserole Courgettes
22	Mixed Grill Salad	Spanish Cod Cauliflower and Spinach
23	Tomato and Cheese Fondue Crispbread	Barbecued Steak Dressed French Beans Apple Soufflé

Day	Lunch/Supper	Dinner
24	Cream of Spinach Soup Bacon and Apple Omelette	Salt Beef in Cider Carrots and Leeks Potatoes
25	Winter Fish Salad Fresh Fruit	Crown Roast Cauliflower, Carrots Onions
26	Macaroni Cheese	Orange and Cucumber Rollmops Green Salad Cheese and Biscuits
27	Sweet Slaw Salad Ham	Stuffed Pork Fillet Baked Potatoes Leeks
28	Shepherds' Soufflé Fresh Fruit	French Veal Cutlets Courgettes and Tomatoes

Slimming the man of the family

Putting the man of the family on to a reducing diet can be psychologically difficult for both husband and wife. The man may feel disturbed by the plan because he is used to thinking of himself as the breadwinner, the support of the whole family, without acknowledging that this is usually now a mental rather than a purely physical task. He does not need huge meals to keep up his strength, but may feel obscurely that he could become run-down without them. The wife will be upset because her natural instinct is to feed him well, as a practical demonstration of her affection: cutting down on someone's food rations is a very new and sophisticated way of showing love.

But it is essential for the family man to bring his weight down to a reasonable level if he wants to enjoy a healthy and comfortable life and avoid premature ageing. His co-operation is of the first importance; a man will not succeed in losing weight unless he is really anxious to do so. It may be difficult for him to keep to his diet at lunchtime. That is when the temptation to ignore his slimming plans and keep up with his friends will be at its strongest. If possible, the best answer is to provide him with an interesting packed lunch. In this way he keeps control of his diet in his own hands. If he has to eat out, he should refer to the section on eating in a restaurant and remember its advice.

If the midday meal is taken out, you must keep a tighter rein on the two remaining meals, breakfast and supper. Starch-reduced bread or crispbread and low-fat spreads instead of butter or margarine will help at breakfast, and sweeteners can replace sugar. A satisfying but sensible breakfast may also prevent a man from over-indulging at lunchtime. The evening meal should not be too heavy, as there is little opportunity to work off its effects afterwards.

Perhaps the most difficult decision for the male dieter to make is what to do about alcohol. The earnest dieter will substitute fruit juice or mineral water for alcohol whenever possible, but it is not easy to cut it out altogether. The best thing is to avoid the occasions where you know you will have to drink, if this is socially possible. It is better to be doing something else—going to the pictures, playing golf or gardening, than to stand in a pub feeling sorry for yourself over one glass of tonic water. But if you must drink, consult the alcohol chart at the back of this book and choose a drink that is low in calories.

Adaptable dinner plans

The evening meal assumes particular importance if some members of the family have only a packed lunch at midday or if just one person is slimming. We have devised alternative dinner menus to cover these varying circumstances. The first are intended for families where the children have a packed lunch and need a substantial evening meal, but where the father is trying to slim. The second set is intended for families where the children have their midday meal at home and the father has a business lunch and so no one needs a very large meal in the evening.

The important thing in the first category is to choose dishes which will provide a full and nourishing meal if rice or potatoes is added, but be tasty for the father who must leave out the carbohydrates for his diet. The child's needs can be satisfied by giving him larger helpings, the father's slimming programme will not be harmed since the main part of the dish is non-fattening.

In the second category, none of the family needs a very large evening meal. The dishes suggested here are appetising but not too filling. They consist, generally, of a single course, since there is no need for starters or finishers if this is the third good meal of the day.

Two-way dinner menus

(A month's suggestions for ways of providing adequate nutrition for the children who have taken a packed lunch to school and so require a substantial evening meal, and at the same time contributing to father's slimming programme by omitting such things as potatoes.)

Day   Two-way dinner menus

1	Veal Cutlets Cole Slaw Creamed Potatoes	11	Stewed Heart Cabbage Steamed Potatoes
2	Ham Casserole Jacket Potatoes Courgettes	12	Spanish Cutlets Dressed French Beans
3	Beef and Mushroom Sweet and Sour Rice Green salad	13	Tournedos with Mushrooms Vegetable Salad
4	Ham and Cheese Rolls Pasta Salad Endive	14	Kidney Casserole Broccoli Grilled Tomatoes
5	Fish à la Portugaise Cress Pickled Beets Creamed Potatoes	15	Roast Beef Roast Potatoes French Beans
6	Oriental Chicken Rice Green Salad	16	Baked Bream with Lemon and Cress Red Cabbage Salad
7	Lamb Cutlets Espagnole Asparagus Spears Tomatoes	17	Grilled Entrecôte Steak Roquefort Butter Grilled Tomatoes Atlantic Salad
8	Braised Kidney with Ham Carrots Potatoes	18	Goulash with Sauerkraut Carrots Boiled Potatoes
9	Pork Chops with Apple Jacket Potatoes Broccoli	19	Lamb Paprika Spinach Creamed Potatoes
10	Chinese Omelette Grilled Tomatoes Belmont Salad	20	Grilled Plaice with Lemon Butter Salad Niçoise

Day Two-way dinner menus

21 Braised Livers in Wine
   Baked Courgettes and
   Aubergines

22 Gammon and Mushroom
   Bake
   Baked Tomatoes
   Cress

23 Rolled Herrings in
   Wine Sauce
   Leeks with Lemon Butter
   Broccoli

24 Continental Meat Loaf
   Buttered Noodles
   Tossed Green Salad

25 Grilled Sole with Grapes
   Rice Salad
   Dressed French Beans

26 Roast Loin of Veal
   Broccoli
   Roast Potatoes

27 Kofta
   Rice
   Green Bean Salad

28 Bordeaux Chicken
   Courgettes
   Creamed Potatoes

A month's menus to help slimming fathers

(For the family where children are able to have their midday meal at home and the father has a main meal at a canteen or restaurant.)

Day	Midday Meal	Supper
1	Veal and Sausage Casserole Cabbage Baked Tomatoes	Spanish Stuffed Onions and Tomato Sauce Ryvita and Cheese Fresh Fruit
2	Liver Française Broccoli Carrots Fresh Fruit	Cheese and Leek Soup Winter Fish Salad
3	Barbecued Steak Jacket Potatoes Green Beans	Courgettes in Cheese Sauce Crispbreads Fresh Fruit
4	Carbonade of Pork Creamed Potatoes Spinach	Scrambled Bacon and Corn Green Salad Fresh Fruit

Day	Midday Meal	Supper
5	Uccelli Scappari Courgettes Minted Potatoes	Soused Herrings Salad Tomatoes
6	Chicken Maryland Ensalada Isabella	Mushroom Casserole Sliced Cold Meat Fresh Fruit
7	Fish Curry Rice Cucumber, Pepper and Cress Salad	Greek Moussaka Celery Crispbreads Fruit
8	Ragoût of Lamb Boiled Potatoes Brussels Sprouts	Veal and Ham Pie Waldorf Salad
9	Austrian Beef Goulash Rice Broccoli	Baked Haddock with Mushrooms Orange and Celery Salad
10	Minced Chicken Loaf Minted Potatoes Cauliflower Salad	French Onion Soup Grilled Ham Steak with Pineapple
11	Stuffed Breast of Lamb Roast Potatoes Spinach and Carrots	Baked Eggs and Mushrooms Green Salad
12	Savoury Meatballs in Casserole Noodles Algerian Salad	Halibut and Cucumber Mornay Fresh Fruit
13	Chicken Louisette French Beans Grilled Tomatoes	Celery and Onion Soup Ox Tongue Cheese and Carrot Salad
14	Devilled Tongue Rice Broccoli	Country Soup Chicken and Grape Salad
15	Mushroom-stuffed Meat Loaf Jacket Potatoes Cabbage	Maryland Soufflé Cole Slaw Bowl Fresh Fruit

Day	Midday Meal	Supper
16	Lamb Paprika Noodles French Beans	Cold Meat Loaf Cheese and Pineapple Salad
17	Coq au Vin Minted Potatoes Spinach	Hollandaise Soup Ham Omelette
18	Devonshire Fish with Mushrooms Mixed Vegetables	Braised Kidney, Tomato and Bacon Fresh Fruit
19	Barbecued Lamb Chops Creamed Potatoes Courgettes	Cock-a-Leekie Soup Crispbread Fresh Fruit
20	Oriental Chicken Rice Asparagus	Cod Cutlet Cream Poinsettia Salad
21	Continental Meat Loaf Tomato and Onion Bake	Shirred Eggs with Chicken Livers Apple and Celery Salad
22	Cold Meat Loaf Potato Salad Green Beans	Mulligatawny Soup Ryvita Fresh Fruit
23	Grilled Salmon Cutlets Courgettes Potatoes	Hamburger Steaks Spinach Fresh Fruit or Stewed Fruit
24	Burgundy Beef Jacket Potatoes Baked Tomatoes	Kidney Soup Chicken and Ham Salad
25	Italian Veal Casserole Carrots and Beans	Grilled Mackerel Leek and Lemon Salad
26	Pork and Pineapple Curry Rice	Ratatouille Niçoise Crispbreads
27	Poached Haddock and Shrimp Sauce Pickled Beets Boiled Potatoes	Chilli-burgers Apple and Cabbage Salad

Day	Midday Meal	Supper
28	Liver Rolls Broccoli Diced Potatoes	Shrimp and Mushroom Chowder Melba Toast Fresh Fruit

Slimming the overweight child

The reasons *why* some children are overweight are discussed in the introduction to this section. But there is no doubt that parents with fat children should try to make them lose weight for the children's sake. The younger child is entirely dependent on his parents for his food, so it is up to them to see that he is put on a proper reducing diet, and that other members of the family—including grandparents—understand why the diet is important and why it must be followed.

The parents must set about the diet in a positive fashion, explaining to the child the benefits of being slim and of being able to run and play like other children. They will have to offer unqualified encouragement and affection, lest the child should mistakenly interpret his reduced rations as a punishment. This danger can be averted if one of the parents can join in the diet, making it a mother-and-daughter or father-and-son effort. The child's progress should be carefully recorded and praised, so that he feels he is doing something worthwhile. And, above all, he should be encouraged to take as much exercise as possible.

The child's diet has to be modified with great care. He will still need large amounts of protein foods, as he will still be growing upwards if not outwards. There is probably no need to cut down on the body-building foods. He will be able to lose weight effectively simply by cutting down rigorously on all the sweet and starchy ones. Sweets should be vetoed, likewise ice lollies, ice cream and sweet drinks. Apples, oranges or celery can be offered for between-meal munching, and cups of Bovril, Marmite, PLJ lemon juice or unsweetened fruit juice instead of lemonade. An artificial sweetener can be used in tea, or you might be able to persuade the child to take unsweetened tea—a better alternative.

Lastly, as with all children, to distract is better than to forbid. If you can get him interested in a new hobby which will demand all his pocket money, such as collecting of some sort, it will save him spending all his allowance on sweets and tuck. And if you can keep him occupied and happy with outings and games, or even just by letting him help around the house, it will help to take his mind off his appetite at critical times.

Breakfast

(No cereals, no bread)
Fruit Juice or fresh or stewed Fruit
(sweetened with artificial sweeteners)

Grilled Tomatoes, Grilled Bacon
Eggs (boiled, poached or scrambled)
or Grilled or Poached Fish

Starch-reduced Crispbread and
Butter; Marmite

A fortnight's menus for the overweight child

Other meals

No pie crusts or dumplings and no puddings; half-helpings only of potatoes, rice or noodles. Give double helpings of green vegetables, cauliflower, onions, tomatoes, etc.; provide fresh fruit or stewed fruit, low-fat yoghurt, egg custard or cheese to replace puddings.

Unthickened soups can be added *if necessary*.

Day	Main Meal	Supper/Lunch
1	Belted Sausage Casserole French Beans, Carrots Fresh Fruit Salad	Gardener's Broth Chinese Omelette Fresh Fruit/Milk Drink
2	Smothered Pork Chop Courgettes Potato	Golden Fish Green Salad Fresh Fruit/Milk Drink
3	Grilled Cod Steak Grilled Tomato Cauliflower and Cheese Sauce	Stuffed Cabbage Leaves Starch-reduced Crispbread Fresh Fruit/Milk Drink
4	Hamburger Steaks Pickled Beets Leeks Cheese	Chicken Soup Scrambled Eggs Fresh Fruit
5	Grilled Chicken Joint Green Beans Sorrento Baked Egg Custard and Fruit	Sliced Cold Meat Hot-weather Green Salad Fresh Fruit Milk Drink

Day	Main Meal	Supper/Lunch
6	Lamb Paprika Noodles Courgettes Fresh Fruit	French Onion Soup Salade Niçoise Fresh Fruit
7	Stuffed Onions Cabbage Tomatoes Fresh Fruit	Greek Moussaka Fresh Fruit
8	Grilled Mackerel Glorified Apple Salad Banana Nut Cream	Baked Stuffed Aubergine Fresh Fruit Milk Drink
9	Italian Veal Casserole Broccoli Creamed Potatoes Fresh Fruit	Cheese Grilled Fish Apple and Tomato Salad Milk Drink
10	Lamb Kebabs Rice Green Salad Cheese	Celery Noodle Soup 'Main Dish' Salad Bowl Milk Drink
11	Grilled Steak Belgian Cucumber Grilled Tomatoes Cheese	Cod en Cocotte Sweet Pepper Salad Milk Drink
12	Pork Chop with Creamed Cabbage Small Jacket Potato Carrots Fresh Fruit	Marrow and Tomato Bake Tossed Winter Slaw Milk Drink
13	French-Style Roast Chicken French Beans Baked Tomatoes Fresh Fruit	Spinach with Poached Eggs Fresh Fruit Milk Drink
14	Fish Provençale Rice Green Salad Cheese	Chicken Slices with Pear and Grape Salad Milk Drink

PART TWO

Keeping slim

Those lucky enough, sensible enough or persevering enough to be slim are making the best contribution they can towards a healthy life. There is not a great deal you can do to avoid meeting with an infection, or having an accident, but you *can* exercise complete control over what you eat. The most outstanding medical problems today are those associated with degeneration, with the ageing of the body through a life-time's wear and tear. By being slim, getting slim and remaining slim, you can stop that wear and tear setting in before its time. The fat body ages quickly. Keep your family slim and they will live a little longer and a lot better.

There are no absolute rules, because how much we can eat depends entirely on our own system.

This varies not just between different age groups and sexes, but from one man to another. It is unfair but true that one person can stuff away food and never put on a superfluous ounce, while another gains weight if he eats just a little too much. No one really knows why this is so. Some people just burn up more of the food they eat than others, and have none left to turn into fat. So there can be no hard-and-fast rules about what to eat. It is simply a matter of finding out what one's individual requirements are and making sure they are not exceeded. (For a general guide, see the chart on pages 53–54.)

A Good Beginning

The most important thing is to start as you mean to go on. Any newly-married wife should promise herself never to let her husband or herself become podgy. It is far, far easier never to put weight on than to struggle to get it off. And the best time to start sensible eating, as with so many things, is in the cradle.

It may be hard at first to believe that there is any need to be concerned about a bouncing baby. Most mothers are far more concerned about whether their new baby will thrive, than whether it will thrive too well. But the most recent evidence has shown that almost half the fat babies grow into fat children. And of children overweight at the age of five, four out of five will be overweight all the rest of their lives. So it is well to start at the beginning.

The mother of a new-born baby is under tremendous material and emotional pressure, and may also be spending long hours alone in the house for the first time in her life. It is natural that she should feel anxious about doing the best for her baby, and in these difficult circumstances it is easy to equate an impressive weight gain with good health. Doctors often say that it is impossible to overfeed a healthy baby and this is true for the first four to six months. But after this the baby can easily take more than it needs, and it will turn the excess food into fat. And if a baby grows accustomed to eating too much at this stage, it will be setting a pattern that will be extremely difficult to break in later years.

What's more, the fat baby gets caught up in a vicious web. Because he is fat he will be less active in his cot and will start to walk much later. This lack of exercise makes him fatter still, which makes him take less exercise, and so on in a dangerous spiral.

Family circumstances also contribute, of course. An American survey found that if one parent was fat, 40 per cent of the children were also fat, and if both parents were fat the figure jumped to 80 per cent. Heredity, as we've already seen, is partly responsible. If a parent has a stocky frame, the child may inherit this and it can't then be altered. Children show a remarkable correlation with their parents' weights, even if they are brought up apart from them. Similarly, identical twins separated at birth will still weigh almost exactly the same as each other in later years, whereas an adopted child shows little correlation with the weight of the parents who adopted him. But while heredity may predispose a child towards fatness, the eating patterns he learns at home will determine whether he does actually become fat, or manages to avoid it.

The reasons *why* mothers overfeed their children are complicated, and governed largely by emotion. It is sometimes just a sign of their anxiety to nourish the baby adequately. Often it is because the mother does not measure the powder for bottle feeds accurately enough and adds a little bit more thinking it will do the baby good and give him a good start in life. Some mothers overfeed because they miss the feeling of the child's dependance they had while he was still attached by the umbilical cord.

Whatever the reason, this overfeeding gives a baby a poor start in life and should be avoided. The mother could start by ignoring the current practice of increasing the baby's intake of carbohydrate at the expense of protein and fat through replacing milk by high carbohydrate cereal foods, often before the child is four months old. This tendency should be resisted, especially if the baby is already showing signs of fat.

Another useful thing the mother can do is to avoid giving the child sugar in his first cups of tea. Sweetening his drinks will only give him a life-long taste for sugar, a taste which in some cases can only be called addictive, so much does the appetite crave it. The British are the largest

48

Swiss Steak (see page 136)

sweet consumers in the world. We eat 140 calories (586 joules) worth of sweets and chocolates every day, enough to put on 10 lb (4.5 kg) of fat a year. If you can help to prevent this craving by not starting your baby off with a sweet tooth, you will be doing him a life-long favour.

What foods does a child need?

The foods a small child particularly needs are all those connected with growth. Children need a higher proportion of protein to carbohydrate than adults, since it is protein that builds up tissue. They should be given lots of meat and fish, green vegetables and fruit, and all dairy products. Milk is especially important, because it provides calcium to build sturdy bones and strong teeth, so children should be given all the free milk and school milk they are entitled to. If they find milk drinks monotonous, they can be tempted with milk puddings and with flavoured milk shakes.

While seeing that the child gets all the good food he needs to help him grow, it is unwise to be too strict about insisting that he always cleans his plate. Mothers sometimes get very fixed ideas that the child should never leave any food on the plate, and may make it a disciplinary matter. But unless a child is being wilfully naughty, his natural appetite will tell him when he has had enough. Making him force down extra food will not do him any good, and may throw his appetite-control mechanism permanently out of joint, so that he becomes used to unnecessarily large helpings of food. Your child is not a dustbin. Of course, if the child does leave some of his food, he should not be given sweets a little while later—allowing this will only teach him to leave the protein foods which are good for him so that he can eat the sweet foods which are not.

The taste for sweet, fattening foods can also be countered by giving the child lots of savoury things. Children often show an appreciation of savoury food at a surprisingly early age, if they get the chance to try it. They usually love anything with cheese, tomato or onion, and most children think that cocktail sausages were invented specially for them. More and more often people find at children's parties that the jellies and cakes are ignored while the cheese-and-pineapple-on-sticks is fought over. Since the savoury foods are generally more nourishing and less fattening, the taste for them should be discreetly encouraged.

The teenager's meals

The teenager needs rather different food from his younger brother or sister. He will not be growing as fast; indeed he may have more or less stopped. But bones, muscles and tissues are still being built and strengthened. And most teenagers lead a frenziedly active life that takes in school or work, sports and games, dancing (more demanding now than

49

Pot-au-feu (see page 101)

ever before), shopping and window-shopping, and much visiting of friends.

At this time of life it may be hard to get them to sit down long enough to eat a proper meal. Yet they need a balanced diet, or they will soon be run down and bad-tempered—teenage temperament may sometimes just be due to a simple lack of protein. It is best to insist on a proper breakfast; for one thing, this is usually the one time of the day you can guarantee to see them. Secondly, when they are still half-asleep and compliant they are more likely to do as you want and eat a sensible meal. Cereal and milk; eggs and bacon, sausages or fish; fruit juice, tea or coffee, will all start them off on the right foot. And with a proper breakfast inside them they will be less tempted to eat fattening sandwiches or biscuits half-way through the morning. (This last holds true for everyone in the family.)

It may take quite a bit of ingenuity to get food into them at other times. But no matter how much time has to be spent getting ready to go out, you should be able to persuade them to drink a bowl of thick, nourishing soup with perhaps a piece of bread and cheese. Try to keep up the milk habit— that will provide lots of the protein they need. And watch your daughter especially, to see that if she has decided to lose weight, she is doing so sensibly and not just cutting down indiscriminately. As your children enter their teens, you should be able to teach them the principles of a sensible diet. If they understand how important it is to have a proper balance of foods, it will stand them in good stead all their lives.

No surplus for 'Sir'

The man of the house probably needs no encouragement to eat heartily. In fact, this is likely to be exactly his problem. If he has been brought up to think that a good meal is one that leaves him feeling stuffed, it may be hard at first to convince him that your balanced meals are actually planned with his good at heart. But remember the risks. If you can prevent him putting on weight, you will be saving him from all the ills that overweight people face: premature ageing and the increased risk of an early death.

A man's needs depend not only on his build but on his occupation. If he has a hard manual job, he will need quite a lot more to eat than the man who drives to work, goes upstairs in the lift, sits behind a desk all day and has a secretary to run his errands. Many men have a hot meal at midday and another in the evening when they come home. If this is the case, the evening meal should not be too large, for there is little opportunity to work it off afterwards. If he wants only one main meal a day, it is better for him to take this at lunchtime for the same reason, so that much of the food intake will be used up in energy before the night. If he cannot eat at midday, it is better to have the evening meal fairly early in the evening—and if you can persuade him to take the dog for a walk before he goes to bed, so much the better.

The man who uses up a lot of energy in his job can afford to eat more than anyone else. Bus conductors, for example, can eat more than bus drivers. In fact, in a demanding physical job a man will *need* more to remain well. One of the best sources of energy in this respect is bread. It provides carbohydrates for energy and is also an important source of protein and vitamins. If your husband needs a fair amount of solid food, it will do no harm to give him sandwiches for his lunch, though a hot canteen meal would probably be better. This man may also carry more weight than the usual height and weight charts recommend without needing to worry, as the excess will be due to muscle and not fat. But as soon as he stops work, he will need less food, or the excess will immediately turn to fat. On holiday and in retirement he will have to readjust his eating pattern. Many men put on weight when they retire, but they can avoid this by cutting down on their food intake and trying to keep up with some exercise.

Domestic doldrums

The most difficult person to cater for is the housewife at home. She is the person most likely to eat unwisely, largely because the best incentive to a good meal is good company. The lonely housewife finds it hard to summon up the enthusiasm to take pains over her meals. She is also surrounded by the maximum temptation, with cupboards full of food on every side. It is so easy simply to make a cup of instant coffee and a sandwich, or worse still, take a bun or a hunk of cake—easy but wrong.

Many women fall into the trap of thinking that as housewives they lead such active lives they can work off most of the food they eat. But in fact this is a fallacy. Many of the housewife's jobs are more or less sedentary. She will spend a lot of time standing quietly at the sink, by the washing-machine, sitting at the ironing-board or at a table preparing food. It takes a whole hour of washing dishes to burn up the calories provided by one egg; over half an hour's bed-making to burn up four ounces of white bread, half an hour's window-cleaning to burn up a single portion of potatoes.

The housewife must learn to take as much trouble over herself as over the rest of her family. She can start by joining them in a proper breakfast. It needn't be fattening. A poached egg is just as tasty as a fried egg, but won't add as much weight. Fruit juice can be more appetising than cereal. And an artificial sweetener can be used, if necessary, in those endless cups of coffee—but it's better to try to cut down on the drinks. Not because

51

they're dangerous in themselves, but because the temptation to nibble something with them is so strong.

If the housewife makes herself a good lunch it fulfills the double purpose of giving her sufficient energy to cope with her afternoon's work and also making her less likely to join the children at tea. If the wife is going to share an evening dinner with her husband, she shouldn't eat with the children as well, especially if they are having cakes or biscuits. The best way of avoiding this trap is to have a well-balanced lunch to deaden the appetite.

Part of the wife's trouble is that it seems a lot of fuss to cook for one. But there are some short cuts: an omelette is almost no trouble to make and if she accompanies it with a little salad it will make a very satisfactory meal. The salad will taste better if it is served with French dressing; it's quite easy to make up a bottleful of this at the beginning of the week and use a little every day. It makes the meal so much more appetising. A piece of fresh fruit would round off the meal nicely. And, in the summer, it would be a good idea to have milk instead of tea or coffee occasionally—it's good for adults as well as for children and takes no preparation at all.

Wise words for the expectant mother

The woman who is pregnant is a rather special case. She will naturally expect to put on weight, and she will tend to eat large amounts to be quite sure there is sufficient for the baby. But it is unwise to allow fat to accumulate haphazardly at this time, and the pregnant wife should watch her weight. Otherwise she will be very disheartened after the birth, when she finds none of her clothes fit her because so much of her extra weight has become permanent fat.

The average increase in weight is about 27 pounds (12.5 kg), but some doctors think this is too high. Some of the weight is due to increased fluid retention, which will right itself afterwards, but some (about 8.8 pounds, 4 kg) is fat. This fat store is designed to sustain the mother during lactation, but unfortunately as few mothers feed their babies, or do so for only short periods, a large fat store is unnecessary and should if possible be limited by sensible eating. Excessive weight gain in pregnancy can be dangerous to the foetus. In one series of 43 pregnancies in overweight women, there were five stillbirths, six forceps deliveries, three Caesarian sections and eight cases of toxaemia.

The pregnant wife should try to eat only as much as she did before, but concentrating especially on the body-building protein foods. Her doctor will advise on diet and see that she has all the extra vitamins and iron she needs, and she herself should see that she doesn't over-indulge on sweet foods. She may feel that at this time she is entitled to a little spoiling, but this shouldn't take the form of boxes of chocolates. Flowers would be a lot less dangerous!

In general, the most important thing is to remember to eat as many varied things as possible. The more mixed your diet, the better chance it has of giving you all the nourishment you need. Freshness is also important—the vitamins in food can be easily lost. Overcooking food and keeping it warm for long periods can destroy every scrap of vitamins it once possessed. Fresh fruit and vegetables are especially important in this respect.

Take your time

Finally, it is important to get used to knowing when you have had enough. It takes about ten minutes for the food you have eaten to reach your stomach and have an effect. So next time you think of having a dessert, try waiting a few minutes. You will probably find you don't want it by then. An American experiment discovered that most fat people eat not because they feel the pangs of hunger, but because they are triggered off by external things: their watch tells them it's lunchtime; they are in a restaurant and feel they must have three courses; they are worried about something or frustrated. We should only eat when our stomach tells us it is time. And when our stomach is reasonably full, we should stop. Taking more than we need is one of the gravest health problems of our time. With food, it's the quality, not the quantity, that counts.

Calorie requirements throughout life

Age range	Occupational category	Calories	Joules
Men			
18 up to 35 years	Sedentary	2700	11297
	Moderately active	3000	12552
	Very active	3600	15062
35 up to 65 years	Sedentary	2600	10878
	Moderately active	2900	12134
	Very active	3600	15062
65 up to 75 years	Sedentary	2350	9832
75 and over	Sedentary	2100	8786
Women			
18 up to 55 years	Most occupations	2200	9205
	Very active	2500	10460
55 up to 75 years	Sedentary	2050	8577
75 and over	Sedentary	1900	7950
Pregnancy, 3–9 months		2400	10042
Breast feeding		2700	11297

Age Range	Calories	Joules	Age Range	Calories	Joules
Schoolboys			*Boys and Girls*		
9 up to 12 years	2500	10460	0 up to 1 year	800	3347
12 up to 15 years	2800	11715	1 up to 2 years	1200	5021
15 up to 18 years	3000	12552	2 up to 3 years	1400	5858
Schoolgirls			3 up to 5 years	1600	6694
9 up to 12 years	2300	9623	5 up to 7 years	1800	7531
12 up to 15 years	2300	9623	7 up to 9 years	2100	8786
15 up to 18 years	2300	9623			

The number of calories you need each day is governed by how much energy you use up plus about 1500–6276 joules just to keep the body ticking over.

The fatter you are the shorter your life will be. The death rate goes up by 13 per cent for every 10 per cent by which an individual exceeds his ideal weight for his build. On average the mortality rate rises from about $1\frac{1}{2}$ times the expected rate among people up to 45 per cent overweight, to nearly 3 times the expected rate among those who are 60–74 per cent overweight. This excess mortality is largely accounted for by deaths from degenerative diseases of the heart, arteries and kidneys; diabetes and certain disorders of the liver, biliary tract and bowels. Diabetes is the biggest single threat to the obese—deaths from this condition among people who are overweight are about four times more frequent than among the rest of the population.

Weight by the inch

MEN—desirable weights, stripped, for those aged 25 and over

Height		Small frame			Medium frame			Large frame		
ft. in.	(cm)	st. lb.	st. lb.	(kg)	st. lb.	st. lb.	(kg)	st. lb.	st. lb.	(kg)
5 1	155	7 9 —	8 3	49-52	8 1 —	8 12	51-56	8 9 —	9 10	55-62
5 2	157	7 12 —	8 6	50-54	8 4 —	9 2	53-58	8 12 —	9 13	56-63
5 3	160	8 1 —	8 9	51-55	8 7 —	9 5	54-60	9 1 —	10 3	58-65
5 4	162	8 4 —	8 12	53-56	8 10 —	9 8	55-61	9 4 —	10 7	59-67
5 5	165	8 7 —	9 2	54-58	8 13 —	9 12	57-63	9 7 —	10 11	60-68
5 6	167	8 11 —	9 6	56-60	9 3 —	10 2	59-64	9 11 —	11 2	62-71
5 7	170	9 1 —	9 10	58-62	9 7 —	10 7	60-67	10 2 —	11 7	64-73
5 8	172	9 5 —	10 0	60-64	9 11 —	10 11	62-68	10 6 —	11 11	66-75
5 9	175	9 9 —	10 5	61-66	10 1 —	11 1	64-70	10 10 —	12 1	68-77
5 10	177	9 13 —	10 9	63-68	10 5 —	11 6	66-73	11 0 —	12 6	70-80
5 11	180	10 3 —	10 13	65-69	10 9 —	11 11	68-75	11 5 —	12 11	72-81
6 0	182	10 7 —	11 3	67-71	10 13 —	12 2	69-77	11 9 —	13 2	74-83
6 1	185	10 11 —	11 8	68-74	11 3 —	12 7	71-79	12 0 —	13 7	76-86
6 2	188	11 1 —	11 12	70-75	11 8 —	12 12	74-82	12 5 —	13 12	79-88
6 3	190	11 5 —	12 2	72-77	11 13 —	13 3	76-84	12 9 —	14 3	80-90

These charts are based on a survey carried out in America by 26 assurance companies, and are a valuable guide to what would be a healthy weight. Most of the research into the relationship between weight and mortality has naturally been done by the life assurance companies, but their figures are not absolutes. Dr Robert Brackenbridge, an expert on life assurance, says: 'In this country, if a man is 10 lb. overweight but otherwise has a history of good health, the assurance companies would be lenient'.

Weight by the inch

WOMEN—desirable weights, stripped, for those aged 25 and over

Height		Small frame			Medium frame			Large frame		
ft. in.	(cm)	st. lb.	st. lb.	(kg)	st. lb.	st. lb.	(kg)	st. lb.	st. lb.	(kg)
4 8	142	6 5 –	6 11	35-38	6 9 –	7 6	37-47	7 3 –	8 4	46-53
4 9	145	6 7 –	7 0	36-45	6 11 –	7 9	38-49	7 5 –	8 7	47-54
4 10	147	6 9 –	7 3	37-46	7 0 –	7 12	45-50	7 8 –	8 10	48-55
4 11	150	6 12 –	7 6	38-47	7 3 –	8 1	46-51	7 11 –	8 13	49-57
5 0	152	7 1 –	7 9	45-49	7 6 –	8 4	47-53	8 0 –	9 2	51-58
5 1	155	7 4 –	7 12	46-50	7 9 –	8 7	49-54	8 3 –	9 5	52-60
5 2	158	7 7 –	8 1	48-51	7 12 –	8 11	50-56	8 6 –	9 9	54-61
5 3	160	7 10 –	8 4	49-53	8 1 –	9 1	51-58	8 10 –	9 13	55-63
5 4	163	7 13 –	8 8	50-54	8 5 –	9 6	53-60	9 0 –	10 3	57-65
5 5	165	8 5 –	8 12	53-56	8 9 –	9 10	55-62	9 4 –	10 7	59-67
5 6	168	8 7 –	9 2	54-58	8 13 –	10 0	57-64	9 8 –	10 11	61-68
5 7	170	8 11 –	9 6	56-60	9 3 –	10 4	59-65	9 12 –	11 1	63-70
5 8	173	9 1 –	9 11	58-62	9 7 –	10 8	60-67	10 2 –	11 6	64-73
5 9	175	9 5 –	10 1	60-64	9 11 –	10 12	62-69	10 6 –	11 11	66-75
5 10	178	9 9 –	10 5	61-66	10 1 –	11 2	64-71	10 10 –	12 2	68-77

Planning menus for keeping slim

No woman wants to be tied to a guide-book for the rest of her life. She will want to let her imagination help her when she plans a meal, and to cater for her own family's particular preferences. But while she is still learning the knack of planning well-balanced meals that will nourish but not fatten, these suggested menus will be very useful. (And the recipe for every important dish mentioned is given in Part Four, the quantities being adjusted for the particular menu.)

For anyone who has seldom before planned a meal more than an hour or two in advance, it is worth pausing to consider the advantages of a weekly menu. Probably the chief blessing is that it allows you to strike a better nutritional balance, with the shortages of one day compensated for on the next. It also avoids repetition, so there is no danger of having cabbage three times in one week or of falling into the trap of always eating cold ham on Saturday.

Planning ahead also means that food can be used more efficiently and left-overs taken care of easily. You can add a few shrimps to a garnish without feeling guilty and extravagant if you know that the rest of the packet or tin will provide the main course for the following day; or you may add a couple of egg yolks to a sauce secure in the knowledge that the whites will be used up at the next meal. You will also be able, at times, to cook double quantities, once you know what your future requirements are, and so economise on time and fuel.

The most important part of meal-planning is to see that the menus suit your special needs. This is why we have divided our menus into different categories, as the meals devised for a large family with several school-children could not easily be adapted to the person living in a bed-sitter, with limited storage and cooking facilities. The sort of life you lead also affects the sort of meals you require. Everyone needs the protective foods, but the amount of energy-giving food you should eat obviously depends on how much energy you use up each day.

Finally, in considering the composition of a meal, the appearance and presentation are also important. A meal that looks appetising will be tackled with more enthusiasm than an equally nutritious meal that looks drab. Contrasts of colour and texture are important.

Nothing to Excess

The key to all our menus is balance. A balanced diet is a healthy diet; *all* the nutrients—proteins, fats; carbohydrates, minerals, vitamins, roughage and water—are essential to the human body. None of them can be eliminated entirely, but they should be kept in balance with each other. If you are overweight you should review your eating habits to see which way the balance is tipped. You will almost certainly find that your intake of carbohydrates plus fats is greater than your intake of all the other nutrients put together. The balance has to be readjusted.

Both carbohydrates and fats are a mixture of advantages and disadvantages. A certain proportion of both is essential in the diet, just as too much of either is a mistake. Carbohydrate foods, for example, are cheaper than fats or animal proteins and so provide a good source of energy at less expense. They are also needed to help the body utilise protein, and they can be converted into heat and energy very quickly indeed.

The drawbacks of carbohydrate foods are, first, that they do not contain sufficient vitamins for our needs, so that anyone eating a largely carbohydrate diet runs the risk of going short of vital vitamins; secondly, they are often eaten in excess of need and turn into fat and, thirdly, they can be indigestible if eaten in large quantities and are also a major cause of tooth decay.

Fats provide concentrated energy, giving a large capacity for a small bulk. They also act as a carrier within the body for vitamins A, D, E and K, and are a necessary agent in the absorption of these vitamins. They satisfy hunger more efficiently than any other foodstuff because they are absorbed more slowly, and this slows down the absorption of all the other constituents of the meal as well, so the body remains satisfied for a longer period. They also play an important part in the presentation of a meal, as they make many other foods—such as bread with butter or salad with dressing—more palatable.

The chief drawback to using fats in the diet is that if they are eaten in over-large quantities they can lead to obesity. And an excessive intake of fat can actually hinder the absorption of the vitamins the fat carries, as the body cannot deal effectively with such quantities. But fats are not taken in excessive quantities so often as are carbohydrates, because they have such a high satiety value. Most people simply cannot stomach large amounts. Although they are potentially as likely to lead to obesity as carbohydrates, in practice they are unlikely to be taken to excess. There are exceptions to this—when they are taken as an accompaniment to excess carbohydrates, as butter on bread or baked potatoes or the fat included in pastries, potato crisps and chipped or sauté potatoes. In these cases, a low carbohydrate diet would automatically lead to a reduction in the fat intake as well.

To avoid taking either fat or carbohydrates in harmful quantities, you must ensure that your daily menu contains adequate helpings of the other chief foods. Opposite is the chart, with recommended helpings, of the foods you should try to eat daily to maintain a balanced diet.

58

Daily requirements

Milk	Pre-school children, $1\frac{1}{2}$ to $1\frac{3}{4}$ pints (350 ml–1 litre) School children and adolescents, not less than $1\frac{1}{2}$ pints (850 ml) Adults, 1 pint (600 ml) Expectant and nursing mothers, $1\frac{3}{4}$ pints (1 litre)
Cheese	1 oz. (25–30 g) daily
Eggs	Three to five a week whenever practicable
Meat, fish	A generous serving daily. Serve liver or kidney once weekly if possible
Potatoes	A serving daily, especially for adolescents
Vegetables	Generous servings daily
Fruit	Use raw fruit or tomatoes daily. All fruits are valuable
Butter/Margarine/Fats/Oils	1 oz. (25–30 g) daily for the average adult Pre-school children need little Adolescents and heavy manual workers need more than the average adult—$1\frac{1}{2}$ oz. (40 g) Adults should restrain their appetite for fatty foods
Bread	1–2 oz. (30–55 g) daily. Adolescents may require an extra ounce or so.

The servings of the different types of food given above show the requirements of normal, healthy people leading a fairly active life. Certain special categories of people, however, have slightly modified needs.

Children obviously need rather different food from their parents, as they are still growing and need extra quantities of the body-building foods. Children under five require 1 ounce (25–30 g) of meat, fish, or liver daily, $1\frac{1}{2}$ to $1\frac{3}{4}$ pints (850 ml–1 litre) of milk daily, and three to four eggs a week. You must also include food that requires chewing to develop their teeth and jaws—making a child eat up his crusts is still worthwhile. They usually prefer meals that are simply presented, and should not be given food that is too highly seasoned, nor too much fried food, as there is a limit to the amount of fat they can absorb. Try also to avoid offering pastry, biscuits, cakes, confectionery and heavy puddings. Go back to the list of daily servings and see if you couldn't give them fruit instead.

Adolescents need more food than adults, particularly food to give them energy. Boys of 16 to 18 and girls of 14 to 16 will eat about one-quarter as much again as an adult. Girls of 16 and over need less food than boys of that age. Teenagers should be given large quantities of green vegetables, some root vegetables and some potatoes, but cakes and sweets should be limited. Food to keep them going during the day is especially necessary; a good breakfast will go a long way towards eliminating mid-morning snacks. The hormonal and emotional disturbances of adolescence may interfere with the growing child's eating habits, so it is important to see that the extra food the teenager needs is taken in the form of body-building proteins rather than as comforting but fattening carbohydrates.

The adolescent's social life will affect his evening eating habits. It is best if he can have a substantial evening meal that includes milk, meat, potatoes and vegetables, cheese and fruit. The danger is that he will go off to the local pub for beer and a pie or to a bowling alley for soft drinks, sandwiches and crisps. This pattern can probably only be avoided by teaching the teenager the principles of sound nutrition and giving him every opportunity at home to put them into practice. At this age he is perfectly capable of realising that it is better to have a good meal at home before setting out for the evening than to exist on a badly designed diet — but he will tend to follow the line of least resistance.

The evening meal is especially important if the midday one is taken away from home. The school dinner is all too often the subject of bad jokes, and compensated for at a local tuckshop, while the teenager at work with not much money to spare may be having only a snack at lunchtime, padded out by bread rolls and pastries. In either case the high carbohydrate intake of the lunch should be balanced out by a high-protein evening meal. Teenagers should also continue to drink milk every day: at this age they need it even more than younger children, because their protein, calcium and vitamin requirements are greater. Since cold milk also quenches the thirst, it has the additional advantage of reducing the temptation to buy sweetened fruit drinks or fizzy lemonade.

Pregnant and nursing mothers need to watch their diet, but the danger is that they may over-estimate their needs at this time. They do not need additional amounts of energy foods, as the period of pregnancy especially is often a time of reduced activity, since the mother has difficulty in moving about. The intake of carbohydrates and fats should not go up, and the pregnant mother must beware of putting on unnecessary fat. But milk consumption must, naturally, be increased, to about $1\frac{3}{4}$ pints (1 litre) daily. This should be taken in milky, not sugary drinks, in custards and milk puddings. If the mother finds it really difficult to tolerate milk, she should make up her allowance by increasing her cheese consumption. Other protein foods such as meat, fish, eggs, fruit and green vegetables should be increased slightly, as there is a special need for body-building foods.

Elderly people need the same quality of food as other adults, but the quantity they need varies. Protective foods are still very necessary, but the energy requirement will probably be reduced. Older people are usually less active, so they don't need as much food as they did in the prime of life. The food that suits them best is readily digestible, fairly low in fat, with moderate protein allowances and a high vitamin and mineral content. The protein is required simply for maintenance, rather than for building the body tissues, and can be supplied by milk, eggs and lean meat. Rich desserts, soups and sauces should be avoided, and the intake of butter, cream and bacon watched. The very elderly may find chewing a problem, and then soft foods such as minced meat, flaked fish and creamed foods will be more acceptable than tough grills and roasts. Desserts should be simple—usually milk-based, with added fruit. Vitamin C is essential for the elderly.

Month's menus for young married couple

(both working and taking midday meal out, so evening meal only is shown; for breakfast see notes below)

Young newly married couples are in the best position to enjoy a good diet, as they can start from scratch to build up the sort of food pattern they want, and they have complete control over what they choose, with only themselves to please. They don't have to bother about keeping their menus simple to please a child, or avoiding exotic dishes to satisfy an un-adventurous parent; they can experiment with all the foods in the world to find the ones that please them most.

They should use the daily servings set out on page 59 as a guide, aiming to see that some food in each category is included every day. Once this pattern has been established, they can modify it at different stages in their lives—during pregnancy, feeding subsequent children, taking care of elderly relatives or during periods of sickness—without changing the basic structure of the diet.

The menus that follow here do not include desserts, as these seldom add anything except carbohydrate to the meal, and should be avoided by anyone wanting to remain slim. Instead, the meal can be rounded off with cheese or fresh fruit, though of course a dessert can be enjoyed occasionally without disrupting the whole of the established pattern, so long as it does not become a habit.

Breakfast

Chilled Orange Juice	Fresh Fruit	Glass of PLJ
Poached Egg on Toast	Boiled Egg	Grilled Kipper
Toast/Butter/Spread	Toast/Butter/Spread	Toast/Butter/Spread
Tea/Coffee/Milk	Tea/Coffee/Milk	Tea/Coffee/Milk

It cannot be repeated too often that this is an essential meal, but it is also very much a matter of personal taste. These examples show the kind of things to aim at—as you see, they need not take long to prepare. Build up on the basics of fruit, protein, with a little carbohydrate.

Day Dinner

1 Grilled Rump Steak
Brazilian Salad
Potatoes

2 Orange-braised Pork Chops
Courgettes   Steamed Potatoes

3 Chicken and Pepper Pie
Asparagus Spears

4 Liver Hot-Pot
Cabbage
Jacket Potatoes

5 Ham Salad
Pickled Beets

6 Soused Herrings
Baked Potato   Cole Slaw

7 Pineapple Lamb Casserole
Rice   Tomato and Watercress

8 Escalopes Fines Herbes
Broad Beans
Potatoes   Tomatoes

9 French Beef and Olive Casserole
Noodles   Endive Salad

10 Fish Provençale
Rice
Green Salad

11 Pork Chops with Apple
Tossed Green Salad

12 Devonshire Squab Pie
Baked Tomatoes
Apple and Celery Salad

13 Swiss Steak
Baked Potatoes   Broccoli

14 Indonesian Fish
Rice   Omelette Garnish

15 Vegetable Platter with
Beef Balls

16 Chicken Maryland
Baked Tomatoes   French Beans

17 Curried Lamb
Green Salad
Carrots

18 Ham Montmorency
Baked Potatoes   Broccoli

19 Meatballs Sweet and Sour
Rice   Green Salad

20 Fish Braised in Cider
Brussels Sprouts   Potatoes

21 Roast Beef
Roast Potatoes
Leeks   Pumpkin

22 Beef Potato Bake
Vegetable Salad

23 Liver Piquant
Beans   Tomatoes

24 Carbonade of Beef
Baked Potatoes
Broccoli

25 Grilled Chicken Joints
Orange and Celery Salad
Minted Potatoes   Watercress

26 Smothered Pork Chop
Green Salad   Noodles

27 Chicken Rice Pimiento
Leek and Lemon Salad

28 Lamb Cutlets with Barbecue
Sauce   Creamed Potatoes
French Beans

Month's menus for very active couple with teenage family
(According to circumstances, the larger 'dinner' meal can be taken at midday or in the evening, and the lighter one switched to the other time.)

62

People who lead very active lives and habitually use up large amounts of energy every day usually eat the right amount of food instinctively. They need an increased supply of fuel to sustain them in their activities, and this stimulates their appetite, so that intake and output are balanced.

Their extra requirements affect also the kind of food they should eat. The active family's food pattern must be based in the first place, like everyone else's, on the foods needed for body-building and maintenance. These protein foods are needed simply to keep the body ticking over, and are absolutely essential. But the extra energy output of active people means that, in addition to the food needed to maintain the body in good repair, they need food for energy. Such people can eat more carbohydrates than usual without putting on weight, because they burn them up in their activities; the extra starch is turned into fuel immediately and never stored as fatty tissue. For this reason, the menu suggestions given here include toast regularly for breakfast and potatoes—or a substitute—every evening. So long as the family remains energetic, these will do no harm. Incidentally, it is assumed that the lunch/supper meal will include tea, coffee or a milk drink.

Breakfast

This meal can be very similar to the one suggested for the young married couple. However, adolescents need to keep up a high milk consumption, so they should use milk frequently as a drink, or have it with their stewed fruit. Yeast or meat extracts, too, should be used frequently, as they are good sources of the B vitamins.

Some sample menus are given, but once again you will of course base the meal on the dishes you enjoy and find it easy to prepare in a hurry, while trying to keep to the basic scheme.

Chilled Fruit Juice
Grilled Sausage
   and Tomato
Toast/Butter/Spread
Tea/Coffee/Milk

Fresh Fruit
Poached Egg on Cheese Toast
Toast/Butter/Spread
Tea/Coffee/Milk

Grapefruit Halves
Bacon and Eggs
Toast/Butter/Spread
Tea/Coffee/Milk

Day	Lunch/Supper	Dinner
1	Grilled Cod Steaks Crunchy Salad Bread Rolls	Hamburger Steaks Roast Potatoes Green Beans Tomatoes Apple Crumble and Custard

Day	Lunch/Supper	Dinner
2	Quiche Anglaise Tomato Salad	Burgundy Beef Baked Potatoes Broccoli Fruit Whip
3	Salerno Fish Mushroom Salad Fresh Fruit	Stuffed Lamb Chops Minted Potatoes Cole Slaw Peach and Orange Flan
4	Savoury Pancakes Green Salad	Crumbed Brains Harvard Beets Cress Creamed Potatoes Blackberry Whip
5	Cheese and Leek Soup Open Sandwiches	Malayan Curried Beef and Rice Spring Salad Banana Nut Cream
6	Cheese Soufflé Tossed Mixed Salad	Baked Haddock with Tartare Sauce French Beans Sautéed Potatoes Fresh Fruit
7	Scalloped Potatoes Cucumber and Tomato Salad	Orange-Apple Steak Broccoli Baked Custard Fruit
8	Leek and Bacon Savoury Bread Rolls Fresh Fruit	Colonial Goose Roast Potatoes Cauliflower French Beans Apricot Sponge
9	Beef Potato Bake Sweet Pepper Salad Cheese	Baked Mackerel Jacket Potatoes Sautéed Courgettes Fresh Fruit Salad
10	Welsh Rarebit de Luxe Endive and Tomato Salad Fresh Fruit	Cold Lamb Potato Salad Carrots Broccoli Honeycomb Castles
11	Stuffed Peppers Cheese Bread Rolls	Chicken Marengo Rice Green Bean Salad Fresh Fruit
12	Savoury Fish Stew Noodles Fresh Fruit	Veal and Mushroom Rolls Braised Celery Strawberry Sponge

Day	Lunch/Supper	Dinner
13	Country Soup Spanish Omelette Fresh Fruit	Belted Sausage Casserole Baked Potatoes Spinach Cheese and Biscuits
14	Baked Cheese Fondue Cole Slaw Fresh Fruit	Barbecued Lamb Chops Broccoli Potatoes Banana Sherbet
15	Ratatouille Niçoise Crispbread and Cheese	Veal Cutlets Sweet Corn Tomatoes Minted Potatoes Fresh Fruit
16	Savoury Baked Eggs Mixed Vegetable Salad	Pork Liver Loaf Roast Potatoes Pumpkin Spinach Cheese and Biscuits
17	Fruit, Nut and Cheese Salad Cold Meat Loaf	Baked Haddock with Mushrooms Baked Potatoes Broccoli Crispy Top
18	Stuffed Marrow and Tomato Sauce Tossed Green Salad	Chicken Catalonian Style Buttered Noodles Dressed French Beans Fresh Fruit
19	Risotto Green Salad	Braised Liver with Bacon Grilled Tomatoes Cauliflower Raspberry Crème
20	Tomato and Fish Salad French Bread	Silverside with Carrots Potatoes Cabbage Queen of Puddings
21	Homestead Fry Leek and Lemon Salad	Tipsy Chops Baked Tomatoes Cauliflower Baked Apples and Orange Sauce
22	Hunter's Harvest Stew Fresh Fruit	Shish Kebabs Rice Green Salad Cheese and Biscuits
23	Cheese and Asparagus Flan Lettuce and Tomato Salad	Zesty Haddock Broccoli Noodles Orange Mousse
24	Sliced Luncheon Meat Rice, Celery and Apple Salad	Veal and Mushroom Rolls Brussels Sprouts Carrots Fresh Fruit
25	Pizza Napoletana Apple and Celery Salad	Barbecued Chicken Casserole Minted Potatoes French Beans Fresh Fruit Salad

Day	Lunch/Supper	Dinner
26	Macaroni Cheese Apple and Celery Salad	Goulash Noodles Spinach Spiced Pear Grill
27	Gammon and Mushroom Bake Endive and Tomato Salad Crispbread and Cheese	Chicken and Pepper Pie Celery Potatoes Carrots Plum and Orange Salad
28	Cheese Omelette Waldorf Salad	Rabbit Hot-Pot Courgettes Tomatoes Rhubarb Almond Crème

A month's menus for the bed-sitter cook

(Supper dishes for one, prepared with limited cooking facilities.)

One of the most difficult situations for anyone wishing to eat well is to live in a bed-sitter. The cooking facilities usually consist of a single gas ring near the floor, a ring and a grill, or a small electric oven and hot-plate. And the bed-sitter that has a refrigerator is rare indeed, yet the bed-sitter tenant has a special need for somewhere to store food as it is difficult to use up large quantities at once. All too often there will be three-quarters of a cabbage left over, or the remains of half a pound of sausages or a packet of bacon.

The difficulties of cooking in a bed-sitter make it all too likely that the girl (or man) will give up in despair and live on beans on toast. Yet the bed-sitter tenant is usually a young person just starting out to work, and needing a full and nourishing diet. Breakfast is the first essential, and need not take much time or preparation. An egg can be boiled while you are getting up (the great advantage of living in one room is that you can actually cook as you dress). Just fruit juice, an egg and a slice of toast will start the day off well.

People living in bed-sitters should try to have a proper midday meal if this is at all possible, as this will simplify the evening catering. But if you do have only a snack at lunch, then the evening meal *must* provide all the rest of the essential foods. It is best to aim at one satisfying dish rather than at a number, which will always seem too much trouble to make for one. Fresh fruit or a piece of cheese will always serve for a dessert and will give valuable vitamins or protein. Similarly, there is little point in trying to start your meal off with soup if you have no oven in which to keep the main course hot while you eat it. Concentrate your energy on to one very good main course such as a casserole—the dish that every bed-sitter cook comes to rely on in the end. And try never to get into the habit of thinking that it's not worth cooking just for one. Everybody needs to eat well, and though it may take a little more effort, it will always be worthwhile.

Day	Supper
1	Cream of Tomato Soup Ham and Cheese Salad Tea or Coffee
2	Liver and Bacon Kebabs Tomato and Cucumber Salad Tea, Coffee or Milk
3	Fish and Bacon Chowder Ryvita Fresh Fruit Tea or Coffee
4	Mushroom Omelette Grapefruit Slaw Tea, Coffee or Milk
5	Spicy Rarebit Fresh Fruit Tea or Coffee
6	Grilled Cod Steaks Belmont Salad Cheese and Biscuits Tea or Coffee
7	Rabbit and Bacon Blanquette French Beans Fresh Fruit Tea, Coffee or Milk
8	Crab Salad Mornay Fresh Fruit Salad Tea or Coffee
9	Shish Kebabs Apple and Celery Salad Tea, Coffee or Milk
10	Grilled Lamb Chops California Salad Cheese and Biscuits Tea or Coffee
11	Ham and Cheese Rolls Sweet and Sour Cucumber Salad Tea, Coffee or Milk
12	Portuguese Plaice Rice, Pimiento and Tomato Salad Tea, Coffee or Milk
13	Grilled Ham and Pineapple Endive and Tomato Salad Tea, Coffee or Milk
14	Braised Kidney with Tomatoes and Mushrooms Apple and Celery Salad Tea, Coffee or Milk
15	Carrot Soup Chicken Joint Salad Royale Tea or Coffee
16	Mediterranean Omelette Green Salad Fresh Fruit Tea or Coffee
17	Rice and Meat Salad Ryvita and Cheese Tea or Coffee
18	Grilled Pork Chop with Mushrooms Fresh Fruit Tea, Coffee or Milk
19	Fish Olives with Cheesy Mustard Sauce Cucumber Salad Fresh Fruit Tea or Coffee
20	Scrambled Eggs and Kidney Fresh Fruit Tea or Coffee
21	Spanish Cod Fresh Fruit Tea, Coffee or Milk
22	Leek and Liver Casserole Fresh Fruit Tea, Coffee or Milk

Day	Supper	26	Chop Suey

Day Supper

23 Haddock Rarebit
Dressed French Beans
Fresh Fruit
Tea or Coffee

24 Grilled Steak and Tomatoes
Cheese and Biscuits
Tea or Coffee

25 Smothered Pork Chop
French Beans
Tea, Coffee or Milk

26 Chop Suey
Fresh Fruit
Tea, Coffee or Milk

27 Tomato Bouillon
Chicken Mandarin Salad
Cheese and Biscuits
Tea or Coffee

28 Veal, Ham and Mushroom
Fricassee
Broccoli
Fresh Fruit
Tea or Coffee

Good health on a budget

(A month's full menus based on less expensive foods.)

The housewife who has to count every penny before she spends it will inevitably have to plan her family's meals more carefully. But a limited income need not prevent her from providing sensible meals. The best foods are undoubtedly expensive, especially if there is a large family to cater for, so it is important to modify the diet slightly and use more of the cheaper protein foods such as eggs, milk and cheese. The cheaper cuts of meat will also be useful; price is not necessarily the best guide to meat, which tends to be high in price if it is tender and cheap if it is tough. Yet the tough meat may be equally nutritious and better flavoured, and it can easily be made tender by slow and careful cooking. A pound of shin of beef gives the same food value as a pound of beef topside, at lower cost.

In addition to the cheaper cuts of meat, the economical housewife can add heart, liver, kidney and sweetbreads into the family menu; fish, too, gives generous helpings of protein, minerals and vitamins and is sometimes cheaper than meat. Fresh vegetables and fruit will come down in price when they are in season, and are always cheaper, pound for pound, than meat. They should be used in large quantities in the tight-budget diet to add bulk. Potatoes must not be forgotten, as they provide essential nourishment, but they should not be used in more than one dish a day. Pulses can be used in moderation in soups, etc., to give added food value and staying power.

It may be difficult to stretch the budget to include all the milk that is needed, and adults anyway are often reluctant to drink it. But the housewife on a budget can use dried skim milk in cooking without any great expense and go some way towards fulfilling the demands of a balanced diet. In the menus which follow we assume that the lunch/supper meal will include tea, coffee or a milk drink.

68

Breakfast Fruit Juice, and Egg in some
form *or*
Stewed Fruit with Cereal and Milk
Toast/Butter/Spread
Tea/Coffee/Milk

Day	Lunch/Supper	Dinner
1	Mulligatawny Soup— Crispbread Cheddar Cheese Salad Fresh Fruit	Goulash Noodles, Courgettes
2	Cheese Omelette Tossed Green Salad	Marinaded Lamb Kebabs Rice Cole Slaw
3	Celery Noodle Soup Kentucky Salad	Cider-baked Herrings Baked Tomatoes Broccoli, Potatoes
4	Baked Celery Cheese Sliced Luncheon Meat	Chicken Casserole Baked Potatoes, Spinach
5	Egg Flip and Potato Pie Green Salad	Haddock Roly-Poly Brussels Sprouts Carrots
6	Welsh Rarebit de Luxe Health Salad	Roast Leg of Lamb Baked Onions and Potatoes Creamed Pumpkin Peas
7	Sliced Lamb Whirligig Salad	Russian Casseroled Beefsteak Cauliflower with Cheese Sauce Baked Tomatoes
8	Tomato Plaice Fillets Crispbread or Rolls Fresh Fruit	Curried Lamb Rice, Tossed Green Salad
9	Cheese and Mushroom Soufflé Salad Anna	Heart Hot-pot Creamed Potatoes French Beans
10	Country Soup Open Sandwiches	Grilled Cod Steaks Rice, Celery and Apple Salad
11	Cheese and Chopped Ham Salad Bread Rolls, Fruit	Liver and Bacon Casserole Cabbage Pickled Beets

Day	Lunch/Supper	Dinner
12	Stuffed Marrow with Sauce Crispbread Fresh Fruit	Meat Loaf Baked Potatoes Tomato and Onion Bake
13	Cold Meat Loaf Pear and Ginger Salad	Chicken Marengo Courgettes Carrots
14	Carrot Soup Open Sandwich	Halibut Mozzarella Orange and Celery Salad Brussels Sprouts
15	Cheese and Egg Pie Fresh Fruit	Minted Breast of Lamb Potatoes, French Beans Baked Tomatoes
16	Herring Salad Orange Mousse	Belted Sausage Casserole Jacket Potatoes, Broccoli
17	Pot-au-Feu Crispbread Fresh Fruit	Chicken and Tongue Loaf Spinach with Cheese Potatoes
18	Sliced Chicken and Tongue Loaf Green Salad Fresh Fruit	Fish and Bacon Rolls Tomato and Cucumber Salad Potatoes
19	Potato and Cheese Soup Kentucky Salad	Grilled Lamb Chops with Devil's Sauce Brussels Sprouts Carrots
20	Haddock Rarebit Tossed Green Salad	Braised Kidneys with Tomatoes and Mushrooms Creamed Potatoes, French Beans
21	Tomato and Mushroom Omelette Crispbread Fresh Fruit	Kofta Noodles Celery and Green Pepper Salad
22	Cream of Tomato Soup Ham Salad	Spanish Cod with Red Pepper Sauce Cucumber and Tomato Salad Potatoes
23	Cheesy Beef Patties Baked Tomatoes	Beef Olives with Orange Creamed Potatoes Broccoli
24	Cod and Cottage Cheese Cocottes Orange Salad	Finnish Cabbage and Lamb Hot-pot Carrots Watercress

Lunch/Supper	Dinner
25 Cheese and Chopped Ham Salad Bread Roll Fresh Fruit	Baked Stuffed Liver Jacket Potatoes Courgettes
26 Mixed Grill Potato Salad	Curried Fish Rice Tossed Green Salad
27 Cheese and Corn Soufflé Fresh Fruit	Summer Casserole Creamed Potatoes Brussels Sprouts
28 Chicken and Celery Salad Crispbread	Hamburger Steaks Baked Potatoes Green Beans Tomatoes

Two dozen midday meals for the housewife at home

The housewife at home has one advantage over other solitary eaters: she normally has a full-size kitchen at her disposal and a store-cupboard to dip into. Whereas an old-age pensioner living alone may not be able to use just a little bit of lettuce in a salad, or a few mixed vegetables as part of a Spanish omelette because she would not know when the left-overs could be used, the housewife can plan to use such ingredients, knowing the remainder will be used up in the family meals.

She has the additional benefit of choice. A housewife can afford to buy two or three different cheeses, knowing they will all be eaten up before they can go stale, whereas the single girl in a bed-sitter will have to finish all the Cheddar herself before she can risk buying Double Gloucester. The housewife will be able to pick from a number of cans of soup, or decide between bread, crispbread or crackers as an accompaniment.

The chief drawback to the housewife's diet is that she is so used to cooking for other people, she often finds it difficult to be bothered cooking just for one person. But she needs a good diet just as much as the other members of her family. She should try to eat some meat, fish, cheese or eggs every lunchtime. A light but appetising and nourishing lunch will help her to avoid the temptations of elevenses and afternoon tea. And it can give her the opportunity to experiment with tempting new dishes that she thinks her family might enjoy. She should try to think of her lunch as a treat rather than as a chore, a welcome break in the day's routine, when she can rest and enjoy herself. The dishes suggested here will not take long to prepare—we don't want to add to the work—but they can be enjoyed with a favourite radio programme or book to give a necessary rest.

Day	Lunch		
1	Cream of Celery Soup Ryvita and cheese Fresh Fruit Tea or Coffee	13	Grilled Sausages Savoury Grilled Tomatoes Tea or Coffee
2	Grilled Lamb Chop Tomatoes Cheese Tea or Coffee	14	Poached Egg Mornay Fresh Fruit Tea or Coffee
3	Mexican Scramble Fresh Fruit Tea or Coffee	15	Mexicalli Soup Open Sandwiches Tea or Coffee
4	Cold Meat with Green Salad Fresh Fruit Tea or Coffee	16	Sliced Ham White Salad Platter Tea, Coffee or Milk
5	Cheese and Leek Soup Open Sandwich Tea or Coffee	17	Quick Pizza Green Salad Tea or Coffee
6	Eggs Florentine Ryvita and Cheese Tea or Coffee	18	Cheese and Carrot Salad Tea or Coffee
7	Peach Cheese Salad Tea or Coffee	19	Tomato Soup Cheese and Ham Roll Tea or Coffee
8	Ham Omelette Fresh Fruit Tea or Coffee	20	Cauliflower au Gratin Fresh Fruit Tea or Coffee
9	Chilli-burgers Tomatoes Tea or Coffee	21	Kedgeree Orange and Celery Salad Tea or Coffee
10	Curried Eggs Sunshine Salad Tea or Coffee	22	Grilled Gammon with Mushrooms Fresh Fruit Tea or Coffee
11	Frankfurter Salad Tea or Coffee	23	Grapefruit and Shrimp Salad Tea or Coffee
12	Welsh Rarebit de luxe Fresh Fruit Tea or Coffee	24	Egg Salad Tea or Coffee

Packed lunches, with menu suggestions

Packed lunches need very careful planning if they are not to become monotonous and badly-balanced. The carry-out meal should contain as much nourishment as an ordinary one, and be substantial enough to prevent hunger-pangs appearing halfway through the afternoon.

The lunch should include a drink of some description—milk, tea or coffee, fruit juice or soup. These can be varied according to the time of year; hot soup might be very acceptable on a cold winter's day, fruit juice at high summer. The packed lunch should also include fresh fruit in some form. The most suitable are oranges, apples, bananas and grapes. Soft fruit can be messy and peaches, though delicious, are all too often damaged by lunchtime. But a small melon would be very good in the summer if the seeds can be discreetly disposed of.

Sandwiches, of course, provide the commonest basis of the packed lunch and are undoubtedly one of the simplest and easiest ways of packaging food. For those who are actively slimming, starch-reduced bread together with a low-fat spread should be used. The fillings should be varied as often as possible. In addition to simple things such as meat, egg, cheese or ham, many unusual and interesting fillings can be achieved by combining two or more ingredients:

Beef with horseradish sauce, onions, gherkins and French mustard;

Chicken or other white meat with celery, mayonnaise or olives and tomato sauce;

Salmon or smoked salmon with lettuce and lemon juice or cucumber and tomato sauce;

Crab, lobster or other shellfish with cress and cucumber or tomato and mayonnaise;

Smoked cods' roe with tomato, lettuce and lemon juice;

Various kinds of cheese with celery and pickles, chives and parsley or apple and chutney;

Egg—hard-boiled or scrambled—with cream cheese and chopped chives or capers and tomato sauce;

Vegetable mixtures such as mushrooms, tomatoes and parsley; cooked peas, mint and mayonnaise; olives, lettuce and vinegar; pickled onion, cucumber and piquant sauce;

Fruit mixtures such as apple, lemon juice and nutmeg, mashed banana, chopped raisins and orange juice; dates, ginger and chopped apple.

Although the sandwich is the most usual basis of the packed lunch, there are alternatives. Open sandwiches can be served up on a base of wholemeal, ryebread or pumpernickel, spread with butter or a savoury butter and topped and garnished in a variety of ways. Ideally, they should be made on the day they are needed, and it is easier if the components can be packed in individual containers and assembled when they are needed. But if they have to be packed in advance, a shallow container in which the sandwich fits without too much shaking around is best.

73

Toppings for Open Sandwiches

Pâté
Luncheon meat
Black sausage
Cold meats—ham, beef,
lamb, salt beef, etc.

Salami
Hard-boiled egg
Salmon
Herring
Shrimp

Sardines
Anchovies
Cheese

Sliced shredded carrots, radishes, lettuce, cucumber, peppers and onion add colour or contrast.

Good garnishes are herbs, dill, parsley, chives or piped mayonnaise.

Sliced cold meat or pie and salad also provides an easy packed lunch, since it takes little preparation. Left-overs from the previous day's meal, such as a joint of chicken or duck, a slice or two from the Sunday roast, a cold lamb chop, meat loaf, a patty or slice of pie can be accompanied by salad, vegetables or fruit, and parcelled in tinfoil or a strong covered container.

Packed Lunch Suggestions

Mexicalli Soup
Ham and Cheese Rolls
Green Salad and Tomatoes
Fresh Fruit

Mushroom Soup
Chicken Joint
Sunshine Salad
Fresh Fruit

Onion Soup
Ham and Mushroom Patties
Fresh Fruit

Quick Tomato Soup
Chicken and Rice Salad
Fresh Fruit

Chicken Soup
Open Sandwich
Fresh Fruit

Oxtail Soup
Scotch Eggs with Cole Slaw
Fresh Fruit

Carrot Soup
Cheese and Egg Pie
Green Salad
Fresh Fruit

Tomato Bouillon
Sliced Ham with Orange and
Celery Salad
Fresh Fruit

Vichyssoise
Corned Beef and
Asparagus Rolls
Fresh Fruit

Entertaining without putting on weight

(Eight menus covering meals for two, four, six and eight people.)

Some people find it impossible to entertain successfully while actually on a slimming diet. But once you have got your weight down to the level you want, you can start once more to think of food as a treat, and of dinner parties as a pleasure to be shared with friends.

Unless you know your guests extremely well, however, it is safer not to offer a lot of very fattening foods. Even though you no longer have a weight problem, they very well may have. People don't always talk about their diets, especially if they are not trying to lose very much, but it is unwise to assume that all visitors will be happy to eat everything unless you are absolutely sure.

The menus we suggest here do contain some starchy foods—potatoes, rice, toast. These will not put weight on if you don't eat too much or too often, and they are an almost indispensable part of good eating. But we have planned them so that there is not more than one starchy element in each menu. You don't want to follow cream by potatoes by sugar, but a little of what you fancy will do no harm. And, finally, don't insist on your guests having second helpings; they may have a good reason for refusing.

For Two

Watercress Soup
Lobster Thermidor
Dressed French Beans
Raspberry delight

Ham and Melon
Filet Mignon
Grilled Tomatoes
Tossed Green Salad
Cheese Board

For Four

Grilled Grapefruit
Carpet-bag Steak
Brussels Sprouts
Potatoes
Strawberries in Burgundy

Tomato Consommé
Sweet and Sour Pork
Tossed Green Salad
Ginger Fruit Salad

For Six

Chicken Liver Pâté
Grilled Salmon Steaks
Asparagus Spears
Rice Salad
Strawberry Cream

Frozen Pineapple Cocktail
Trout and Almonds
Atlantic Salad
New Potatoes
Summer Fruit Sundae

For Eight

Moulded Prawn Salad
Cherry-glazed Duck
Broccoli   New Potatoes
Apricot and Pineapple Whip

Shrimp Courgettes
Swiss Veal
Tomato and Cucumber Salad
Sunshine Salad
Snow Peaks

What to choose when eating out

A meal at a restaurant can be quite a hazard for anyone who is trying to lose weight or to keep slim. In the first place, everything about the ambiance of a restaurant is specifically designed to encourage you to eat. The relaxed atmosphere, the comfortable chairs and the sense of cultivated enjoyment all conspire to lower your guard and make you feel that some temptations should be succumbed to.

How you react will partly depend on whether you are there as host or guest, for business or pleasure. If you are being taken out to dinner by friends for a special occasion, it would be tactless to insist on keeping rigidly to your individual diet and not accepting the treats they offer. But if it is simply a business occasion, or a meal eaten while out shopping or on a journey, you can bear the principles of your diet in mind when you study the menu.

For the first course, remember that clear soup is less fattening than thick or creamy types, and avoid taking a bread roll with either. Seafood cocktails in a rich mayonnaise dressing are also dangerous, but oysters in season would be safe if you want something fishy. Avocado pears, especially if they are brimming with vinaigrette dressing or filled with shrimp cocktail, should be avoided: a melon or grapefruit would be a better choice or, best of all, fruit or tomato juice. And try to resist an apéritif; save your alcohol allowance for one glass of good wine.

When it comes to selecting the main dish, the principle of simple food, simply presented, should be followed. Although there is a natural tendency to choose in a restaurant the sort of food you find too much trouble to prepare at home, those rich sauces and complicated dishes are also the dishes most likely to prove fattening. Grilled lean meat or fish, with salad, tomatoes or green vegetables in season, can be a delicious alternative. Or you might enjoy a freshly-made omelette. If the ingredients are really first-class, the plain dishes of your diet will be every bit as good as the more complicated ones. You should at all costs avoid thick stews, potatoes in all their forms, rice, pasta and rich dressings.

If you have no choice in the selection of food available, but have to accept a fixed menu, you will just have to eat what is put in front of you and make up for it the next day by eating a little less. But if you have the option, take fresh fruit or cheese instead of a dessert. One piece of fruit is enough, or about one ounce (25 g) cheese with no more than three water biscuits. But don't feel you have to spoil your meal. Once your weight is down to the desired level, an occasional indulgence will not be a hazard as long as the basic pattern of sensible eating is normally observed.

76

Feeding children sensibly

Children are born with a natural appetite for food which the shrewd mother will do everything she can to encourage. Unless she indulges and exaggerates his fads and fancies, there is every reason for the child to grow up enjoying most of the food she offers him, although most children naturally develop some genuine aversions.

They generally prefer to have a regular mealtime, which contributes to their sense of security, and they generally prefer straightforward dishes in which they can recognise all the elements. In one way children are extremely easy to cater for, since they usually have no objection to having the same breakfast day after day. Indeed, they may even ask for it, as they get very attached to familiar routines.

Children need $1\frac{1}{2}$ to $1\frac{3}{4}$ pints (850 ml–1 litre) of milk a day; some meat, poultry or fish; an egg; green and root vegetables once or twice a day, some of them raw; fruit two or three times a day, half of it raw and always including some orange juice; starchy vegetables once or twice a day and whole-grain bread and cereals once or twice a day. A good basic guide is:

Breakfast: Fruit or fruit juice
Cereal
Egg
Milk

(A good substantial breakfast is important. And if the child is tired and unwilling to eat in the morning, this is a sign that breakfast is all the more urgently needed to restore his energy.)

Midday: Meat, fish or poultry (or an extra egg)
Green or root vegetable (cooked or raw)
Potatoes
Raw fruit or, occasionally, pudding
Milk

Evening: A filling dish—cereal, bread or sandwich, potato, soup or egg dish with toast
Vegetables or fruit, raw or cooked
Milk

The milk the child requires need not always be served straight out of the bottle. It can be made up into milk puddings, junkets or soups or heated as a bed-time drink. Cheese is also important: cottage cheese, although containing less calcium than other cheeses, is more easily digested and so can be eaten in larger amounts to compensate. The problem of digestion also affects the child's intake of butter or of fats in cooking. These should be introduced into the diet slowly, as the digestive system takes time to adjust to the absorption of fat.

The young child will find meat difficult to eat at first, so to begin with it should be finely minced. Bacon is not an adequate substitute for meat, as it has a higher fat content and a lower protein content than a comparable amount of lamb. Fish, like meat, should be introduced gradually. The oily kinds should be avoided, and when you are serving fish to a small child, all the bones and skin should be removed.

Vegetables can feature in the child's diet as soon as he starts taking solid food. At first they should be puréed; solid vegetables can be introduced later. Vegetables can also be used liberally in soups. Fruit can be served raw or stewed, but canned fruits should be avoided, as these are preserved in heavy syrups which would be fattening. (This does not apply to canned baby foods, as these are specially prepared.)

Once the child has grown out of the nursery stage, he no longer requires a special diet and can be fitted in with the rest of the family catering. But it would be wise to see that he does not eat too many foods containing refined starches, sugars and fats, such as cakes, pastries and biscuits. These are rich in calories and therefore they do satisfy the appetite, but they do not provide vitamins, minerals and proteins. If the child fills up on these, and leaves out the body-building foods, he will suffer from malnutrition. This is not to say they should be banned completely, but they must be treated with discretion. They can make occasional appearances, especially at birthday parties, but they should not be a regular feature of the diet.

How much do children need?

Imperial measures

	1–2 yrs.	2–3 yrs.	3–5 yrs.	5–7 yrs.	7–9 yrs.	9–12 yrs.	12–14 yrs.	Adult
Milk	$1\frac{1}{3}$ pts.	$1\frac{3}{4}$ pts.	$1\frac{3}{4}$ pts.	$1\frac{3}{4}$ pts.	$1\frac{3}{4}$ pts.	$1\frac{3}{4}$ pts.	$1\frac{3}{4}$ pts.	1 pt.
Eggs *or*	1	1	1	1	1	1	1	1
Meat, fish or liver	1 oz.	1 oz.	1 oz.	1 oz.	$1\frac{1}{2}$ oz.	$2\frac{1}{4}$ oz.	3 oz.	4 oz.
Green vegetables	$1\frac{1}{2}$ oz.	$1\frac{1}{2}$ oz.	$2\frac{3}{4}$ oz.	$3\frac{1}{2}$ oz.	$4\frac{1}{2}$ oz.	$6\frac{1}{2}$ oz.	8 oz.	4 oz.
Potatoes	$\frac{1}{2}$ oz.	1 oz.	$1\frac{3}{4}$ oz.	$2\frac{1}{2}$ oz.	3 oz.	4 oz.	4 oz.	4 oz.
Root vegetables	$\frac{1}{2}$ oz.	1 oz.	$1\frac{3}{4}$ oz.	$2\frac{1}{2}$ oz.	3 oz.	4 oz.	4 oz.	4 oz.
Raw fruit	$3\frac{1}{2}$ oz.	$3\frac{1}{2}$ oz.	$3\frac{1}{2}$ oz.	$3\frac{1}{2}$ oz.	$3\frac{1}{2}$ oz.	$3\frac{1}{2}$ oz.	$3\frac{1}{2}$ oz.	$3\frac{1}{2}$ oz.
Butter	$\frac{1}{4}$ oz.	$\frac{1}{2}$ oz.	$\frac{1}{2}$ oz.	1 oz.	$1\frac{1}{2}$ oz.	2 oz.	2 oz.	1 oz.
Cereals (incl. flour)	1 oz.	1 oz.	$1\frac{1}{4}$ oz.	$1\frac{1}{2}$ oz.	$2\frac{3}{4}$ oz.	$2\frac{3}{4}$ oz.	3 oz.	2 oz.
Bread	2 oz.	$2\frac{1}{4}$ oz.	$2\frac{3}{4}$ oz.	3 oz.	$3\frac{1}{2}$ oz.	4 oz.	4 oz.	2 oz.
Cheese	$\frac{1}{2}$ oz.	$\frac{1}{2}$ oz.	$\frac{1}{2}$ oz.	1 oz.	1 oz.	1 oz.	1 oz.	1 oz.

Metric measures

	1–2 yrs.	2–3 yrs.	3–5 yrs.	5–7 yrs.	7–9 yrs.	9–12 yrs.	12–14 yrs.	Adult
Milk	740 ml	1 litre	1 litre	1 litre	1 litre	1 litre	1 litre	600 ml
Eggs *or*	1	1	1	1	1	1	1	1
Meat, fish or liver	25 g	25 g	25 g	25 g	40 g	60 g	85 g	115 g
Green vegetables	40 g	40 g	75 g	100 g	125 g	185 g	225 g	115 g
Potatoes	15 g	25 g	50 g	70 g	85 g	115 g	115 g	115 g
Root vegetables	15 g	25 g	50 g	70 g	85 g	115 g	115 g	115 g
Raw fruit	100 g	100 g	100 g	100 g	100 g	100 g	100 g	100 g
Butter	7 g	15 g	15 g	25 g	40 g	55 g	55 g	25 g
Cereals (incl. flour)	25 g	25 g	35 g	40 g	75 g	75 g	85 g	55 g
Bread	55 g	60 g	75 g	85 g	100 g	115 g	115 g	55 g
Cheese	15 g	15 g	15 g	25 g	25 g	25 g	25 g	25 g

Fortnight's menus for schoolchildren

Breakfast: As for the rest of family.

Main meal: This varies enormously, particularly when taken at school. However, when it is taken at home, it should consist mainly of high-quality protein with vegetables.

Day	Main Meal	Supper
1	Grilled Lamb Chops Creamed Potatoes Diced Mixed Vegetables Baked Custard	Cream of Pumpkin Soup Sardine and Egg Fingers Fresh Fruit
2	Poached Fish au Gratin Carrots Spinach Stewed Apricots and Custard	Scrambled Egg Nests Sliced Tomato Milk Drink
3	Liver and Bacon Casserole Jacket Potatoes Turnips Peas Apricot Creams	Tomato Soup Cheese Nest Salad Fresh Fruit

Day	Main Meal	Supper
4	Sprats on Skewers Creamed Potatoes Spinach Swede Apple Whip	Cream of Chicken Soup Cheese Picnic Baskets Fresh Fruit
5	Pork and Liver Loaf Brussels Sprouts Potatoes Tomatoes Baked Egg Custard and Fruit	Tuna Salad Milk Drink
6	Casseroled Chicken Baked Potato Cabbage Carrots Fruit Crumble	Macaroni Cheese Green Salad Fresh Fruit
7	Grilled Sausages Jacket Potatoes Beans Cauliflower and Cheese Sauce Baked Apple Surprise	Corn Chowder Toast Fresh Fruit
8	Hunter's Harvest Stew Baked Potatoes Apple Cobbler	Fish Soufflé Orange Salad Milk Drink
9	Chicken Louisette Peas Carrots Potatoes Orange Mousse	Scotch Egg Salad Milk Drink
10	Braised Liver Baked Potato Tomato Cabbage Crispy Top	Split Pea Soup Welsh Rarebit Milk Drink
11	Lamb Hot-pot Courgettes Carrots Baked Apples and Custard	Cauliflower Cheese Apple and Celery Salad Milk Drink
12	Poached Cod Fillets Cheese Sauce Jacket Potatoes French Beans Queen of Puddings	Braised Kidneys Tomato and Cucumber Salad Milk Drink
13	Poacher's Pie Leeks Swedes Fresh Fruit Salad	Cream of Celery Soup Cheese and Chopped Ham Salad
14	Savoury Meatballs in Casserole Brussels Sprouts Spanish Cream	Spaghetti and Egg Casserole Fresh Fruit Milk Drink

Bengal Chicken Curry (see page 161)

PART THREE

Plan your own diet

Here we introduce two different ideas—the Basic Four Diet and a Calorie Counting Diet. Each plan allows 1200 calories (5021 joules) each day for women and 1700 calories (7113 joules) each day for men; this is our only stipulation. By using either of these plans you can choose a flexible diet to suit your own likes and dislikes.

Basic four diet

The basic four diet is built around the four basic food groups—the building blocks of good nutrition. Even if you were not slimming they would still be essential for good health. As a slimmer you must have a certain number of servings from each group every day (see below). Add extras and more servings from the basic groups to fill out the meal for non-slimming members of the family who generally require more calories than this plan allows. If you eat no more than the servings listed below your total consumption will be 1200 calories (5021 joules) for a woman and 1700 calories (7113 joules) for a man.

Your diet plan

The basic four reducing diet provides practical and easily maintained calorie levels for long term reducing. The beauty of the plan is that there are literally hundreds of everyday foods to choose from so that you can fit your diet to your budget and the special food likes and dislikes of the family.

Listed are the food choices—each with its recommended portion and also a small list of 'extras'—those foods which make meals a little more appetising.

The diet plan lists the total servings allowed for each group each day. The menu outline suggests a practical way to distribute the servings among the three meals—this is only a guide, not a rigid menu plan. For example, a woman may not want a protein breakfast and would prefer to have the protein for lunch or supper, or fruit or vegetables may be withdrawn from the meal and eaten as a snack instead. However the rule is that as long as you include the number of servings listed for each group in your diet plan, you will get all you need nutritionally and also reduce.

81

Savoury Pancakes (see page 172)

GROUP I

Meat and Protein rich foods

MEAT:
beef, lamb, pork, veal: 3 oz. (85 g)
brains: 6 oz. (170 g)
liver: 4 oz. (115 g)
kidney: 4 oz. (115 g)
lean ham: 3 oz. (85 g)

SAUSAGES: (grilled) 3 oz. (85 g)

EGGS: 2 medium

POULTRY:
chicken ⎫
turkey ⎬ 4 oz. (115 g)
pheasant ⎭
goose ⎫ 2 oz. (55 g)
duck ⎭

FISH:
cod, haddock, sole, plaice: 8 oz. (225 g)
halibut, trout: 6 oz. (170 g)
herrings, mackerel: 5 oz. (140 g)
shellfish: 6 oz. (170 g)

GROUP II

Fruit and Vegetables

FRUIT: Raw or cooked without sugar.
apple: 1 small
apricot: 2
banana: $\frac{1}{2}$
melon: 4 oz. (115 g)
cherries: 10
grapefruit: $\frac{1}{2}$
grapes: 10
orange: 1 medium
peach: 1 medium
pear: 1 small
plums: 3
rhubarb: 8 oz. (225 g)
berry fruits (strawberries, raspberries, gooseberries): 4 oz. (115 g)
fruit juices:
　　lemon: $\frac{1}{2}$ pint (300 ml)
　　orange, grapefruit: $\frac{1}{4}$ pint (150 ml)
　　tomato: 8 fl. oz. (225 ml)

VEGETABLES: steamed or boiled
asparagus: 5 oz. (140 g)
broad beans: 2 oz. (55 g)
French beans: 8 oz. (225 g)
runner beans: 8 oz. (225 g)
beetroot: 2 oz. (55 g)
broccoli: 6 oz. (170 g)
Brussels sprouts: 5 oz. (140 g)
cabbage:
　　raw: 3 oz. (85 g)
　　cooked: 6 oz. (170 g)
celeriac: 6 oz. (170 g)
celery: 8 oz. (225 g)
lettuce: 6 oz. (170 g)
chicory: 8 oz. (225 g)
cucumber: 6 oz. (170 g)
leeks: 3 oz. (85 g)
mushrooms: 4 oz. (115 g)
onions: 4 oz. (115 g)

carrots: 5 oz. (140 g)
cauliflower: 6 oz. (170 g)
radishes: 4 oz. (115 g)
spinach: 4 oz. (115 g)
parsnips: 1 oz. (25 g)
peas: 2 oz. (55 g)
seakale: 8 oz. (225 g)
swede/turnip: 4 oz. (115 g)

GROUP III

Bread, Cereals, Pasta, and some Vegetables

BREAD: 2 thin slices

CEREALS:

Cornflakes, Shredded Wheat, Rice
Crispies etc.: ½ oz. (14 g)

Oatmeal: 2 level tbsps. (uncooked
weight) (30 ml)

Cornflour, flour: 1½ level tbsps. (22.5
ml)

PASTA: (uncooked weight) ½ oz.
(14 g)

SAGO, RICE, SEMOLINA (uncooked
weight): ½ oz. (14 g)

VEGETABLES:

potatoes ⎫
butter beans – ⎬ 2 oz. (55 g)
haricot beans ⎭

lentils: 1½ oz. (40 g)

crispbreads: 2

Energen rolls: 3

GROUP IV

Milk and Milk Products:

MILK: ¼ pint (150 ml)

Buttermilk, low-fat skimmed milk:
½ pint (300 ml)

Yoghurt (low-fat): ¼ pint (140 g)

BUTTER/MARGARINE: ¼ oz. (7 g)

LOW-FAT SPREAD: ½ oz. (14 g)

CHEESE:

Cheddar, Edam: 1 oz. (25 g)

cottage: 4 oz. (115 g)

EXTRAS:

Oil: 1 tbsp. (15 ml)

Single cream: 2 tbsps. (30 ml)

Soured cream: 2 tbsps. (30 ml)

Pickles and chutneys: 1 level tbsp.
(15 ml)

Bacon: 2 thin rashers, lean ½ oz. (14 g)

Salad Dressing: 1 tbsp. (15 ml)

Dry wine, dry cider: 3 fl. oz. wine
glass (85 ml)

HELPFUL TIPS: Extras can be saved from 1 meal to the next, but remember to keep tabs on the daily total.

Have milk at meals or as a snack—it is not essential to have it at breakfast or lunch.

Roast, grill or braise your meals. Do not add fat unless you count it as extra.

Calorie Counting

Calorie counting to many slimmers is a challenge and an integral part of a successful slimming campaign. They find it very much easier to slim if they can keep a close check on the actual number of calories consumed each day. As this can become a little tedious to even the most dedicated slimmer we have included a number of recipes already calorie counted, comprising 100–500 calories (418–2092 joules). These can form the basis for menu planning. By adding a few ounces of freshly cooked vegetables or salads, a slice or two of cold meats, fruits or cheese—all carefully checked against our chart on pages 230–3 and the notes on menu planning on pages

Diet plan

		WOMEN	MEN
For the day	calories	1200	1700
	joules	5020.8	7112.8
		servings	
Meat + protein rich foods		2	3
Fruit + vegetables			
fruit		3	4
vegetables		4	4
Breads, cereals, pasta + some vegetables		3	4
Milk + milk products		3	4
Extras		2	2
For each meal			
Breakfast			
fruit		1	1
bread/cereal		1	2
milk + milk products		1	1
protein rich food		1	1
Lunch/supper			
meat + protein rich food		—	1
vegetables		2	2
bread/cereals		1	1
fruit		1	2
milk, milk products		1	1
extras		1	1
Dinner			
meat + protein rich food		1	1
vegetables		2	2
bread/cereals etc.		1	1
fruit		1	1
milk, milk products		1	2
extras		1	1

At each meal coffee or tea may be served with milk from the daily allowance.
No sugar should be added.

57–61 a great variety of menus can be built up to fit in with the family life and activities, seasons, time and energy available.

Allow a total calorie count of 1200 calories (5021 joules) each day for women and 1700 calories (7113 joules) per day for men.

---

100 calories per serving

2 dessert apples
2 pears
4 apricots
1 banana
2 grapefruit
½ melon
1 large orange
1 lb. (450 g) strawberries, raspberries, plums

Watercress Soup
Celery and Satsuma Slaw
Teezers Summer Soup
4 oz. (115 g) Jacket Potato

Watercress Soup

2 bunches watercress	salt and pepper
½ oz. (15 g) butter	½ pint (300 ml)
1½ pints (900 ml)	buttermilk
chicken stock	

Wash the watercress and remove any coarse stalks. Reserve a few sprigs for garnish. Lightly cook the rest of the watercress in butter for 2–3 minutes. Add the stock, salt and pepper and simmer for 15–20 minutes. Sieve and return to the heat. Add the buttermilk and re-heat without boiling. Serve garnished with sprigs of watercress. (Serves 4)

Teezers Summer Soup

1 pint (600 ml) natural yoghurt	½ cucumber, peeled and cubed
19-oz. (538-g) can tomato juice	salt and pepper
finely grated rind and juice of 1 lemon	cucumber slices
	lemon slices
	chopped chives

Whisk together the yoghurt and tomato juice. Stir in the lemon rind and juice, cucumber and seasoning. Serve well chilled, garnished with cucumber and lemon slices and sprinkled with a few chopped chives. (Serves 4)

Celery and Satsuma Slaw

2 oz. (55 g) white cabbage, finely shredded	2 sticks celery, scrubbed and chopped
1 satsuma, peeled and segmented	1 tbsp. (15 ml) French dressing chopped parsley

Toss together the cabbage, satsuma segments, celery and dressing. Serve sprinkled with chopped parsley. (Serves 1)

150 calories per serving

Cauliflower Niçoise
Fresh Fruit Salad
Creamed Kidneys
Cream of Celery Soup

Lemony Peas and Celery
Spinach Salad
Coeur à la Crème

Cauliflower Niçoise

1 cauliflower	1–2 cloves garlic,
1 tbsp. (*15 ml*) oil	skinned and crushed
1 small onion,	3 tomatoes, peeled
skinned and	finely grated rind and
chopped	juice of 1 lemon

Break the cauliflower into florets and cook in boiling salted water for 5 minutes. Drain and place in a warm serving dish. Keep hot. Heat the oil and sauté the onion and garlic. Cut the peeled tomatoes into quarters, add to the onion and cook for 3 minutes. Add the lemon juice and cook for a further 2 minutes. Pour over the cauliflower and serve sprinkled with finely grated lemon rind. (Serves 4)

Cream of Celery Soup

1 oz. (*25 g*) butter	2 bay leaves
1 onion, skinned and	1 tbsp. (*15 ml*) flour
chopped	½ pint (*300 ml*) milk
4 sticks celery,	1 oz. (*25 g*) cheese,
scrubbed and	grated
chopped	chopped parsley
1 pint (*600 ml*) stock	

Melt the butter and sauté the onion and celery. Add the stock and bay leaves, cover and simmer until the vegetables are tender then pass them through a sieve or blend until smooth. Return to the pan. Mix the flour to a smooth paste with a little of the milk. Add the remaining milk to the pan, bring to boiling point, stir in the flour and cook at a slow simmer for 5 minutes. Serve piping hot sprinkled with cheese and parsley. (Serves 4)

Fresh Fruit Salad

1 lb. (*450 g*) dessert	liquid sweetener
apples	2 oranges
¼ pint (*150 ml*) water	1 grapefruit

Peel, core and cut the apples into thick slices. Simmer in boiling water for 4 minutes. Remove from the heat and add 1–2 drops liquid sweetener. Peel the oranges and remove all pith. Cut the fruit into thick slices across the segments and add to the apples. Remove all the pith from the rind of ½ orange and cut rind in very fine shreds. Place in boiling water and simmer until tender. Drain and add to the fruits. Peel away the skin and pith of the grapefruit and remove the flesh from between the membranes. Mix all the fruit together and chill. (Serves 4)

Lemony Peas and Celery

1 oz. (*25 g*)	12 oz. (*340 g*)
margarine or butter	shelled or frozen
4 sticks celery,	peas
scrubbed and thinly	2 tsps. (*10 ml*) lemon
sliced	juice
	salt and pepper

Melt the butter or margarine and sauté the celery for 5 minutes. Add the peas and lemon juice and season well with salt and pepper. Cover and cook over a low heat until the peas are cooked. (Serves 4)

Creamed Kidneys

8 lambs' kidneys	2 tsps. (*10 ml*)
¼ pint (*150 ml*) beef	prepared mustard
stock	¼ pint (*140 g*)
4 oz. (*115 g*) mush-	natural yoghurt
rooms, wiped and	salt and pepper
sliced	chopped parsley
1 level tbsp. (*15 ml*)	
tomato paste	

Pour boiling water over the kidneys and leave to stand for 30 minutes. Skin, cut into quarters and remove the cores, place them in a pan with the stock, mushrooms and tomato paste. Cook, covered, for 20 minutes or until just tender. Stir in the mustard and yoghurt. Season to taste and serve sprinkled with a little chopped parsley. (Serves 4)

Spinach Salad

2 oz. (*55 g*) raisins
4 tbsps. (*60 ml*) lemon juice
¾ lb. (*340 g*) fresh spinach, shredded
8 oz. (*225 g*) white cabbage, shredded

3 tbsps. (*45 ml*) salad oil
salt and pepper
1 dessert apple, chopped

Soak the raisins in 2 tbsps. (30 ml) lemon juice until soft and swollen. Add to the prepared vegetables. Mix together the oil, remaining lemon juice, salt and pepper. Whisk with a fork to thicken and add the prepared apple; mix. Pour the dressing over the vegetables. Toss quickly and serve immediately. (Serves 4)

Coeur à la Crème

1 lb. (*450 g*) cottage cheese
½ pint (*280 g*) natural yoghurt
3 level tsps. (*15 ml*) powdered gelatine

3 tbsps. (*45 ml*) water
1 lb. (*450 g*) strawberries or other seasonal fruit

Sieve the cheese and blend it with the yoghurt. Dissolve the gelatine in the usual way and stir into the cheese mixture. Spoon into 6 individual moulds and cover with muslin, held in place with rubber bands. Stand, muslin side down, on a wire tray over a dish. Leave to drain in the refrigerator overnight. Serve with fresh fruit. (Serves 6)

---

200 calories per serving

Casserole of Brussels Sprouts
Stuffed Tomatoes
Prawn and Cottage Cheese Salad

Open Sandwiches
Beef Rolls Confetti

Casserole of Brussels Sprouts

1½ lb. (*700 g*) Brussels sprouts
1 tbsp. (*15 ml*) oil
1 medium onion, skinned and chopped

3 tomatoes, peeled
4 tbsps. water
salt and pepper
4 oz. (*115 g*) cheese, grated

Oven temperature: 325°F., 170°C., mark 3
Wash the sprouts, remove the outer leaves as necessary and cut in half through the stalk; place in a casserole. Heat the oil and sauté the onion until clear then add to the sprouts. Cut the tomatoes into quarters and add with the water. Season well. Cover and cook for 45 minutes. Sprinkle with cheese and bake uncovered for a further 15 minutes or place under a hot grill and cook until golden and bubbling. (Serves 4)

Prawn and Cottage Cheese Salad

8 oz. (*225 g*) peeled prawns
8 oz. (*225 g*) cottage cheese
1 oz. (*25 g*) peanuts, chopped
1 level tbsp. (*15 ml*) chopped onion

1 tbsp. (*15 ml*) lemon juice
1 tbsp. (*15 ml*) oil
salt and pepper
lettuce leaves
tomato wedges
parsley

Mix together the prawns, cheese, nuts and onion in a bowl. Mix together the lemon juice and oil with a little salt and pepper and use to moisten the prawn mixture. Chill well and serve piled into lettuce leaves. Garnish with tomato wedges and parsley. (Serves 4)

Stuffed Tomatoes

4 large ripe tomatoes
8 oz. (*225 g*) cottage
  cheese
1 spring onion,
  chopped
1 stick celery,
  scrubbed and
  chopped

1 dessert apple,
  chopped
freshly ground black
  pepper
2 oz. (*50 g*) cole slaw

Cut the tops off the tomatoes and scoop out the centres; turn them upside down to drain. Mix the remaining ingredients together and season with pepper to taste. Divide the mixture between the tomato cups, replace the lids and serve on a bed of cole slaw. (Serves 2)

Beef Rolls Confetti

10 oz. (*280 g*) shelled
  or frozen peas
10-oz. (about *280-g*)
  can small broad
  beans, drained
10-oz. (about *280-g*)
  can cut green
  beans, drained
1 large onion, skinned
  and grated
3 tbsps. (*45 ml*) wine
  vinegar

1 tbsp. (*15 ml*) grated
  horseradish
few drops Tabasco
  sauce
French dressing
12 thin slices roast beef
1 canned pimiento,
  chopped
watercress for garnish

Cook the peas until just tender, drain and cool. Mix together the peas, beans, onion, vinegar, horseradish and Tabasco and add just enough dressing to moisten. Chill well. Roll up each slice of beef, then place the seam side down; sprinkle with a little dressing and leave to stand for 1 hour. Place the marinaded vegetables on a platter. Top with beef rolls and garnish with watercress and pimiento. (Serves 4)

Cottage Cheese Open Sandwiches

Quantities of fillings for 16–18 open sandwiches:

1 lb. (450 g) cottage cheese; 1 head chicory; ½ lb. (225 g) kipper fillets; 1 lettuce; ¼ lb. (115 g) sliced tongue; 8-oz.

(226-g) can pineapple rings, drained; ¼ lb. (115 g) tomatoes; ¼ lb. (115 g) sliced ham; ½ cucumber; ¼ lb. (115 g) smoked salmon; ¼ lb. (115 g) fresh prawns; ¼ lb. (115 g) salami.

To garnish: lemon, onion, stuffed olives, radishes, parsley, watercress.

Bases: wholemeal, granary, stone ground, white, Hovis, black and rye breads, crispbreads, bridge rolls, pumpernickle.

Kipper fillets: These are best marinated overnight in oil and lemon juice. Butter 4 slices of granary bread, line with chicory, spoon on cottage cheese and arrange thin strips of kipper on top. Garnish with a lemon twist.

Tongue rolls: Butter 2 slices of rye bread. Line with lettuce and spoon on cottage cheese. Top with a roll of tongue and garnish with finely sliced onion rings.

Ham cornets: Butter 3 slices of white bread. Line with lettuce and top with a pineapple ring and slice of tomato. Mix 1 tbsp. (15 ml) chopped chives with 4 oz. (115 g) cottage cheese and spoon into the ham cornets. Place on top of pineapple and tomato. Garnish with a slice of cucumber.

Prawn stars: Butter 2 slices of black bread. Line with cucumber slices, spoon on cottage cheese and arrange shelled prawns in a star shape on top of the cheese. Garnish with slices of stuffed olive.

Salami coils: Butter halves of 2 bridge rolls and line them with lettuce. Fill the salami coils with cottage cheese, place on the lettuce and sprinkle with chopped chives.

Smoked salmon rolls: Butter 3 slices of pumpernickle. Spoon cottage cheese into the centre and arrange a roll of smoked salmon at each end. Garnish with a twist of cucumber.

250 calories per serving

Barbecued Chicken
Sweet Lemon Chicken
Herring Calaisienne
Cauliflower Cheese

Sardine and Beetroot Salad
Cheese and Leek Soup
Tuna Salad

Barbecued Chicken

4 chicken joints (6 oz.,
    170 g, each)
1 level tbsp. (*15 ml*)
    flour
1 tbsp. (*15 ml*) oil
8 oz. (*225 g*) onion,
    skinned and
    chopped

½ pint (*300 ml*)
    tomato juice
salt and pepper
3–4 tsps. (*15–20 ml*)
    Worcestershire sauce
chopped parsley

Coat the joints with flour. Heat the oil in a large shallow pan and sauté the onion until clear. Push to one side and quickly brown the joints. Reduce the heat and add the tomato juice, seasoning and Worcestershire sauce. Cover and simmer for 45 minutes or until the chicken is tender. Remove the joints to a warmed serving dish and rapidly boil the juices to reduce. Pour over the joints and serve sprinkled with a little chopped parsley. (Serves 4)

Sweet Lemon Chicken

4 chicken joints
2 level tbsps. (*30 ml*)
    flour
1 level tsp. (*5 ml*) salt
2 tbsps. (*30 ml*) oil
finely grated rind and
    juice of 1 lemon

2 level tbsps. (*30 ml*)
    tomato paste
¼–½ pint (*150–300
    ml*) stock
6 peppercorns
2 bay leaves
lemon and parsley to
    garnish

Coat the joints with seasoned flour. Heat the oil and quickly brown the chicken. Mix together the lemon juice, rind, tomato paste and ¼ pint (150 ml) stock and pour over the chicken. Add the peppercorns and bay leaves, cover and simmer over a low heat for about 45 minutes until tender, adding a little more stock if necessary. Remove the chicken to a warm serving dish. Reduce the sauce by boiling rapidly. Strain over the chicken and serve

garnished with lemon twists and sprigs of parsley. (Serves 4)

Herring Calaisienne

½ onion, skinned and
    chopped
1 hard-boiled egg,
    shelled and
    chopped
1 tbsp. (15 ml)
    chopped parsley

2 oz. (*55 g*) fresh white
    breadcrumbs
salt and pepper
lemon juice to mix
4 herrings, cleaned
    and boned

Mix all the stuffing ingredients together and divide the mixture between the four fish. Place in an ovenproof dish with a little water, cover and bake in the oven for 20–30 minutes. (Serves 4)

Sardine and Beetroot Salad

2 4½-oz (*124-g*) cans
    sardines, drained
2 eating apples, cored
    and chopped
1 medium beetroot,
    peeled and diced

4 tbsps. (*60 ml*) low-
    calorie salad cream
1 tsp. (*5 ml*) lemon
    juice
salt and pepper
lettuce

Flake the drained sardines and mix with the apple and beetroot. Moisten with the salad cream and lemon juice. Season to taste and serve on a bed of lettuce. (Serves 4)

Cauliflower Cheese

1 medium cauliflower
4 oz. (*115 g*) Cheddar
    cheese, grated

½ pint (*300 ml*) white
    sauce

Break the cauliflower into florets and cook in boiling salted water for 7–10 minutes. Drain. Mix 3 oz. (85 g) cheese with the white sauce and stir to blend. Pour over the cauliflower, sprinkle with the remaining cheese, place under the grill and cook until golden and bubbling. (Serves 4)

Cheese and Leek Soup

1 oz. (*25 g*) butter	4 oz. (*115 g*) Cheddar
2 lb. (*900 g*) leeks,	cheese
sliced	2 lean bacon rashers,
1½ pints (*900 ml*)	grilled and chopped
stock	
salt and pepper	

Melt the butter and sauté the leeks for 5 minutes. Add the stock, season and simmer for 20 minutes. Strain, retaining the liquor. Blend or sieve the leeks, add the liquor and return to the boil. Add the cheese, stirring until completely blended. Re-heat gently without boiling, adjust

seasoning and serve sprinkled with chopped bacon. (Serves 4)

Tuna Salad

7-oz. (*198-g*) can tuna	4 sticks celery, diced
fish	4 tbsps. (*60 ml*)
1 lb. (*450 g*) red-	French dressing
skinned apples	
2 tbsps. (*30 ml*) lemon	
juice	

Drain and flake the fish. Core and dice the apples and sprinkle with lemon juice. Combine the celery with the apples, tuna and dressing and toss lightly. Chill for a few minutes before serving. (Serves 4)

---

300 calories per serving

Stuffed Marrow with Devilled Sauce
Apple Stuffed Kippers
Tomato Fish Bake

Cottage Cheese Baked Potato
Liver with Mushrooms

Stuffed Marrow

3-lb. (*1.5-kg*) marrow	6 oz. (*170 g*) cooked
2 onions, skinned and	rice
sliced	1 tsp. (*5 ml*) chopped
1 oz. (*25 g*) butter	parsley
1 red pepper, seeded	salt and pepper
and sliced	pinch of thyme
½ lb. (*225 g*) mush-	4 hard-boiled eggs
rooms	

For devilled sauce:	1 level tsp. (*5 ml*)
¼ pint (*150 ml*)	paprika
tomato juice	2–3 drops Tabasco
1 tsp. (*5 ml*)	sauce
Worcestershire sauce	¼ level tsp. (*1.25 ml*)
1 bay leaf	salt
1 tbsp. (*15 ml*) butter	
1 level tbsp. (*15 ml*)	
flour	

Oven temperature: 325°F., 170°C., mark 3
Wash the marrow and place it in a greased baking dish with a little water; bake until tender—about ¾ hour.
Fry the onions in butter until golden brown then add the pepper and mush-

rooms and cook for a few minutes. Add the rice, parsley and thyme and season well with salt and pepper. Finally add the eggs. When the marrow is cooked remove a portion of the top for the lid. Scoop out the seeds and fill the centre with the rice mixture. Replace the lid and serve with devilled sauce.
To make the devilled sauce: simmer the tomato juice, Worcestershire sauce and bay leaf for 5 minutes. Melt the butter and blend in the flour and paprika. Cook for 2 minutes then add the tomato mixture, removing the bay leaf. Add the remaining seasonings and serve piping hot. (Serves 4)

Apple Stuffed Kippers

2 pairs kippers	1 apple, cored
¼ lb. (*115 g*) mush-	juice of ½ lemon
rooms	½ level tsp. (*2.5 ml*)
1 oz. (*25 g*) butter	salt
¼ lb. (*115 g*) tomatoes	

Oven temperature: 400°F., 200°C., mark 6
Carefully remove the bones from the kippers. Fold them in half and place with tails uppermost down the centre of an ovenproof dish. Pull the tails back so that the kippers are opened ready for stuffing. Cut the mushrooms into quarters. Melt the butter and sauté the mushrooms. Cut the tomatoes and apples into ½-in. (1.25-cm) dice, add to the mushrooms and mix well. Add the lemon juice and salt. Fill the kippers with the mixture. Fold the tails over again, cover lightly with foil and bake for 20–25 minutes. (Serves 4)

Liver with Mushrooms

1 lb. (*450 g*) lambs' liver	2 cloves garlic, skinned and crushed
1 oz. (*25 g*) flour	½ pint (*300 ml*) tomato juice
1 level tsp. (*5 ml*) salt	8 oz. (*225 g*) mushrooms, sliced
freshly ground black pepper	
2 tbsps. (*30 ml*) oil	
2 onions, skinned and sliced	

Cut the liver into slices ½ in. (1.25 cm) thick and coat with seasoned flour. Heat the oil in a frying pan and quickly brown the liver. Remove to a heated dish and keep warm. Sauté the onions and garlic; add the tomato juice and mushrooms and cook for 2 minutes before returning the liver to the pan. Cover and cook over a gentle heat for about 10 minutes or until the liver is fork tender. (Serves 4)

Cottage Cheese Baked Potato

1 large potato (6 oz., *170 g*)	salt and pepper
1 oz. (*25 g*) cooked ham, chopped	½ level tsp. (*2.5 ml*) made mustard
4 oz. (*115 g*) cottage cheese	watercress garnish

Oven temperature: 400°F., 200°C., mark 6
Scrub the potato and prick with a fork. Place it in the oven and bake for 1 hour or until tender. Cut in half and scoop out the potato and mix with the ham, cheese and seasonings. Pile back into the shell and re-heat for 5 minutes. Serve garnished with watercress. (Serves 1)

Tomato Fish Bake

4 oz. (*115 g*) mushrooms	1 in. (*2.5 cm*) cucumber, diced
1 tsp. (*5 ml*) lemon juice	1 tbsp. (*15 ml*) chopped parsley
salt and pepper	5 tbsps. (*75 ml*) tomato juice
8 oz. (*225 g*) haddock fillet or steak	
¼ small green pepper, chopped	

Oven temperature: 375°F., 190°C., mark 5
Slice the mushrooms and mix with the lemon juice; season with salt and pepper and place in the bottom of a small ovenproof dish. Place the fish on top. Mix together the remaining ingredients and pile on top of the fish. Bake uncovered for 30 minutes. (Serves 1)

---

350 calories per serving

Haddock Provençal
Kipper en Papillotte
Baked Cheese Fondue

Cottage Cheese Omelette
Eggs in Baked Potatoes
Welsh Rarebit

Eggs in Baked Potatoes

4 potatoes, scrubbed (6 oz., *170 g*, each)	salt and pepper
1 oz. (*25 g*) butter	2 tbsps. (*30 ml*) milk
	4 small eggs

Oven temperature: 350°F., 180°C., mark 4
Mark a circle around the tip of each potato with a sharp pointed knife. Bake in centre of the oven for 1–1½ hours until soft. Remove the top, scoop out the inside and

cream it with butter, seasonings, and milk. Half-fill each potato with the creamed potato, break in an egg and return the potato to the oven to cook until the eggs have set (10–15 minutes). Pipe the remaining potato around the edge and brown quickly under grill. (Serves 4)

Haddock Provençal

1½ lb. (700 g) haddock fillet, skinned or 6 frozen haddock steaks, thawed	1 tbsp. (15 ml) chopped parsley
1 oz. (25 g) seasoned flour	1 level tbsp. (15 ml) tomato paste
3 tbsps. (45 ml) oil	¼ pint (150 ml) wine vinegar
2 large onions, skinned and sliced	¼ pint (150 ml) water
1 clove garlic, skinned and crushed	4 oz. (115 g) shelled prawns
	chopped parsley for garnish

Oven temperature: 350°F., 180°C., mark 4
Cut the fillets into 2-in. (5-cm) squares or divide the steaks in two. Coat with seasoned flour. Heat the oil in a frying pan and fry the fish to lightly brown. Place in a shallow casserole. Fry the onion until golden and add to the fish with the garlic and parsley. Mix together the tomato paste, vinegar and water, pour over the fish, cover and bake for 30 minutes. Add the prawns and cook for a further 15 minutes (if using frozen prawns add half way through the cooking time). Serve sprinkled with a little extra freshly chopped parsley. (Serves 3)

Kipper en Papillotte

1 kipper, head removed	salt and pepper
1 tsp. (5 ml) lemon juice	lemon slices and parsley for garnish
2 oz. (55 g) button mushrooms, sliced	

Oven temperature: 400°F., 200°C., mark 6
Sprinkle the kipper with lemon juice. Arrange the mushrooms down the centre, season, enclose loosely in foil and bake for 15 minutes. Remove from foil and serve garnished with lemon and parsley. (Serves 1)

Baked Cheese Fondue

(see colour picture between pages 192, 193)

¼ pint (150 ml) milk	1 egg, separated
½ oz. (15 g) soft breadcrumbs	salt and pepper
1 oz. (25 g) cheese, grated	

Oven temperature: 350°F., 180°C., mark 4
Scald the milk and add the breadcrumbs and cheese, then the lightly beaten egg yolk, salt and pepper. Beat the egg white until stiff and fold it into the cheese mixture. Turn into an individual baking dish and set in a pan of hot water. Bake for ¾–1 hour or until firm when tested with a knife. Serve immediately. (Serves 1)

Cottage Cheese Omelette

2 eggs	¼ level tsp. (1.25 ml) made mustard
1 tbsp. (15 ml) water	
¼ level tsp. (1.25 ml) dried mixed herbs	1 tbsp. (15 ml) chopped chives
salt and pepper	small knob butter
2 oz. (55 g) cottage cheese	

Beat together the eggs, water, herbs and seasonings. Mix together the cheese, mustard and chives. Melt the butter in an omelette pan. Pour in the beaten eggs; stir gently with the back of the prongs of a fork, drawing the mixture from the sides to the centre and letting the liquid egg from the centre run to the sides. When the egg has set, stop stirring, top with cheese mixture and cook for 1 minute until golden underneath. Fold over the omelette, turn on to a warm serving dish and serve immediately. (Serves 1)

Welsh Rarebit

8 oz. (225 g) Cheddar cheese, grated	salt and pepper
1 oz. (25 g) butter	3 tbsps. (45 ml) brown ale
1 level tsp. (5 ml) mustard	4 thin slices toast

Place the cheese, butter, mustard, salt, pepper and ale in a heavy based saucepan and heat very gently until a creamy mixture is obtained. Pour over the toast and put under the grill until golden and bubbling. (Serves 4)

---

400 calories per serving

Lemon Kipper Snack
Spare Ribs Piquante
Beef Hotpot
Trout with Almonds

Roast Beef Dinner
Mixed Grill
Ham Salad
Braised Liver

Lemon Kipper Snack

8 oz. (225 g) kipper fillets	juice and finely grated rind of ½ lemon
2 hard-boiled eggs, chopped	salt and pepper
½ oz. (15 g) butter	4 slices hot toast
½ oz. (15 g) flour	2 oz. (55 g) cheese, grated
¼ pint (150 ml) milk	

Chop the fillets and mix with the egg. Melt the butter and blend in the flour, cook for 1 minute then gradually add the milk, stirring continuously until thick and smooth; add the lemon rind and juice and season to taste. Mix in the fish and egg and spoon on to the toast. Sprinkle with cheese and place under a hot grill until golden and bubbling. (Serves 4)

Spare Ribs Piquante

2 lb. (900 g) pork spare ribs (English cut)	¼ pint (150 ml) stock
2 level tbsps. (30 ml) seasoned flour	2 level tbsps. (30 ml) tomato paste
1 tbsp. (15 ml) oil	4 oz. (115 g) mushrooms, sliced
1 onion, skinned and chopped	¼ pint (140 g) natural yoghurt
1 level tsp. (5 ml) paprika pepper	chopped chives

Oven temperature: 350°F., 180°C., mark 4
Trim any fat and bone from the meat and coat it with seasoned flour. Heat the oil and sear the meat on both sides. Drain on absorbent paper and transfer to a shallow casserole. Sauté the onion in the pan drippings, stir in the paprika and cook for 1–2 minutes. Mix together the stock and paste and pour into the pan, stir to mix then pour over the meat. Cover and cook for 1¼ hours. Add the mushrooms and cook for a further 10 minutes. Heat the yoghurt without boiling; blend it with the casserole and serve sprinkled with chopped chives. (Serves 4)

Trout with Almonds

4 trout	juice of 1 lemon
oil	salt
1½ oz. (40 g) butter	lemon and parsley to garnish
2 oz. (55 g) flaked almonds	

Clean the trout without removing the heads. Brush with oil and grill under a moderate grill for about 2 minutes on each side. Reduce the heat and cook until done. Melt the butter, add the almonds and fry gently until brown. Add the lemon juice and a little salt. Pour the almonds over the cooked trout and serve garnished with a twist of lemon and a sprig of parsley. (Serves 4)

Beef Hotpot

1½ lb. (700 g) blade or chuck steak	1 lb. (450 g) onions, skinned and sliced
salt and pepper	15-oz. (425-g) can tomatoes
2 level tsps. (10 ml) dry mustard	chopped chives
1 oz. (25 g) butter	

Oven temperature: 325°F., 170°C., mark 3
Cut the meat into large chunks. Mix salt, pepper and mustard together and use to coat the meat. Melt the butter and fry the

onions. Layer the meat, onions and tomatoes in a casserole. Cover and bake for about 2½ hours or until the meat is tender. Serve sprinkled with freshly chopped chives. (Serves 4)

Roast Beef Dinner

(per person)
3 oz. *(85 g)* lean roast beef
1 popover
1 4-oz. *(115-g)* roast potato
4 oz. *(115 g)* green beans, boiled

Mixed Grill

(per person)
2 rashers back bacon, grilled
2 tomatoes, grilled
2 large mushrooms, grilled
crispbread

Braised Liver

(per person)
4 oz. *(115 g)* lambs' liver, braised with 1 onion, 8 tbsps. *(90 ml)* stock, 1 tomato, peeled and quartered
4 oz. *(115 g)* potato creamed
4 oz. *(115 g)* Brussels sprouts, boiled

Ham Salad

(per person)
3 oz. *(85 g)* lean ham
3 oz. *(85 g)* new potatoes, boiled
cole slaw: 3 oz. *(85 g)* cabbage, 1 stick celery, ½ dessert apple, 1 tbsp. *(15 ml)* salad cream

Beef Casserole

(per person)
4 oz. *(115 g)* casseroled beef
1 carrot ⎫ cooked
1 onion ⎭ with the meat
4 oz. *(115 g)* broccoli, steamed

---

450 calories per serving

Mixed Grill
Mixed Salad Platter

Potato and Lamb Casserole
Chicken and Bacon Casserole

Potato and Lamb Casserole

1½ lb. *(700 g)* minced cooked lamb
6 oz. *(170 g)* onion, skinned and minced
1 clove garlic, skinned and crushed
salt and pepper
1 lb. *(450 g)* potatoes, peeled and thinly sliced
3 level tbsps. *(45 ml)* tomato paste
½ pint *(300 ml)* stock
pinch ground cinnamon
pinch powdered bay
chopped parsley

Oven temperature: 375°F., 190°C., mark 5
Mix together the lamb, onion, garlic, salt and pepper and place in a casserole in layers with the sliced potato, ending with potato. Mix together the tomato paste, stock, cinnamon and bay. Pour over the potatoes. Bake for 45 minutes or until the potatoes are quite tender. Serve sprinkled with a little chopped parsley. (Serves 4)

Chicken and Bacon Casserole

4 6-oz. *(170-g)* chicken joints
1 oz. *(25 g)* seasoned flour
2 tbsps. *(30 ml)* oil
½ oz. *(15 g)* butter
4 oz. *(115 g)* streaky bacon, chopped
1 onion, skinned and chopped
½ pint *(300 ml)* stock
4 tomatoes, peeled and quartered
2 slices bread
watercress sprigs

Oven temperature: 350°F., 180°C., mark 4
Coat the chicken joints with seasoned flour. Heat the oil and butter together and brown the joints. Drain well and place in a single layer in a shallow casserole. Fry the bacon until the fat runs. Add the onion and sauté until clear. Stir in any flour remaining and cook for 1 minute. Stir in the stock and bring to the boil, stirring. Pour over the chicken, cover

and bake for 45 minutes. Add the prepared tomatoes and cook for a further 15 minutes. Toast the bread, and cut it into quarters and use to garnish, with a few sprigs of watercress. (Serves 4)

Mixed Salad Platter

1 lb. (450 g) cottage cheese
2 fresh peaches, skinned and sliced
juice of ½ lemon
10 oz. (280 g) cooked ham, sliced and rolled
2 oz. (55 g) haricots verts
2 courgettes, sliced

2 oz. (55 g) mushrooms, sliced
1 green pepper, seeded and sliced
1 red pepper, seeded and sliced
2 beetroots, cooked and diced
2 tomatoes, sliced
spring onions
radishes

Heap the cottage cheese into the centre of a platter. Immerse the peach slices in lemon juice, drain, then arrange with the ham rolls around the cheese. Blanch the beans, courgettes and mushrooms in boiling salted water for 2 minutes. Drain, chill and arrange with other salad ingredients around the platter. (Serves 4)

Mixed Grill

(*per person*)
2 sausages, grilled
1 rasher bacon, grilled
2 rings pineapple, grilled

---

500 calories per serving

Cheese Grilled Fish
Marinaded Steak
Spiced Gammon

Cottage Pie
15-oz. (425-g) can Ravioli or Canneloni

Marinaded Steak

1 clove garlic, skinned and crushed
2 tbsps. (30 ml) oil
8 tbsps. (120 ml) red wine

1 level tbsp. (15 ml) tomato paste
¾ lb. (340 g) rump steak
watercress

Combine the garlic, oil, wine and tomato paste and place with the steak in a plastic bag. Leave for 4–5 hours in a cool place. Heat the grill, drain and grill the steak for 5–7 minutes on each side (depending on thickness). Boil the marinade until reduced to about 2 tbsps. and serve as a sauce. Serve garnished with watercress. (Serves 2)

Cottage Pie

8-oz. (about 225-g) can savoury minced beef
3 tomatoes, sliced
garlic salt

freshly ground black pepper
8 oz. (225 g) potato, creamed

Oven temperature: 375°F., 190°C., mark 5
Place the meat in a pie dish and top with tomato slices. Sprinkle with garlic salt and pepper. Top with creamed potatoes and bake until golden. (Serves 2)

Cheese Grilled Fish

1 cod steak
1 small onion, skinned and grated
½ oz. (15 g) butter
2 oz. (55 g) cheese, grated

½ level tsp. (2.5 ml) dry mustard
salt and pepper

Trim the fish and remove the centre bone with a small sharp knife. Mix the remaining ingredients together to form a paste. Grill the fish under a medium heat for 5 minutes, turn and grill the second side for 4 minutes. Cover with the cheese mixture and continue grilling under a moderate heat until the cheese is golden and bubbling. (Serves 1)

Spiced Gammon

8 oz. (*225 g*) gammon steak
oil
1 level tbsp. (*15 ml*) brown sugar
½ level tsp. (*2.5 ml*) dry mustard
¼ level tsp. (*1.25 ml*) mixed spice

Snip the edges of the steak and lightly brush with oil. Place under a hot grill and grill for 5 minutes. Turn and grill for 2 minutes. Mix together the sugar, mustard and spice, sprinkle over the steak and grill for a further 5 minutes until golden and bubbling. (Serves 2)

Ratatouille Niçoise (see page 182)

Recipe File

Appetisers

Frozen Pineapple Cocktail

16-oz. (*454 g*) can of crushed pineapple
½ pint (*300 ml*) unsweetened orange juice
½ pint (*300 ml*) unsweetened grapefruit juice
½ pint (*300 ml*) low-calorie ginger ale
liquid sweetener
mint to garnish (optional)

Mix together the crushed pineapple, fruit juices and ginger ale. Add 2–3 drops of liquid sweetener, pour into an ice-cream tray and freeze. Spoon into glass dishes and garnish with mint, or as desired. (Serves 4–6)

Grapefruit and Orange Cocktail

(*see picture below*)
2 large grapefruit
2 oranges
mint freeze (see recipe)

Halve the grapefruit, using a zig-zag cut to give a decorative edge. Remove the flesh from the halves. Peel and segment the orange, remove the membranes and cut into pieces. Mix with the grapefruit, pile into the grapefruit shells and top with mint freeze. (Serves 4)

Mint Freeze

1 tbsp. (*15 ml*) PLJ lemon juice
1 bottle low-calorie lemonade
2 tbsps. (*30 ml*) finely chopped fresh mint leaves

Grapefruit and Orange Cocktail

Chicken and Grape Salad (*see page 163*)

Mix together, pour into the refrigerator ice tray and freeze to the soft ice stage. (Serves 4, as accompaniment)

Oysters au Naturel

The best varieties of oysters, such as Whitstable or Colchester, should be used to serve raw. Open and beard them, then place on a bed of cracked ice, arranging them so that the pointed end is towards the centre of the dish. Serve with thin slices of brown bread and butter and lemon wedges. Cayenne pepper should be at hand for those who like it.

Ham and Melon

Divide a chilled melon into portions, removing the seeds and fibres. Place a piece of Continental-type ham on each portion and serve.

Ham and Fig Rolls

Trim the rind from some ham or boiled bacon. Cut into pieces about 2 inches by 1 inch, and spread with a layer of cream cheese. Chop some figs and scatter over the cheese, roll up tightly and chill.

Hors d'Oeuvre Platter

(*see picture below*)
Cauliflowers—Blanch quickly in boiling salted water, drain and chill.

Green Beans—Blanch in boiling salted water, drain, chill and toss in a little French dressing.
Asparagus—Cook fresh asparagus for 10–15 minutes, drain and chill. Alternatively, use canned green asparagus.
Carrots—Cut into thin slices; cut each strip almost through, place in chilled water and leave to curl.
Beetroot—Cut cooked beetroot into balls, leave in pickling vinegar overnight and drain well before serving.
Arrange all decoratively on the platter.

Chicken Liver Pâté

(*see colour picture facing page 177*)

2 oz. (*55 g*) butter	1 lb. (*450 g*) chicken
2 bay leaves	livers
pinch of dried thyme	salt and pepper
1 small onion,	stuffed olives and
skinned and	celery sprigs to
chopped	garnish

Melt the butter in a pan, add the bay leaves, thyme and onion, and cook gently for 2–3 minutes. Prepare the chicken livers and cut each into 2–3 pieces. Add to the pan, and simmer gently for 5–7 minutes until the liver is cooked. Remove the bay leaves and mince the liver once or twice, using a fine grinder (the second mincing gives a smoother pâté). Season well and place in a lined loaf tin. Weigh carefully and

Hors d'Oeuvre Platter

98

chill well. Serve garnished with stuffed olives and celery. (Serves 6–8)

Chive Dip Platter

(see colour picture facing page 16)

8-oz. (225-g) carton of cottage cheese	salt and pepper
	1 oz. (25 g) Cheddar cheese, grated
2 tbsps. (30 ml) chopped fresh chives	salad 'dunks'

Combine the cottage cheese, chives, salt and pepper. Place in a dip dish and sprinkle with the shredded cheese. Serve accompanied by cucumber slices, carrot, bamboo shoots, cocktail frankfurters, celery and watercress.

Garlic Dip

(see colour picture facing page 16)

8 oz. (225 g) cottage cheese	2 cloves of garlic
	salt and pepper
¼ pint (150 ml) fat-free yoghurt	salad 'dunks'

Mix the cheese and yoghurt together, beat or blend till the mixture is smooth, then add the garlic, salt and pepper. Leave for at least 1 hour before placing on a platter with lettuce, celery, carrot, small sprigs of cauliflower, apple slices, black and green olives, radishes, cucumber slices, spring onions and tomato quarters.

Crab Dip Platter

(see colour picture facing page 16)

6 oz. (170 g) canned crab-meat	freshly ground pepper
	sliced lemon and parsley to garnish
¼ pint (150 ml) fat-free yoghurt	salad 'dunks'
salt	

Combine the crabmeat and yoghurt, seasoning to taste, then put it into a small dish and chill. Place the dish on a larger platter, garnish, and arrange around it asparagus, celery, tomato quarters, slices of large radishes and apple, black and green olives and spring onions to use as 'dunks'. (Supply cocktail sticks for use with the smaller items.)

Softly-softly

Softly-softly

(see picture above)

1 can of frozen orange juice, partly thawed	1 egg white
	ice cubes
1 tbsp. (15 ml) PLJ	lemon and mint to garnish
½ pint (300 ml) water	

Whisk the orange juice, PLJ, water and egg white together until thoroughly blended. Pour over some ice cubes in a long glass, and garnish with a slice of lemon and a sprig of mint. (Serves 3)

Soups

A good soup must have a pleasing appearance, a well-blended, satisfying flavour and a definite consistency. The temperature is also important—hot soup should be piping hot, a cold one should be served very, very cold.

Thin soups—hot or cold—are served as appetisers at the beginning of a full meal, while thick, heavy soups often form the main course of a luncheon or supper, or the first course of an otherwise light meal. These provide good food value and should be served in generous portions.

Stocks
We give here recipes for the three most commonly used stocks, which can serve as the basis for innumerable soups.

To remove fat from stock
If the stock has cooled in the refrigerator, the fat can be removed from it as a solid cake. Remove any small pieces by wiping the surface of the jelly with a clean cloth dipped in hot water and wrung out. If the stock is warm, skim as much fat as possible from the top and remove the remainder by passing small sheets of absorbent paper across the top, or remove the last traces with a piece of ice wrapped in a cloth.

To clear stock
Allow 1 slightly-beaten egg white and 1 crushed egg shell to each quart of stock. Heat the stock only enough to liquefy it. Add the egg and the shell and mix thoroughly, stirring constantly until the mixture boils. Boil vigorously for a few minutes. Remove from the heat, add $\frac{1}{4}$ pint (150 ml) cold water, leave to settle, then strain carefully.

Brown Stock

1 lb. (*450 g*) marrow bone or knuckle of veal, chopped
1 lb. (*450 g*) shin of beef, cut into pieces
3 pints (*1.5 litre*) water
bouquet garni
1 carrot, peeled and sliced
1 onion, skinned and chopped
1 stick of celery, scrubbed and sliced
$\frac{1}{2}$ level tbsp. (*7.5 ml*) salt

To give a good flavour and colour, brown the bones and meat in the oven (exact temperature of no importance) before using them. Put them into a large saucepan with the rest of the ingredients, bring to the boil and remove any fat from the top with a spoon. Simmer for 4–5 hours with a lid on the pan. Strain, and when cold, skim off any more fat. Any stock not used at once may be kept in a cool place for not longer than 2 or 3 days; boil up each day, if not stored in a refrigerator.

White Stock

2 lb. (*1 kg*) knuckle of veal or veal or mutton bones
4 pints (*2 litres*) cold water
little lemon juice (optional)
1 onion, skinned and sliced
2 carrots, peeled and sliced
bouquet garni
2 level tsps. (*10 ml*) salt

Put the bones into a large pan, add the

cold water and lemon juice, bring to the boil and remove any scum that rises. Add the vegetables, bouquet garni and salt, re-boil, cover with a lid and simmer for 4 hours. Strain, and when cold remove any fat. Keep as for brown stock.

Fish Stock

1 cod's head or fish bones and trimmings	bouquet garni
cold water	1 onion, skinned and sliced
salt	

Clean the cod's head or wash the fish trimmings. Put in a saucepan, cover with water, add some salt, bring to the boil and skim. Reduce the heat and add the bouquet garni and onion. Cover, simmer for 40 minutes and strain. Use on the same day, or store in the refrigerator for not more than 2 days.

Bouquet Garni

Most soups are improved by the addition of a small bunch of herbs, called a 'faggot' or 'bouquet garni'. The herbs can be made into a small bunch or tied up in muslin, so that they are easily removed before the soup is served.

bay leaf	⎫	tied in a
sprig of parsley	⎬	small piece
sprig of thyme		of leek
few peppercorns	⎭	leaf

You can, of course, choose other herbs, or include some dried 'mixed herbs'.

Pot-au-feu

(see colour picture facing page 49)

1½ pints (*1 litre*) well-flavoured stock	3 leeks, sliced
½ lb. (*225 g*) chuck steak, cut into cubes	small cauliflower, broken into florets
4 carrots, diced	4 oz. (*115 g*) peas
2 bay leaves	2 tomatoes, skinned and diced
sprig of rosemary	salt and pepper
2 tbsps. (*30 ml*) long-grain rice	pinch of cayenne

Put the stock in a saucepan, add the steak and carrots, with the bay leaves and rosemary. Bring to the boil and simmer gently for 1–1½ hours. Add the rice, leeks, cauliflower and peas and simmer for 15–20 minutes. Remove the bay leaves. Finally, add the tomatoes and seasonings. Serve piping hot. (Serves 4–6)

Ox Tail Soup

1 ox tail	2 quarts (*2 litres*) stock or water
2 rashers of bacon	
1½ oz. (*40 g*) dripping	bouquet garni
2 onions	salt and pepper
2 carrots	1½ oz. (*40 g*) flour
4 outside stalks of celery	2 tsps. (*10 ml*) Worcestershire sauce (optional)
1 small turnip	

Wipe the ox tail, and cut it into joints if this has not already been done. Fry the cut-up bacon, then remove from the pan. Add the dripping, and when it is hot fry the meat on all sides, then remove this also. Slice and fry the vegetables, then return the ox tail and bacon to the pan, adding the stock or water, the bouquet garni and some salt and pepper. Cover, and simmer very gently for 3–4 hours; strain into a bowl and leave until the next day.

Remove all fat from the surface of the soup, and thicken it by stirring in the flour, blended with a little cold stock or water. Add some sauce if desired, and adjust the seasoning as necessary.

The meat may be served separately, or it may be shredded or sieved and added to the finished soup before serving. (Serves 6–8)

Scotch Broth

1½ lb. (*700 g*) neck of mutton	1 onion
	2 leeks
2 quarts (*2 litres*) water	2 carrots
	1 small turnip
salt and pepper	3 pieces of celery
6 oz. (*170 g*) pearl barley	chopped parsley

Trim the fat from the mutton, put the meat into a pan with the water and bring slowly to the boil; remove the scum and add salt, pepper and the washed barley. Cover, and simmer gently for about 1 hour. Prepare the vegetables, cutting them into dice or thin slices, and add to the soup. Cook for a further hour, then take out the meat, remove it from the bones and cut it into small pieces; return these to the pan, with a generous quantity of freshly chopped parsley. (Serves 6–8)

Kidney Soup

½ lb. (*225 g*) kidneys	salt and pepper
1–2 rashers of bacon	bouquet garni
1 onion, sliced	¼ pint (*150 ml*) milk
1 carrot, diced	
2 pints (*1 litre*) stock or water	

Skin, core and cut up the kidney; rind and dice the bacon. Heat the bacon until the fat runs, add the kidney and fry for a few minutes, then remove, add the onion and carrot and sauté until they are lightly cooked. Add the stock, salt, pepper, bacon, kidney and bouquet garni, bring to the boil and simmer till tender—about 1 hour. Remove the bouquet garni, add the milk and boil for 2–3 minutes before serving. (Serves 4)

Chicken Soup

1 chicken carcass	6 peppercorns
1 carrot, peeled	2 cloves
1 onion, skinned	salt and pepper
2–3 sticks of celery	chopped parsley

Remove any remaining pieces of meat from the bones, then break these up and put into a pan with the cut-up vegetables, spices and seasoning. Cover with water and simmer gently for about 2 hours. Strain, add the pieces of meat and the parsley, re-boil and serve. (Serves 4)

Cock-a-leekie

1 boiling fowl, about 2½ lb. (*1 kg*)	4 leeks, sliced
2 pints (*1 litre*) stock or water	salt and pepper
	6 prunes (optional)

Cover the fowl with stock or water and add the leeks and seasoning. Bring to the boil and simmer gently for 3½ hours, until tender. Remove the chicken from the stock, carve off the meat and cut into fairly large pieces. Serve the soup with the chicken pieces in it, or serve the soup on its own, with the chicken as a main course.

If prunes are used, soak them overnight in cold water, halve and stone them and add to the stock 30 minutes before the end of the cooking. (Serves 4–6)

Mulligatawny Soup

1 onion, chopped	2 cloves
1 carrot, grated	1 level tsp. (*5 ml*) curry powder
½ lb. (*200 g*) tomatoes, chopped	1 tbsp. (*15 ml*) chopped parsley
½ green pepper, seeded and chopped	salt and pepper
2 sticks of celery, chopped	1 oz. (*25 g*) cornflour
1 apple, grated	¼ pint (*150 ml*) milk
1 oz. (*25 g*) butter	leftovers of cold cooked chicken
1¾ pints (*1 litre*) chicken stock	1 oz. (*25 g*) rice, ready cooked

Sauté the vegetables and apple in the butter for 5 minutes. Add the stock, flavourings and seasonings and simmer for 2–2½ hours, then sieve. Blend the cornflour with the milk and stir it into the soup. Add the chicken (cut into neat pieces) and the rice, and re-boil to thicken. (Serves 4–6)

Finnan Haddock Soup

2 carrots	½ pint (*300 ml*) fish liquor
4 sticks of celery	
bouquet garni	salt and pepper
1 lb. (*450 g*) Finnan haddock	ground nutmeg or mace
½ oz. (*15 g*) butter	chopped parsley
½ oz. (*15 g*) flour	
¾ pint (*375 ml*) skimmed milk	

Cut up the vegetables, put into a pan with sufficient water to cover and a bouquet garni of fresh herbs, simmer for about 20 minutes, then add the fish. Simmer until the fish and vegetables are tender, then strain off and reserve the liquor. Remove the backbone from the haddock, and put the fish and vegetables through a sieve. Make a thin white sauce, using the butter, flour, milk and fish liquor; season with salt, pepper and a little ground nutmeg or mace, add the fish purée, and serve with a little chopped parsley sprinkled on top. (Serves 4)

Fish and Bacon Chowder

¼ lb. (*115 g*) fresh   8-oz. (*225-g*) can
   haddock   of tomatoes
1 rasher of bacon   salt and pepper
½ oz. (*15 g*) butter   1 bay leaf
1 onion, skinned and   1 clove
   sliced
1 potato, peeled and
   sliced

Skin the fish and simmer the skins in ¼ pint (150 ml) water to make stock. Fry the bacon until the fat runs, add the butter, then the onion and fry gently. Add the sliced potato and the boned, chopped fish. Beat the tomatoes to a thick purée, combine with the fish mixture and add the seasoning and flavourings. Simmer gently for ½–¾ hour. Remove the bay leaf and clove and garnish with parsley before serving. (Serves 1)

Shrimp and Mushroom Chowder

(*see picture on right*)
1 onion   1 pint (*600 ml*) milk
½ oz. (*15 g*) butter   salt and pepper
¼ lb. (*115 g*) mush-   4 oz. (*115 g*) shrimps
   rooms   chopped parsley
2 medium-sized
   potatoes, peeled and
   sliced

Slice the onion and fry gently in the butter without browning. Add the mushrooms and potatoes and cover with the milk. Season well and simmer gently for about 15 minutes. Add the shrimps, and serve very hot, garnished with chopped parsley. (Serves 2–3)

Note: For 4 servings, use 2 onions, ½ oz. (15 g) butter, 6 oz. (170 g) mushrooms, 3 medium-sized potatoes, 1½–2 pints (1 litre) milk and 6 oz. (170 g) shrimps, with seasoning and parsley.

Shrimp and Mushroom Chowder

Fish Chowder

2 rashers of lean   2 potatoes, peeled
   bacon, chopped   and diced
1 onion, skinned and   ½ pint (*300 ml*) fish
   sliced   stock
1 lb. (*450 g*) fresh   salt and pepper
   haddock, cooked   bay leaf
   and flaked   2 cloves
14-oz. (*395-g*) can of   ¼ pint (*150 ml*) milk
   tomatoes   chopped parsley

Fry the bacon until the fat runs, add the onion and sauté until clear. Add the fish, tomatoes and potatoes, with the stock and seasonings, and simmer gently for ½ hour. Add the milk and remove the bay leaf and cloves, then re-heat gently. Serve sprinkled with parsley. (Serves 4)

Hollandaise Soup

1 chicken bouillon   2 egg yolks
   cube   ¼ pint (*150 ml*) milk
1½ pints (*1 litre*) water   1 tbsp. (*15 ml*) single
2 carrots, diced   cream
4 tbsps. (*60 ml*) green   salt and pepper
   peas

Dissolve the bouillon cube in the water and cook the vegetables in this stock.

Strain the liquid. Mix the eggs and milk together and strain into the stock, then re-heat, but do not boil. Remove from the heat, add the cooked vegetables and cream and season to taste. (Serves 4)

Appetiser Soup

1¼ pints (700 ml) water	2 stalks of celery, cut into ½-in. (1.25-cm) lengths
1 beef stock cube	
1 chicken stock cube	3 whole peppercorns
15-oz. (425-g) can tomatoes	¼ level tsp. (1.25 ml) dried sage
1 medium-sized onion, skinned and chopped	salt black pepper grated Parmesan cheese to garnish
4 oz. (115 g) carrots, peeled and thinly sliced	

Put the water into a saucepan, then add the stock cubes, tomatoes, onion, carrot, celery, peppercorns and sage. Mix well, bring to the boil, cover and simmer gently for 1 hour. Adjust the seasonings and serve sprinkled with Parmesan cheese. (Serves 4)

Carrot Soup

9 oz. (255 g) carrots, sliced	1 pint (600 ml) good thin white sauce
2 oz. (55 g) butter	¼ pint (150 ml) cultured buttermilk
pinch of salt	
1 pint (600 ml) stock	

Sauté the carrots in half the butter with some salt for 15 minutes. Add the stock, and cook together until the carrots are tender, then pass them through a sieve and add the white sauce. Bring to the boil and test the seasoning. When about to serve, add the remaining butter and the buttermilk; re-heat without boiling. (Serves 4–6)

Celery Soup

1 head of celery	2 oz. (55 g) fat
1½ pints (900 ml) chicken stock	1½ oz. (40 g) plain flour
½ pint (300 ml) milk	
1 onion, skinned and sliced	

Cut up the celery and cook it in the chicken stock until tender, then sieve. Place the milk and onion in a small pan and bring to the boil. Remove the onion and add the flavoured milk to the celery purée. Melt the fat in a pan, add the flour and blend together. Gradually add the purée, re-heat and season to taste. (Serves 4)

Note: If you have no chicken stock available use water in making this soup.

Bortsch (Beetroot Soup)

(*See picture right*)

¼ oz. (7 g) dripping	1½–2 pints (1 litre) stock
1 large raw beetroot, grated	salt and pepper
1 carrot	2 bay leaves
1 onion	pinch of mixed herbs
¾ lb. (340 g) red cabbage	yoghurt
2 tomatoes	chopped parsley to garnish

Melt the dripping and fry the grated beetroot lightly for 5 minutes. Chop or grate all the other vegetables, and add to the beetroot with the stock, seasoning, and herbs. Bring to the boil, remove any scum on the surface, and continue to cook for about 2 hours. Remove the bay leaves. Serve each portion with a spoonful of yoghurt and a sprinkling of parsley. (Serves 4)

Celery Noodle Soup

1 head of celery	salt and pepper
1 onion	½ pint (300 ml) skimmed milk
2 oz. (55 g) dripping	1 oz. (25 g) noodles
2 pints (1 litre) stock or water	

Wash the celery and cut it into small pieces. Chop the onion and sauté it with the celery in the hot fat. Add the liquid and seasonings, simmer gently till the celery is tender, then sieve and add the milk. Bring to the boil before serving and add the cooked noodles. (Serves 4–5)

Other pasta may be used instead of noodles: tiny letters of the alphabet look effective.

Bortsch (Beetroot soup)

Celery and Onion Soup

1 head of celery	½ pint (*300 ml*) meat
½ lb. (*225 g*) onions	stock and 1 pint
pinch of tarragon	(*600 ml*) water (or
pinch of chervil or	1½ pints (*900 ml*)
parsley	beef cube stock)
salt and pepper	

Cut the celery up small; slice or dice the onions, and place in a large pan. Add the herbs, seasoning, meat stock and water, bring to the boil, then simmer for 1 hour. Sieve and re-heat. (Serves 4)

Corn Chowder

1 oz. (*25 g*) butter	½–1 level tsp. (*2.5–5*
1 large onion, skinned	*ml*) salt
and sliced	pepper
4 oz. (*115 g*) bacon,	12-oz. (*340-g*) can of
diced	whole corn kernels
2 lb. (*1 kg*) old	¾ pint (*375 ml*) milk
potatoes, peeled and	grated cheese and
diced	chopped parsley
¼ pint (*150 ml*)	
boiling water	

Melt the butter in a large saucepan, add the onion and fry until golden-brown, then add the pieces of bacon and fry lightly. Add the potatoes, water, salt and pepper, bring to the boil and simmer for about 15 minutes. Put in the corn and simmer for a further 5 minutes, or until the vegetables are tender. Pour in the milk and re-heat. Serve sprinkled with grated cheese and garnished with parsley. (Serves 4)

Cucumber Soup

(*see colour picture between pages 192, 193*)

½ a cucumber, cut	½ pint (*300 ml*)
into chunks	cultured buttermilk
½ a green pepper,	salt and pepper
seeded and cut up	chopped chives

Blend the cucumber and green pepper together in a blender until a fine consistency is reached. (Alternatively, steam the cucumber and pepper until tender, then sieve and chill.) Add the chilled buttermilk and season to taste. Serve in glasses, garnished with chopped chives. (Serves 2–3)

Country Soup

4 potatoes, peeled	pinch dried basil
and diced	1 bay leaf
2 carrots, peeled and	2 level tsps. (*10 ml*)
thinly sliced	salt
2 medium-sized	¼ level tsp. (*1.25 ml*)
onions, skinned and	pepper
sliced	milk
few lettuce leaves	butter
few celery leaves	chopped parsley

Place the vegetables, lettuce, celery, flavourings and seasoning in a saucepan; cover with cold water (about 1 pint, 600 ml). Bring to the boil, reduce the heat and simmer, covered, for 1 hour. Press the mixture through a food mill or strainer, or purée in an electric blender. Measure the purée, and for every 3 cups add 1 cup of milk. Heat thoroughly. To serve, top with a small piece of butter and sprinkle with parsley. (Serves 4)

Carrot Consommé

(*see picture page 106*)

½ lb. (*225 g*) lean	2–3 peppercorns
beef	salt
1 onion	½ lb. (*225 g*) carrots,
1 carrot	cut into matchstick
2 sticks of celery	strips
1 pint (*600 ml*) stock	juice of ½ lemon
or water	

Mince or chop the beef very finely. Prepare and slice the onion, carrot and celery and put all together in a pan, with the stock or water and the seasonings. Bring to the boil and simmer for about $1\frac{1}{2}$ hours. Strain the soup, add the carrot matchsticks and lemon juice and simmer until the carrots are tender. Adjust the seasoning before serving. (Serves 2–3)

Gardener's Broth

1 rasher of bacon	1–2 tomatoes
1 oz. (*25 g*) butter	a few leaves of
2–3 small onions, sliced	spinach or young cabbage
2–3 small carrots, sliced	2–3 runner beans
1 young turnip or a piece of turnip, sliced	salt and pepper
	pinch of mixed herbs
	1 oz. (*25 g*) macaroni
$1\frac{1}{2}$ pints (*900 ml*) stock or water	grated cheese
	chopped parsley

Rind and dice the bacon, put it in a pan with the butter and onions, and sauté for a few minutes. Add the carrot and turnip and sauté for about the same time.

Add the stock or water and bring to the boil. Add the rest of the vegetables, cut up, and also the seasoning, herbs and macaroni, then cover and simmer for 1 hour, or until the vegetables are tender. Serve with cheese and parsley. (Serves 4)

Mushroom Bouillon
(see colour picture facing page 144)

2 carrots	1 level tsp. (*5 ml*) salt
2 leeks	pepper
2 sprigs of parsley	$\frac{1}{2}$ lb. (*225 g*) fresh
1 bay leaf	mushrooms
$\frac{1}{4}$ tsp. (*1.25 ml*) dried thyme	chopped parsley to garnish
$1\frac{1}{2}$ pints (*900 ml*) beef stock	

Place all ingredients except the mushrooms in a pan, bring to the boil and simmer until the vegetables are soft; strain. Slice the mushrooms very thinly and add to the strained liquor. Cover and simmer for 30 minutes. Season to taste and sprinkle with parsley. (Serves 4)

Carrot Consommé

Mexicalli Soup

(*see colour picture facing page 192*)

3–4 red peppers, seeded and sliced	6 tomatoes, skinned
3 medium-sized onions, skinned and sliced	1½ pints (*900 ml*) chicken stock
	freshly ground pepper
	¼ pint (*150 ml*) milk

Place the peppers, onion, tomatoes and stock in a large pan, bring to the boil and simmer until the vegetables are tender. Drain, retaining the liquor. Sieve or blend the vegetables, mix with the liquor, add some pepper and the milk and bring back to the boil. (Serves 4)

Potato and Cheese Soup

1½ lb. (*700 g*) potatoes	¼ pint (*150 ml*) milk
2 pints (*1 litre*) stock	2 tbsps. (*30 ml*) chopped parsley
salt and pepper	2–3 tbsps. (*30–45 ml*) finely grated Cheddar cheese
½ oz. (*15 g*) flour or cornflour	

Slice the potatoes thinly and cook in the seasoned stock until soft, then mash them with a fork. Stir in the flour, blended with the milk. Season, then bring to the boil; if required, add more milk. Pour into a hot tureen and sprinkle over the parsley mixed with the finely grated cheese. (Serves 4)

Cream of Pumpkin Soup

2 small onions, chopped	salt and pepper
1 oz. (*25 g*) butter	2 eggs, beaten
3 lb. (*1.3 kg*) pumpkin, cooked and sieved	1 pint (*600 ml*) milk
	little grated cheese
1 pint (*600 ml*) water	chopped parsley (optional)

Fry the onions lightly in the butter and put into a pan with the sieved pumpkin, water and seasonings; simmer for about 2 hours. Mix the eggs with the milk, add to the soup, and heat very gently for a further few minutes to cook the egg, taking care to prevent curdling. Add the cheese and the parsley (if used) just before serving. (Serves 6)

French Onion Soup

French Onion Soup

1 oz. (*25 g*) butter	salt
1½ lb. (*700 g*) onions, sliced	freshly ground pepper
2 pints (*1 litre*) beef stock	3 oz. (*85 g*) well-flavoured Cheddar cheese, grated

Melt the butter and brown the onions. Add the stock, salt and pepper and simmer until the onions are translucent. Adjust the seasoning, sprinkle with cheese and place under a hot grill until golden-brown. (Serves 4)

Split Pea Soup

8 oz. (*225 g*) dried split peas, soaked overnight in cold water	1 ham bone, or some scraps of bacon
3 pints (*2 litres*) boiling water	1 level tsp. (*5 ml*) dried sage
1 onion, finely chopped	2 level tsps. (*10 ml*) salt
	½ level tsp. (*2.5 ml*) pepper

Drain the peas and add the boiling water, onion, ham bone or bacon scraps, sage and seasonings. Simmer for 2 hours, until the peas are tender. Remove the ham bone before serving the soup. (Serves 6)

The water in which the bacon or ham has been cooked may be used for making this soup; if it is very salty, no extra salt will be required.

Cream of Spinach Soup

1 lb. (*450 g*) spinach
1½ pints (*900 ml*)
  stock
1 tbsp. (*15 ml*) lemon
  juice
salt and pepper
½ pint (*300 ml*)
  buttermilk
Worcestershire sauce

Cook the spinach in the boiling stock, with the lemon juice, salt and pepper, for 20 minutes. Sieve or blend; add the buttermilk and heat gently. Add a little Worcestershire sauce and adjust the seasoning. (Serves 4)

Tomato Bouillon

15-oz. (*425-g*) can
  tomato juice and an
  equal quantity of
  chicken stock made
  from bouillon cubes
1 small slice of onion,
  chopped
1 stick of celery,
  chopped
2 cloves
6 peppercorns
1 tbsp. (*15 ml*) lemon
  juice
salt and pepper
lemon slices or
  yoghurt, to garnish
  (optional)

Put the tomato juice into a saucepan, and use the can to measure the hot water for making up the chicken stock. Heat the stock, tomato juice, onion, celery, and spices for 10–15 minutes, then strain. Add the lemon juice and salt and pepper to taste. Serve hot or cold, with a slice of lemon or a swirl of yoghurt. (Serves 4)

Tomato Consommé

(*see colour picture facing page 176*)

3 level tbsps. (*45 ml*)
  gelatine
1 chicken stock cube
¾ pint (*375 ml*)
  boiling water
19-oz. (*538-g*) can of
  tomato juice
1–2 tbsps. (*15–30 ml*)
  lemon juice
Angostura bitters
salt and pepper
mint freeze (see p.
  97) and lemon
  wedges to garnish

Dissolve the gelatine and the stock cube in the boiling water. Add the tomato juice, lemon juice and a few drops of bitters, and season with salt and pepper. Leave in a cool place to set. Chop, and pile into glasses. Garnish with mint freeze and lemon wedges. (Serves 6)

Cream of Tomato Soup

1 onion, chopped
1 oz. (*25 g*) butter
8-oz. (*226-g*) can of
  tomatoes
2 tbsps. (*30 ml*) water
salt and pepper
¼ pint (*150 ml*) milk

Sauté the onion in the butter until clear. Add the tomatoes and 2 tbsps. (30 ml) water, season with salt and pepper and blend or sieve. Add the milk, adjust the seasoning and re-heat without boiling. (Serves 1)

Quick Tomato Soup

15-oz. (*425-g*) can of
  tomatoes
1 onion, chopped
1 oz. (*25 g*) butter
½ oz. (*15 g*) flour
½ pint (*300 ml*) milk
salt and pepper

Empty the tomatoes into a saucepan, add the onion and simmer for 10–15 minutes, then sieve. Add the butter, then the flour blended with the milk; stir until boiling and add seasoning to taste. (Serves 3–4)

Vegetable Cocktail Soup (chilled)

(*see picture right*)

4 leeks, cut up finely
1 onion, chopped
1 medium-sized
  potato, sliced
salt and pepper
1½ pints (*900 ml*)
  chicken stock
½ pint (*300 ml*)
  cultured buttermilk
chopped chives

Simmer the leeks, onion and potato with some seasoning in the stock. When tender, sieve or blend. Stir in the buttermilk and chill. Serve sprinkled with chopped chives. (Serves 4)

Crème Vichyssoise

4 leeks
2 oz. (*55 g*) butter
1 onion, chopped
salt and pepper
2 pints (*1 litre*)
  chicken stock
2 potatoes, thinly
  sliced
⅓ pint (*200 ml*) single
  cream
chives to garnish

Prepare the leeks, cut up finely and cook gently for 10 minutes in the butter, together with the onion and seasonings; do not allow to brown. Add the stock and potatoes, and cook until the vegetables are tender, then sieve. Adjust the seasoning, stir in the cream and chill. Sprinkle with chopped chives before serving. (Serves 4)

Cauliflower and Bacon Soup

1 tbsp. (*15 ml*) oil
4 rashers lean bacon, rinded and chopped
1 onion, skinned and chopped
2 carrots, chopped

8 oz. (*225 g*) cauliflower florets
2 sticks celery, chopped
1½ pints (*900 ml*) chicken stock
salt and pepper

Vegetable Cocktail Soup (chilled)

Heat the oil in a large saucepan and lightly fry the bacon and vegetables for 5 minutes. Drain off any excess fat and add the stock. Bring to the boil and simmer for 15 minutes. Adjust seasoning and then liquidise all but a quarter of the soup. Mix all together again and serve hot, garnished with chopped parsley. (Serves 4)

Fish

Fish differs from meat in texture as well as flavour and requires shorter cooking times. The flavour, being rather delicate, is best brought out by skilful combination with other foods; crisp vegetables of decided flavour and colour are a good contrast to the soft texture and the mild flavour of most fish.

When fish is bought whole—with skin, bones, head and tail, etc., intact—then allow 1 lb. (450 g) for 2 people; if bought as steaks, 1 lb. (450 g) will serve 3, 1 lb. (450 g) of fillets will serve 4.

When possible, buy fish on the day you intend to use it; if it is stored overnight in the refrigerator, wrap it securely in foil and place it in a plastic bag to prevent the odour permeating throughout the refrigerator. All fish should be washed before cooking, any scales or blood, etc., being removed.

The method of cooking depends on the type of fish—white, non-oily varieties are usually improved by the addition of a little butter or oil, or by being served with a sauce. Darker, oily fish are best grilled or baked. In general, fish requires only a short cooking time; it is done if the flesh will separate easily into flakes when tested with the point of a knife.

White fish are plaice, turbot, halibut, haddock, hake and cod, etc.

Oily fish are herrings, mackerel, sprats, salmon, etc.

Recipes for a couple of sauces to serve with fish and also for Lemon Butter are given at the end of the chapter.

Seasons for Fresh Fish

While nearly all sea fish are seasonable the year round, they are least so at spawning time and immediately after it, and best from some time after one spawning to before the next: the eggs and milt are formed at the expense of fat and flesh, and fish which are just 'shotten' are therefore of poor quality. The seasons when fish are most preferred vary in some localities.

Baked Bream

Oven temperature: 350°F., 180°C., mark 4
Choose a large fresh-water bream of about 3–4 lb (1–2 kg). Wash it, without removing the head, and wrap it in thin slices of bacon. Put it in a roasting tin and bake until tender (about 40 minutes), basting it frequently. When it is cooked, the bacon fat will have melted and the fish will be a nice golden colour. Put it in a dish; remove bacon. Heat ¼ pint (150 ml) soured cream, pour over fish and sprinkle with pepper. Garnish with lemon. (Serves 4–5)

Cod en Cocotte

1 small onion	salt and pepper
½ oz. (15 g) butter	1 tbsp. (15 ml)
1 cod cutlet, skinned	cheese, finely grated
1 large tomato, skinned	

Oven temperature: 350°F., 180°C., mark 4
Chop the onion finely, fry it in the fat, and put it into an individual ovenproof dish. Put the cod cutlet on top, with the tomato. Season, then sprinkle with the grated cheese. Bake for 20–30 minutes, until the fish is cooked. (Serves 1)

Grilled Cod Steaks

(*see picture below*)
Wipe the fish and brush lightly with oil. Season with salt and pepper and cook under a moderate grill for 10–15 minutes, turning once. Serve with Belgian cucumber. (See recipe in Vegetables chapter)

Spanish Cod

1 oz. (25 g) rice	1 clove of garlic,
½ pint (300 ml) water	skinned and crushed
oil	salt and pepper
1 small onion,	3 tbsps. (45 ml) dry
skinned and sliced	white wine or stock
1 cod steak	chopped parsley
2 tomatoes, skinned and sliced	

Cook the rice in boiling water for 10 minutes, then drain. Heat the oil and sauté the onion. Add the fish, tomatoes, garlic, seasoning and wine, cover and simmer gently for 15–20 minutes. Lift the fish on to a warmed plate. Add some parsley to the liquor, stir well and pour over the fish. (Serves 1)

Grilled Cod Steaks

Cod Cutlet Cream

2 oz. (*55 g*) butter
4 cod cutlets
4 oz. (*115 g*) onion,
  thinly sliced
6 oz. (*170 g*) mush-
  rooms, sliced
salt and pepper
¼ pint (*150 ml*)
  soured cream
dash of Tabasco sauce
pinch of dried basil
1 tbsp. (*15 ml*)
  chopped chives

Brush cod with a little melted butter and grill until tender. Gently cook the onion in remaining butter until tender but not coloured; add the mushrooms and cook for 2 minutes. Season with salt and pepper, pour in the soured cream, and add the Tabasco and basil. Heat gently until the sauce is really hot but not boiling. Place the cutlets on a hot serving dish and pour the sauce over; sprinkle with chopped chives. (Serves 4)

Spanish Cod with Red Pepper Sauce

1½ lb. (*700 g*) fresh
  cod fillet
2 red peppers
1 clove of garlic
½ pint (*300 ml*) fish
  stock or water
1 tbsp. (*15 ml*)
  vinegar
4 tbsps. (*60 ml*) oil
salt
chopped parsley

Skin the fish and cut it into pieces. Halve the peppers, scoop out the seeds and cook the cases in boiling salted water for 5 minutes, then drain and chop them finely. Skin and chop the garlic. Mix the red peppers and garlic together and crush them well, using the back of a wooden spoon. Choose a suitable-sized pan to cook the fish in; put in the pepper mixture, stock, vinegar, oil and salt to taste. Bring this liquid to boiling point, add the fish and cook very gently until it is tender. Drain the fish and keep it hot in a serving dish. Boil the liquid until it is reduced by half, pour over the fish and sprinkle with chopped parsley. Serve at once. (Serves 4)

Simple Baked Haddock

Oven temperature: 350°F., 180°C., mark 4
Wash or wipe the fish and place in an ovenproof dish. Add 2 tbsps. (30 ml) milk,

2 tbsps. (30 ml) dry white wine and a bouquet garni. Cover and bake for 20–30 minutes.

Cod and Cottage Cheese Cocottes

2 medium eggs,
  beaten
1 oz. (*25 g*) soft white
  breadcrumbs
2 tbsps. (*30 ml*) hot
  milk
8 oz. (*226 g*) cottage
  cheese
¼ lb. (*115 g*) cod
few drops of
  Worcestershire sauce
salt and pepper
slices of green pepper
  or a few sliced
  stuffed olives to
  garnish

Oven temperature: 375°F., 190°C., mark 5
Add the eggs to the breadcrumbs, then stir in the remaining ingredients and mix thoroughly; season well to taste. Divide the mixture equally between 4 well-greased individual dishes. Stand the dishes in a baking tin containing about 1 inch of water and bake towards the top of the oven for about 35 minutes, or till set and firm. Garnish each with sliced green pepper or sliced stuffed olive. Serve hot. (Serves 4)

Note: The mixture can, of course, be baked in one casserole, if preferred.

Baked Haddock with Mushrooms

haddock weighing
  2–3 lb. (*1–1.5 kg*)
1 tbsp. (*15 ml*) butter
4 small onions,
  skinned and
  chopped
1 clove of garlic,
  crushed
6 mushrooms,
  chopped
1 tomato, skinned
  and sliced
2 tbsps. (*30 ml*) soft
  breadcrumbs
2 eggs
crumbs to coat fish

Oven temperature: 350°F., 180°C., mark 4
Clean the haddock without removing the head. Melt the butter and sauté the onions. Add the garlic and mushrooms and cook for 3–4 minutes, then add the tomato and crumbs. Remove from the heat, quickly beat in 1 egg and cool. Stuff the haddock with the mixture and secure with skewers. Lightly beat the

Spanish Cream (see page 197), Grape Jelly (see page 196), Apricot Creams (see page 194), Raspberry Delight (see page 197)

remaining egg and coat the fish, then dust with crumbs. Place in a lightly greased baking tin, and bake for about 30 minutes. Remove the skewers and serve the fish on a platter, with baked potatoes and broccoli. (Serves 4)

Zesty Haddock

1½ lb. (*700 g*) fresh or frozen haddock fillet
salt and pepper
¼ pint (*140 g*) soured cream
¼ level tsp. (*1.25 ml*) dry mustard
¼ level tsp. (*1.25 ml*) ground ginger
thyme
paprika
chopped parsley to garnish

Oven temperature: 350°F., 180°C., mark 4
Divide the haddock into 4 serving portions and place in a lightly greased shallow baking dish. Season with salt and pepper. Mix together the cream, mustard, ginger and thyme and spread over the fish. Bake for 20–25 minutes. Serve immediately, topped with paprika and parsley. (Serves 4)

Poached Haddock and Shrimp Sauce

1 haddock (2lb., *1 kg*)
½ level tsp. (*2.5 ml*) salt
2 tbsps. (*30 ml*) chopped celery
1 tbsp. (*15 ml*) chopped onion
sprig of parsley
few peppercorns
1 oz. (*25 g*) flour
1 oz. (*25 g*) margarine
2 tbsps. (*30 ml*) shelled shrimps
lemon and watercress to garnish

First fillet the haddock, then cut each fillet in half lengthwise. Cover the bones, head and trimmings with cold water, add salt and bring slowly to the boil, then skim and add the celery, onion, parsley and peppercorns. Simmer for about 1 hour, then strain into a shallow pan and add the fish fillets, folded in three; bring to the boil and simmer for about 10 minutes. When the fish is cooked, keep it hot on a dish. Thicken the liquor by stirring in the flour and margarine, worked together; add the shrimps and pour the sauce over the fish. Garnish with lemon and watercress. (Serves 3–4)

This shrimp sauce is good with many different kinds of fish.

Scotch Haddock

1 lb. (*450 g*) cooked smoked haddock
1 oz. (*25 g*) butter
cayenne pepper
lemon juice
chopped parsley
4 eggs
tomato to garnish

Remove all bones from the fish and flake the flesh. Heat the butter and lightly sauté the fish. Add the seasoning, lemon juice and some of the parsley. Beat the eggs and pour over the fish. Heat gently, stirring occasionally, until scrambled. Serve sprinkled with parsley and garnished with tomato wedges. (Serves 4)

Haddock Rarebit

knob of butter
2 tbsps. (*30 ml*) milk
2 oz. (*55 g*) grated cheese
mustard
4 oz. (*115 g*) cooked smoked haddock, flaked
1 slice of toast

Melt the butter and add the milk, cheese and mustard. Stir all together until the cheese melts, then add the haddock. Continue to heat gently. Pour the mixture over a slice of toast and grill for 1–2 minutes, until golden. (Serves 1)

Haddock Roly-poly

(see picture page 114)

1 lb. (*450 g*) flaky pastry
1 lb. (*450 g*) haddock fillets, steamed
4 rashers of lean bacon, chopped
8 oz. (*225 g*) mushrooms, sliced
salt and pepper
beaten egg to glaze
lemon and parsley to garnish

Oven temperature: 425°F., 220°C., mark 7
Roll out the pastry on a lightly floured board to form an oblong about 15 by 12 inches (38 × 30 cm). Skin and flake the haddock. Fry the bacon and drain on absorbent paper. Sauté the mushrooms in the bacon fat, then allow to cool. Spread the fish, bacon, mushrooms and seasoning

113

Summer Party Punch (see page 199)

Haddock Roly-poly

over the pastry, and roll up tightly, sealing with egg. Place on a large baking sheet, brush lightly with egg and bake for about 30 minutes. Serve cut in slices, accompanied by lemon wedges and garnished with parsley. (Serves 4)

Halibut and Cucumber Mornay

4 halibut steaks	½ a cucumber, peeled
salt and pepper	and diced
6 peppercorns	¼ pint (*150 ml*)
parsley	cultured buttermilk
¼ pint (*150 ml*) dry	4 oz. (*115 g*) cheese,
cider	grated

Oven temperature: 350°F., 180°C., mark 4
Wash and trim the steaks. Place in an ovenproof dish or casserole, with some seasoning and parsley, and pour the cider over. Cover with foil and bake for about 20 minutes. Simmer the cucumber in the buttermilk, with salt and pepper, for 10 minutes. When the fish is cooked, remove the peppercorns and parsley and pour the cucumber mixture over. Sprinkle with cheese and grill. (Serves 4)

Halibut Mozzarella

4 steaks of halibut	slices of Mozzarella
olive oil	or Cheddar cheese
salt and pepper	parsley to garnish
2 tomatoes	

Heat the grill. Brush the halibut steaks over with olive oil and sprinkle with salt and pepper. Cut the tomatoes into 3 slices crossways and brush them with oil. Grill the fish for 5 minutes on the first side, turn it over and grill for a further 4 minutes; add the tomato slices. Place the sliced cheese on top of the fish steaks and put these under the grill, so that the cheese melts and becomes lightly browned. Serve with the grilled sliced tomato and garnish with sprigs of parsley. (Serves 4)

114

Devilled Herrings

4 herrings
1 oz. (25 g) butter
2 level tsps. (10 ml)
  curry paste

½ level tsp. (2.5 ml)
  curry powder
little lemon juice
lemon to garnish

Clean and fillet the herrings. Cream the butter and work in the curry paste, powder and lemon juice. Spread over the fish and grill. Serve at once on a hot dish, garnished with cut lemon. (Serves 4)

Cider-baked Herrings

4 herrings
salt and pepper
½ pint (300 ml) cider,
  approx.
1 level tbsp. (15 ml)
  mixed pickling spice

4 bay leaves
2 small onions, cut
  into rings
parsley to garnish

Oven temperature: 300°F., 150°C., mark 1
Clean, split and fillet the herrings. Season well with salt and pepper and roll them up, skin inwards, beginning at the tail. Place them neatly and fairly close together in an ovenproof dish. Cover with cider and sprinkle with the pickling spice. Decorate with bay leaves and rings of onion. Cover with foil and bake for about 1½ hours. Garnish with parsley. (Serves 4)

Soused Herring

4 herrings, cleaned
  thoroughly
juice of 3 lemons
6 tbsps. (90 ml) dry
  white wine
½ pint (300 ml) water

6 peppercorns
1 bay leaf
½ level tsp. (2.5 ml)
  salt
1 onion, thinly sliced

Oven temperature: 350°F., 180°C., mark 4
Place the prepared fish in an ovenproof dish. Pour in the liquids to cover the fish and add the seasonings. Cover and bake very slowly for ¾ hour. When the fish is cooked, strain the liquid and pour it back over the herrings. Serve cold. (Serves 4)

Rolled Herrings in Wine Sauce

1½ lb. (700 g) fresh
  herrings
salt
juice of 1 lemon
1½ oz. (40 g)
  margarine
1½ oz. (40 g) flour
4–5 tbsps. (60–75 ml)
  white wine

¾ pint (375 ml)
  cultured buttermilk
  or milk
1–2 tbsps. (15–30 ml)
  chopped bacon
1–2 gherkins,
  chopped

Bone the herrings, salt them and sprinkle some lemon juice over. Make a sauce with the fat, flour, wine and buttermilk. Mix the bacon and gherkins together,

Cider-baked Herrings

place some on each herring fillet and roll the fillets, securing them with cocktail sticks or fine string. Simmer them for about 20 minutes in the wine sauce, remove the cocktail sticks or string and serve with mashed potatoes and baked tomatoes. (Serves 4)

Herring Salad

6 herring fillets, cooked and cooled	chopped chives
	salt and pepper
2 boiled potatoes	lemon dressing
½ a cucumber	lettuce
2 red-skinned apples	

Cut the fish, potatoes, cucumber and apples into even-shaped dice. Add the chives, salt and pepper and toss in the lemon dressing. Serve in lettuce cups. (Serves 4)

Orange and Cucumber Rollmops
(see picture p. 117)

2 large oranges	2-in. (5-cm) piece of cucumber
8 rollmop herrings, drained	

Remove the pith and peel from the oranges, and segment them so that all membranes are removed. Cut each segment into half, then cut the cucumber into ½-inch (1-cm) dice and mix with the orange segments. Open the rollmops; if they are filled with onion, this may if you like be chopped and added to the filling. Use half the filling to stuff the rollmops, roll up tightly and place, with the tails sticking in the air, down the centre of an oblong dish. Arrange the remaining orange and cucumber pieces on either side. (Serves 4)

Monks' Mackerel

4 medium-sized mackerel, oven-ready	2 level tsps. (10 ml) dried herbs
oil	12 black olives
2 onions, chopped	salt and pepper
2 bay leaves	lemon wedges
4 tsps. (20 ml) lemon juice	

Oven temperature: 350°F., 180°C., mark 4
Place the mackerel in a greased baking dish and cover with the onion, bay leaves, lemon juice, herbs and olives. Season well with salt and pepper. Cover and bake for 30–40 minutes. Remove the bay leaves. Serve with lemon wedges. (Serves 4)

Grilled Mackerel

Clean and score the fish. Brush with oil, then cook on both sides under a hot grill; allow 15–20 minutes in all. Serve on a hot dish with grilled tomatoes, lemon and parsley or maître d'hôtel butter.

Baked Mackerel
(see colour picture facing page 17)

4 mackerel, prepared	4 oz. (115 g) mushrooms, sliced
2 shallots, finely sliced	juice of 1 lemon
4 medium-sized tomatoes, skinned and sliced	lemon and dill for garnish

Oven temperature: 350°F., 180°C., mark 4
Lightly oil 4 sheets of foil, place 1 mackerel on each sheet and add some of the shallots, tomatoes, mushrooms and lemon juice. Parcel up the tin foil, place the fish on a baking sheet and bake for about 30 minutes. Garnish. (Serves 4)

Grilled Plaice

1 small plaice per person	1 level tbsp. (15 ml) tomato paste
1 tbsp. (15 ml) oil	salt and pepper

Clean the fish and remove the head and fins. Wash and dry it thoroughly. Mix together the oil, tomato paste and seasonings. Brush the fish with the mixture and grill it under a hot grill for 8–10 minutes, turning it once. Serve with lemon butter.

Portuguese Plaice

1 tsp. (5 ml) chopped chives	2 fillets of plaice
	a little white wine
1 tomato	salt and pepper

Oven temperature: 350°F., 180°C., mark 4
Chop the chives; skin and slice the tomato. Place in an ovenproof dish. Fold each fish fillet in three and lay them on the tomato; cover the tomato and fish with wine, add some salt and pepper, and bake for 25 minutes. (Serves 1)

Tomato Plaice Fillets

8 small plaice fillets	salt and pepper
tartare sauce	chopped parsley
8 slices of processed cheese (optional)	toast triangles
8-oz. (*226-g*) can tomatoes	

Oven temperature: 350°F., 180°C., mark 4
Skin and wash the plaice fillets, spread with Tartare sauce, then if desired wrap each fillet round a slice of processed cheese; fix with a skewer, and place in a greased pie dish. Sieve the canned tomatoes, season and pour round the fish. Bake for 20–30 minutes. Sprinkle with chopped parsley and serve with triangles of toast. (Serves 4)

Grilled Salmon

(see colour picture facing page 177)

3 salmon cutlets	a little butter
salad oil	3 tomatoes
4 oz. (*115 g*) button mushrooms	maître d'hôtel butter
	parsley or watercress

Wipe the salmon and brush all over with oil. Put on to a hot greased grid and grill for about 10 minutes on one side, then turn carefully and cook the other side, again brushing with oil. Peel the mushrooms and sauté in a little butter; grill the halved tomatoes. Serve the salmon on a hot dish, with a small pat of maître d'hôtel butter on each cutlet, and garnish with parsley or watercress and the grilled tomato halves. Arrange the button mushrooms in neat groups between the cutlets. (Serves 3)

Salmon Salad

7-oz. (*198-g*) can of salmon, flaked	3 sticks of celery, chopped
1 apple, cored and chopped	freshly ground pepper
½ tsp. (*2.5 ml*) onion juice	¼ pint (*150 ml*) tomato dressing

Mix all the ingredients together, chill, and serve on a bed of lettuce. (Serves 2)

Sardine and Egg Fingers

Mash 3–4 sardines, season with salt and pepper, and add a few drops of vinegar (if this is popular). Spread on strips of buttered toast or bread and butter and decorate with slices of hard-boiled egg and small sprigs of parsley. (Serves 2)

Orange and Cucumber Rollmops

Sole with Mushrooms

2 sole, filletted	1 oz. (*25 g*) butter
2 shallots, chopped	4 oz. (*115 g*) button
3 tbsps. (*45 ml*) dry	mushrooms, sliced
white wine	juice of ½ a lemon
1 bay leaf	lemon wedges
salt and pepper	parsley to garnish

Oven temperature: 350°F., 180°C., mark 4
Wash the fillets, roll up (skin side inside) and place in an ovenproof dish, with the shallots, wine, bay lea and seasonings. Cover and bake for about 30 minutes. Melt the butter and sauté the mushrooms, add the lemon juice and simmer for 1–2 minutes. Lift the fillets out on to a serving dish, add the mushrooms; garnish with lemon and parsley. (Serves 4)

Grilled Sole and Grapes

1 lemon sole per	lemon juice
person	grapes and parsley to
oil	garnish
salt and pepper	

Brush the sole very lightly with a little oil, sprinkle with salt and pepper, and grill. Squeeze the lemon juice over the fish, and serve garnished with grapes and parsley sprigs.

Lobster Thermidor

2 small cooked	4 tbsps. (*60 ml*) white
lobsters (½ lb., *225 g*	wine
each)	¼ pint (*140 g*) soured
2 oz. (*55 g*) butter	cream
1 tbsp. (*15 ml*)	3 level tbsps. grated
chopped shallot	Parmesan cheese
2 tbsps. (*30 ml*)	mustard, salt and
chopped parsley	paprika pepper
1–2 tsps. (*5–10 ml*)	
chopped tarragon	

Remove the lobster meat from the shells, chop the claw and head meat roughly and cut the tail meat into thick slices. Melt 1 oz. (25 g) butter in a saucepan and add the shallot, parsley and tarragon. After a few minutes add the wine and simmer for 5 minutes, then add the soured cream. Add the lobster meat to the sauce, with 1 tbsp. (15 ml) of the cheese,

the remaining butter in small pieces, and mustard, salt and paprika to taste. Arrange the mixture in the shells, sprinkle with the remaining cheese and put under the grill to brown the top quickly. Serve at once. (Serves 2)

Sprats on Skewers

Wash the sprats and dry them thoroughly, then toss in seasoned flour. Take some small skewers and thread 6–8 sprats on each, sticking the skewers through each head and pushing the sprats close together. Fry in hot fat, turning them when browned on the underside, and drain on paper. Garnish with wedges of lemon.

Moulded Prawn Salad
(*see colour picture facing page 208*)

2 level tbsps. (*30 ml*)	1 tbsp. (*15 ml*)
gelatine	chopped chives
¼ pint (*150 ml*) water	½ level tsp. (*2.5 ml*)
1 pint (*600 ml*) low-	salt
fat yoghurt	freshly ground pepper
1 tbsp. (*15 ml*) lemon	a pinch of chilli powder
juice	lemon and whole
8 oz. (*225 g*) prepared	prawns to garnish
prawns	
2 sticks of celery,	
chopped	

Dissolve the gelatine in the water in the usual way. Mix together the yoghurt and lemon juice; add the prawns, celery and chives, with the seasonings. Stir in the gelatine mixture, then pour into individual moulds, or one mould, and leave in a cold place. When set, turn out on to a serving dish and garnish with lemon wedges and whole prawns. (Serves 8)

Shrimp Courgettes
(*see colour picture facing page 209*)

8 even-sized	freshly ground pepper
courgettes	2 tbsps. (*30 ml*)
a 7-oz. (*198-g*) can of	cheese dressing
shrimps	
1 tbsp. (*15 ml*) lemon	
juice	

Remove a thin slice lengthwise from each

courgette and scoop out the seeds. Blanch for 3–4 minutes in boiling water and cool. Fill with shrimps, add some lemon juice and sprinkle with freshly ground black pepper. Top with dressing and chill before serving. (Serves 8)

Apple-stuffed Kippers

(see picture below)

2 pairs of kippers	1 apple, cored
¼ lb. (*115 g*) button mushrooms	juice of ½ lemon
1 oz. (*25 g*) butter	½ level tsp. (*2.5 ml*) salt
¼ lb. (*115 g*) tomatoes	

Oven temperature: 425°F., 220°C., mark 7
Carefully remove the bones from the kippers. Fold in half and place, tails uppermost, down the centre of an oblong ovenproof dish. Pull the tails back, so that kippers are opened ready for filling. To make the stuffing: Wash the mushrooms and cut into quarters. Melt the butter in a saucepan, add the mushrooms and toss over the heat for few seconds. Cut the tomatoes and apple into ½-inch pieces, add to the mushrooms and mix well. Add the lemon juice and salt. Fill the kippers with this mixture and fold the tails over again. Cover with foil and bake for 20–25 minutes. Serve hot. (Serves 4)

Fish Olives (made with Whiting)

2 fillets of whiting	a little margarine
salt and pepper	parsley
dried sage	
¼ lb. (*115 g*) sausage-meat	

Oven temperature: 350°F., 180°C., mark 4
Skin the fillets, season and add some sage. Put a portion of sausage-meat on each fillet, roll up and put in a greased dish. Dot with a little margarine, cover and bake for 20 minutes. Garnish with parsley and serve with mustard sauce. (Serves 1)

Golden Fish

1 egg	salt and pepper
4 oz. white fish fillet	chopped parsley
¼ pint (*150 ml*) cheese sauce	(optional)
	toast

Hard-boil the egg (cook for 10 minutes). At the same time, cover the fish with cold water, bring slowly to the boil, cover with a lid, turn off the heat and leave for 5 minutes. Meanwhile, make the sauce: shell and chop the egg; drain, skin and chop the fish, and add both to the cheese sauce. Add seasoning to taste, and parsley if used. Re-heat, and serve with toast. (Serves 1)

Apple-stuffed Kippers

Fish Pie

1½ lb. (*700 g*) cod fillet
2 oz. (*55 g*) prawns, shelled
2 eggs, hard-boiled
½ pint (*300 ml*) white sauce
½ lb. (*225 g*) mashed potato
egg to glaze

Oven temperature: 400°F., 200°C., mark 6
Cook the cod, then remove all bones and skin and flake the fish. Put it in a casserole, together with the prawns and sliced eggs, and cover with the sauce. Cream the potato, adding a little milk if necessary, and cover the pie with it. Brush the potato with the egg and bake for 35 minutes. (Serves 4)

Cheese-Grilled Fish

1 cod or hake steak
a small piece of onion, grated (optional)
½ oz. (*15 g*) butter
2 oz. (*55 g*) cheese, grated
½ level tsp. (*2.5 ml*) dry mustard
salt and pepper

Trim the fins from the fish and remove the centre bone with a small, sharp knife. Mix the remaining ingredients together to form a paste. Grill the fish under a medium heat for about 5 minutes, then turn it over and grill on the second side for about 4 minutes. Cover with the cheese mixture and continue grilling under a good heat until the cheese is golden and bubbling. For variety, serve with pickled red cabbage or beetroot. (Serves 1)

Poached Fish au Gratin

1 lb. (*450 g*) white fish fillets—hake, bream, haddock, plaice, etc.
salt and pepper
lemon juice
¾ pint (*375 ml*) fish stock
½ pint (*300 ml*) white sauce
2 oz. (*55 g*) cheese, grated
browned bread-crumbs
shavings of butter

If the fillets are thin, fold them in half after removing the dark skin. Grease a frying pan or casserole and add the fish. Sprinkle with salt, pepper and a squeeze of lemon juice and pour in just enough hot fish stock to cover. (If no fish stock is available, use half milk and half water.) Bring to simmering point, then poach the fish very gently for not more than 10 minutes; drain, and put into a shallow heatproof dish. Make the sauce, using some of the fish liquor and milk, season well and when of a good coating consistency, add most of the cheese. Pour the sauce over the fish, and sprinkle over the top the rest of the cheese mixed with some browned crumbs. Dot with shavings of butter or margarine and put under a hot grill to melt and brown the cheese. (Serves 3)

Fish Soufflé

½ lb. (*225 g*) cooked smoked fish
¼ lb. (*115 g*) cooked potatoes
1 oz. (*25 g*) butter or margarine
1 oz. (*25 g*) cheese, grated
2–3 tbsps. (*30–45 ml*) milk
salt and pepper
1 egg yolk and 2 whites
watercress to garnish

Oven temperature: 400°F., 200°C., mark 6
Flake the fish finely and mash the potatoes. Melt the fat, add the potatoes and finely grated cheese, and beat well. Add enough milk to make the mixture light and creamy; add the fish, season and mix well. Cool the mixture slightly and add the egg yolk, then lightly fold in the stiffly whisked egg whites. Put into a greased 6-inch (15-cm) soufflé dish and bake for about 30 minutes. Serve immediately, garnished with watercress. (Serves 2)

Fish Provençale

1 onion, skinned and chopped
½–1 green pepper, seeded and chopped
2–3 oz. (*60–80 g*) streaky bacon, chopped
1 oz. (*25 g*) butter
1 lb. (*450 g*) fillet of cod or haddock, skinned
seasoned flour
15-oz. (*425-g*) can tomatoes, drained
1 bay leaf
salt and pepper

Fry the onion, pepper and bacon gently in the butter for 5–10 minutes, until soft but not coloured. Wash and dry the fish and cut into 1-inch (2.5-cm) cubes. Toss the cubes in seasoned flour and fry with the vegetables for a further 2–3 minutes. Stir in the tomatoes, bay leaf and seasoning, bring to the boil, stirring gently, cover with a lid and simmer for 10–15 minutes, until the fish and vegetables are cooked. (Serves 4)

Fish à la Portugaise

1 onion	salt and pepper
2 tomatoes	juice of 1 lemon
1 green pepper	$\frac{1}{4}$ pint (*150 ml*) water
$1\frac{1}{2}$ lb. (*700 g*) white fish	

Oven temperature: 350°F., 180°C., mark 4
Slice the onion and tomatoes; seed and slice the green pepper. Put a layer of vegetables in the bottom of a casserole, next a layer of fish, then the rest of the vegetables. Season, and add the lemon juice and water. Cover and bake for 30 minutes. (Serves 4)

Devonshire Fish with Mushrooms

1 lb. (*450 g*) cod fillet	$\frac{1}{2}$ pint (*300 ml*) dry cider
salt and pepper	
1 tomato, skinned and sliced	$\frac{3}{4}$ oz. (*20 g*) fat
	$\frac{1}{2}$ oz. (*15 g*) flour
2 rashers of bacon, cut up	lemon and parsley
4 oz. (*115 g*) mush-rooms, sliced	

Oven temperature: 400°F., 200°C., mark 6
Cut up the cod, put in a dish with some salt and pepper and add the tomato, bacon and mushrooms. Almost cover the fish with cider, cover the dish with grease-proof paper and bake for $\frac{1}{2}$ hour. Strain off the liquor and use to make a sauce with the fat and flour; season, and pour over the fish. Garnish with lemon and parsley. (Serves 3)

Fish Braised in Cider

1 lb. (*450 g*) white fish fillet	salt and pepper
	$\frac{1}{4}$ pint (*150 ml*) cider
3 carrots	1 level tbsp. (*15 ml*) flour
3 onions	
butter	
mixed herbs	

Oven temperature: 350°F., 180°C., mark 4
Wipe the fish and cut into portions. Cut up the carrots and onions and sauté them in some butter, add the herbs and put them in a casserole. Season with salt and pepper and place the fish on the top. Add the cider, cover and bake until the fish and vegetables are tender—about 40 minutes. Drain the cider from the vegetables and use to make a sauce. Melt $\frac{1}{2}$ oz. (*15 g*) butter, add the flour, cook for 1–2 minutes over a low heat, then gradually add the cider. To serve, pour the sauce over the fish. (Serves 2)

Indonesian Fish

1 lb. (*450 g*) white fish	1 tbsp. (*15 ml*) butter
	$\frac{1}{2}$ level tsp. (*2.5 ml*) salt
1 red pepper, halved and seeded	1 level tsp. (*5 ml*) turmeric
$\frac{1}{2}$ lb. (*225 g*) onions, skinned	$\frac{3}{4}$ pint (*375 ml*) milk
$\frac{1}{4}$ oz. (*10 g*) root ginger	

Wash the fish and cut it into serving pieces. Cut the red pepper into fine strips and slice the onions; fry these lightly with the bruised ginger in butter, add salt and turmeric and fry for a few minutes longer. Pour in the milk and bring to the boil. Lay the fish in the mixture and simmer gently for 15 minutes, until tender. Remove the ginger and serve immediately. (Serves 2)

Salerno Fish (Italian)

4 fillets of hake or cod cutlets	chopped parsley
	1 level tsp. (*5 ml*) flour
1 tbsp. (*15 ml*) oil	
1 clove of garlic, skinned and crushed	2–3 tbsps. (*30–45 ml*) stock
1 tsp. (*5 ml*) chopped chives	salt and pepper
	parsley to garnish
6 mushrooms, sliced	
1 tbsp. (*15 ml*)	

Prepare the fillets. Heat the oil in a saucepan, add the garlic, chives, mush-rooms and parsley, and cook for a few minutes. Stir in the flour and cook for a further 3 minutes. Very slowly add the stock, salt and pepper and bring to the boil. Cover and simmer gently for 10 minutes. Meanwhile, grill the fish, put into a hot dish and cover with the sauce. Garnish with parsley. (Serves 4)

Curried Fish

1½ lb. (*700 g*) white fish, cooked (haddock, cod or hake)	1 pint (*600 ml*) stock
	2 tsps. (*10 ml*) chutney
	1 oz. (*25 g*) sultanas
1 oz. (*25 g*) butter	1 tsp. (*5 ml*) lemon
2 medium-sized onions, skinned and chopped	juice
	salt and pepper
	boiled rice, hard-
1 oz. (*25 g*) flour	boiled egg and
1 level tbsp. (*15 ml*) curry powder	parsley to garnish

Remove the skin and bones from the fish and flake it. Melt the butter and sauté the chopped onions, then add the flour and the curry powder and cook for 2 minutes over a low heat. Add the liquid (use fish stock if available) and simmer for about 20 minutes, then add the remaining ingredients and stir in the flaked fish. Serve the curry surrounded with boiled rice and decorated with hard-boiled egg and parsley. (Serves 4)

Fish and Bacon Rolls

8 back rashers of bacon	salt and pepper
	lemon juice
8 small fillets of plaice	sprigs of parsley

Oven temperature: 350°F., 180°C., mark 4
Remove the bacon rinds and flatten the rashers with the back of a knife on a board. Put a plaice fillet on each rasher, add salt and pepper and a squeeze of lemon juice. Roll up the stuffed rashers and bake for about 25 minutes. Garnish with parsley sprigs. (Serves 4)

Savoury Fish Stew

2 lb. (*1 kg*) mackerel	1 clove of garlic, skinned and crushed
1 oz. (*25 g*) seasoned flour	¼ pint (*150 ml*) vinegar
2 tsps. (*10 ml*) olive oil	3 level tsps. (*15 ml*) tomato paste
2–3 onions, sliced	
chopped parsley	

Prepare the fish and cut into 2-inch (5-cm) lengths. Coat with seasoned flour and fry in hot olive oil, then remove. Fry the onions until clear, and add the parsley, garlic and fish. Pour in the vinegar, tomato paste and sufficient water to cover, bring to the boil and simmer very gently for ½ hour, taking care not to break up the fish. Serve hot, with noodles. (Serves 4)

Tomato and Fish Moulded Salad

4 level tsps. (*20 ml*) powdered gelatine	cooked peas
	1½ lb. (*700 g*) cooked white fish
artificial sweetener to taste	¼ pint (*150 ml*) good white sauce
1 tsp. (*5 ml*) piquant table sauce	chopped chives, shrimps and water-
salt and pepper	cress to garnish
1 pint (*600 ml*) tomato juice	

Dissolve the gelatine in a little hot water. Mix the sweetener, piquant sauce, salt, pepper and tomato juice, and add the gelatine. Pour a little of this mixture into a damp ring mould, add the peas, then the rest of the liquid, and allow to set. Turn out on to a dish, and fill the centre of the mould with the fish, bound to-gether with white sauce. Garnish with chopped chives, shrimps and watercress. (Serves 4)

Winter Fish Salad

1 lettuce	2 tbsps. (*30 ml*) chopped gherkins
1 lb. (*450 g*) cooked cod	salad dressing
2 tbsps. (*30 ml*) cooked peas	watercress, cooked peas and cauliflower
4 tbsps. (*60 ml*) chopped cooked cauliflower	sprigs to garnish
4 tomatoes, chopped	

Arrange the lettuce round the edge of a dish, mix the other ingredients and place in the centre, then garnish. (Serves 4)

Note: For 2 servings, merely halve all the quantities.

Mustard Sauce

2 oz. (*55 g*) margarine	½ pint (*300 ml*) water
1 oz. (*25 g*) flour	4 tbsps. (*60 ml*) vinegar
1 level tsp. (*5 ml*) dry mustard	salt and pepper

Melt the fat, mix in the flour and mustard lightly, add the water gradually, then mix in the vinegar, salt and pepper. Stir and boil gently for 2–3 minutes, until the sauce has thickened.
Serve with herrings, made-up fish dishes and so on.

Lemon Butter

1 oz. (*25 g*) butter	salt
1 tsp. (*5 ml*) lemon juice	freshly ground pepper

Cream all the ingredients together, form into round pats and chill thoroughly. Serve with baked or grilled fish.

Tartare Sauce

¼ pint (*150 ml*) mayonnaise or salad cream	2 tsps. (*10 ml*) chopped gherkins
1 tsp. (*5 ml*) chopped tarragon or chives	2 tsps. (*10 ml*) chopped parsley
2 tsps. (*10 ml*) chopped capers	1 tbsp. (*15 ml*) lemon juice or tarragon vinegar

Mix all the ingredients well, then leave the sauce to stand for at least 1 hour before serving, to allow the flavours to blend. Serve with baked, grilled or poached fish.

Maître d'Hôtel Butter

2 tsps. (*10 ml*) chopped parsley	1 oz. (*25 g*) butter
squeeze of lemon juice	salt
	cayenne pepper

Mix all the ingredients together. Leave in a cool place to become firm before serving. (Makes 4 portions.)

Meat

Meats are important for both their nutritive value and their palatability. An excellent source of protein, meat generally forms the basis for the main dish in the principal meal of the day.

The appearance of meat is a good index to its quality.

Beef: The choicest beef is usually 'ripened'—that is, it has been allowed to hang in refrigerated storage to develop flavour and tenderness. Its grain is velvety, the colour dark, with creamy-white fat, and the tissues well marbled with fat.

Good beef (as opposed to 'choice') is a clear, bright red, with a smooth, fine and firm texture. The outer layer of fat, while thinner than that of 'choice', is of good depth, brittle and flaky.

Veal: Flesh is light pink, fine-grained, with little marbling. Usually contains considerable moisture and connective tissue.

Lamb: Flesh is pink and fine-grained, and the fat is clear white, solid and brittle. Bone should be pink rather than white.

Mutton: Flesh is dark red, with hard, white fat, the bone white and slightly flinty.

Pork: Flesh is almost greyish-white, well-streaked with fat and covered by soft white fat.

Amount to Buy

The quantity depends on the cut. Where the meat has a high proportion of bone, allow $\frac{1}{2}$ lb. (225 g) per serving, but where the lean proportion is high (e.g., leg of lamb), then 1 lb. (450 g) will serve about 3 people.

Storage

Remove the wrappings, place the meat on a plate and store it in a refrigerator. If no refrigerator is available, wrap it lightly and store in a cool, well-ventilated place.

Roasting meat

Meat is roasted either at the traditional high temperature in a hot oven (425°F., 220°C., mark 7), when the joint is seared quickly on the outside, giving a good, meaty flavour, or at a lower temperature in a fairly hot oven (375°F., 190°C., mark 5) when the joint is more moist, there is less shrinkage and (since the fibres are broken down) the meat is more tender, though the flavour may not be so good.

Arrange the shelves in the oven so that the meat is in the centre. Put the joint in the roasting tin so that the largest cut surfaces are exposed and the thickest layer of fat is on top; this automatically bastes the joint. If the fat is rather meagre, top the meat with 2 oz. (55 g) dripping or lard. Don't prick the meat with a fork or anything sharp while it is cooking or you will lose some of the juices. If you turn or lift the joint, use two spoons.

Stewing

This is a long, slow method of cooking in a liquid which is kept at simmering point (205°F., 96°C.); it is particularly suitable for cheaper pieces of meat. The meat is cut up and vegetables are usually added. Since all the liquid is served, none of the flavour or food value is lost. A good, strong pan or casserole is needed to avoid burning; it should have a tightly fitting lid to prevent evaporation. Keep the temperature below boiling point—this is important, as boiling often causes meat to become tough. It is often easier to achieve this by cooking the stew in a casserole in the oven.

To obtain a good colour when making a brown stew, the meat and vegetables are fried in hot fat until they are lightly browned before the liquid is added.

Boiling

Although, technically speaking, boiling is cooking in a liquid at 212°F., 100°C., meat is actually simmered at about the same temperature as for stewing—205°F., 96°C. The joint is barely covered with cold water, brought slowly to boiling point, covered with a tightly fitting lid and simmered gently throughout the whole of the cooking time given in the particular recipe. Root vegetables are usually added to give extra flavour.

Grilling

A quick method of cooking food under a grill or over a hot fire, which is suitable only for the best quality types of meats—chiefly tender chops, steaks, liver, kidneys, gammon and back bacon rashers. The poorer cuts remain tough, as the fibres cannot be broken down quickly enough. Season the meat with salt and pepper and brush it with melted fat or oil before cooking. The grill should be made really hot before the cooking is begun.

Many meats are greatly improved if they are first marinaded for at least 2 hours. Mix 2 parts salad oil with 1 part vinegar or lemon juice, add a little chopped onion and some salt and pepper and keep turning the meat in this mixture.

Sauces for meat
A few useful recipes appear at the end of this chapter.

Roast Crown of Lamb

(*see picture below*)

Oven temperature: 350°F., 180°C., mark 4
Buy 2 pieces of the best end of neck, each
with 6–7 cutlets (taken if possible from
the opposite sides of the animal, though
this is not essential). They should be
chopped—not chined—and sliced between the bones about half-way down,
the ends of the bones being scraped clean.
Trim neatly and bend round to form a
crown, securing it with skewers and
string. Twist some pieces of buttered
paper round each of the exposed bones
to prevent their burning. Roast, allowing
30 minutes to the lb. (450 g), plus 30
minutes. Serve with cutlet frills on the
ends of the bones to form 'jewels'.
Just before serving, fill the centre of the
joint with vegetables such as peas and
diced carrots.

Parcha Seek Kabob

2 lb. (*1 kg*) best end	1 level tsp. (*5 ml*)
of neck or breast of	cardomom powder
mutton	1 level tsp. (*5 ml*)
1 large onion	cumin powder
1 clove of garlic	salt and pepper
4 green chillies	oil
1 level tsp. (*5 ml*)	
ground ginger	

Oven temperature: 400°F., 200°C., mark 6
Ask the butcher to bone and roll the
meat. Mince the onion, garlic and
chillies and mix with the spices and
seasoning. Unroll the meat, spread the
mixture over it and re-roll, then secure
with a skewer. Place on a grid in a baking
dish, brush with oil, and roast for 1 hour.
(Serves 4)

Stuffed Breast of Lamb

1 onion, skinned	pepper
1 apple, peeled	2 breasts of lamb,
4 oz. (*115 g*) bread-	boned and trimmed
crumbs	1 level tsp. (*5 ml*)
½ level tsp. (*2.5 ml*)	ground ginger
rosemary	1 level tsp. (*5 ml*) dry
salt	mustard

Oven temperature: 350°F., 180°C., mark 4
Grate the onion and apple and mix with
the breadcrumbs. Add the rosemary, salt
and pepper, with sufficient water to bind.
Spread this mixture over the boned side
of the breasts, roll up tightly and secure
with skewers. Mix the ginger, mustard,
and some salt and pepper, and rub into
the lamb. Place in a shallow baking dish
and bake uncovered for about $1\frac{1}{2}$–$1\frac{3}{4}$
hours. (Serves 3–4)

Roast Crown of Lamb

126

Minted Breast of Lamb

2 breasts of lamb, boned	1 oz. (25 g) bread-crumbs
2 large cooking apples, peeled	salt and pepper
2 tbsps. (30 ml) chopped mint	

Oven temperature : 350°F., 180°C., mark 4
Trim the breasts of lamb, removing the excess fat. Coarsely grate the apple and mix with the mint and breadcrumbs. Spread over each breast, roll up tightly and secure with skewers or string. Season, put in a shallow baking dish and bake uncovered for about 1½ hours. (Serves 4)

Colonial Goose

(see colour picture facing page 145)

4–5 lb. (2–2.5 kg) leg of lamb, boned	1 clove of garlic, skinned and crushed
¾ lb. (340 g) pork, minced	1 tbsp. (15 ml) chopped parsley
1 onion, skinned and finely chopped or grated	1 egg, lightly beaten
	1 tbsp. (15 ml) dry white wine
salt and pepper	

Oven temperature : 350°F., 180°C., mark 4
Wipe the leg of lamb. Mix together the pork, onion, seasoning, flavourings, egg and wine. Fill the cavity left by the bone and truss firmly. Place in a baking dish with 1 pint (600 ml) water and cook, allowing 25–30 minutes per lb. (50–60 mins/kg). (Serves 6–8)

Lamb Cutlets with Espagnole Sauce

4 lamb cutlets	½ a swede
2 oz. (55 g) mush-rooms	1 tomato
2–3 tomatoes	a little fat
watercress	½ pint (300 ml) stock
	bouquet garni
	salt and pepper
For the Sauce :	1 tbsp. (15 ml) red wine
2 carrots	

Skin and trim the cutlets. Cut up the carrots, swede and mushroom stalks (leaving the caps whole). Sauté the cut-up vegetables, mushroom stalks and tomato in the fat. Add the stock, bouquet garni and seasonings, and leave to simmer until reduced. Meanwhile, grill the cutlets for 6–7 minutes. Remove the bouquet garni from the sauce and add the wine; re-heat, and serve in a sauceboat. Grill the mush-room caps and 2–3 tomatoes to use as a garnish. Place the cutlets diagonally across an oval plate, add some cutlet frills, surround with the grilled tomatoes and mushrooms and garnish with water-cress. (Serves 4)

Grilled Cutlets with Gooseberry Sauce

(see colour picture facing page 144)

8 small lamb cutlets, trimmed	water
oil	¼ oz. (10 g) butter
salt and pepper	saccharin tablets
½ lb. (225 g) goose-berries	nutmeg

Brush the chops with a little oil and season. Place under a hot grill and cook for 2–3 minutes on one side, until lightly browned; turn and grill on the other side. Continue cooking the chops, turn-ing them frequently, until the meat is cooked through. To make the sauce, stew the gooseberries in a little water until tender; drain, then sieve, add the butter and saccharin, and grated nut-meg to taste. (Serves 4)

Spanish Cutlets

4–6 lamb cutlets	2 medium-sized onions
olive oil	
salt and pepper	2–3 tomatoes, skinned
4 oz. (115 g) bacon rashers	

Oven temperature : 350°F., 180°C., mark 4
Brush the cutlets with oil and grill for about 2 minutes on each side, then put in a casserole and season well. Fry the cut-up bacon in the oil, together with the sliced onions; when the onions begin to brown, add the chopped tomatoes, season well, and cook for about 10 minutes. Pour this sauce over the cutlets and cook in the oven for about 30 minutes. (Serves 4)

Stuffed Lamb Chops

Stuffed Lamb Chops

(*see picture above*)

4 thick loin chops	1 oz. (*30 g*) mush-
1 kidney, skinned and	rooms, chopped
chopped	salt and pepper

Oven temperature: 375°F., 190°C., mark 5
Cut along the edge of the meat of each
chop to form a pocket. Mix together the
kidney and mushrooms, season with salt
and pepper and fill the pockets in the
chops. Place on a lightly greased baking
dish and cook for 30–40 minutes. Serve
with cooked onion rings. (Serves 4)

Curried Lamb

4 chump chops	1 level tsp. (*5 ml*)
1 tbsp. (*15 ml*) oil	turmeric
2 onions, skinned and	1 level tsp. (*5 ml*)
sliced	curry powder
3 cloves of garlic,	1 level tsp. (*5 ml*) salt
skinned and crushed	¼–½ level tsp. (*1.25–*
1 level tsp. (*5 ml*)	*2.5 ml*) chilli powder
ground ginger	4 tomatoes, skinned
1 red pepper, seeded	and sliced
and chopped	½ pint (*300 ml*) stock

Trim the chops, removing the excess fat.
Heat the oil and sauté the onions, garlic,
ginger and red pepper. Add the turmeric,
curry powder, salt and chilli powder, mix
well, add the chops and brown them.
Add the tomatoes and stock, cover, bring
to the boil and simmer until the meat is
tender. Remove the lid to evaporate off
any excess gravy. (Serves 4)

Barbecued Lamb Chops

4–6 middle loin chops	1 level tsp. (*5 ml*)
pepper	celery seed
1 lemon, sliced	4 tbsps. (*60 ml*)
1 onion, chopped	Worcestershire sauce
4 tbsps. (*60 ml*)	5½-oz. (*165-g*) can of
vinegar	tomato juice
1 level tsp. (*5 ml*) salt	¼ pint (*150 ml*) water
1 level tsp. (*5 ml*)	few drops Tabasco
chilli powder	sauce

Oven temperature: 350°F., 180°C., mark 4
Arrange the chops in a shallow baking
dish and sprinkle with pepper. On each
chop put a slice of lemon and a little
chopped onion. Mix all the remaining
ingredients together and add to the
chops. Bake for 30–45 minutes, basting
the chops frequently with the sauce.
(Serves 4)

Pineapple Lamb Casserole

2 lamb chops	salt and pepper
4 chipolata sausages	¼ pint (*150 ml*)
2 slices of pineapple	unsweetened pine-
2 oz. (*55 g*) mush-	apple juice
rooms	

Oven temperature: 350°F., 180°C., mark 4
Trim the chops and grill until golden-
brown, then lightly grill the sausages.
Place the chops in a casserole, lay a slice
of pineapple on each chop and add the
sausages. Prepare the mushrooms, leaving them whole, add to the casserole and
sprinkle with salt and pepper. Pour in
the pineapple juice, cover and bake for
about 1 hour, or until the chops are
tender. (Serves 2)

Lamb Paprika

1½ lb. (*700 g*) middle	1 tbsp. (*15 ml*)
or best end of neck	chopped parsley
1 oz. (*25 g*) butter	1–2 level tsps. (*10 ml*)
6 oz. (*170 g*) onion,	paprika pepper
skinned and minced	salt
1 lb. (*450 g*)	¼ pint (*140 g*)
tomatoes, skinned	soured cream or
and sliced	yoghurt

Chine the meat and trim away any

128

excess fat, then cut into chops. Heat the butter and brown the chops on both sides; remove from the pan, and fry the onion in the fat until beginning to brown. Add the tomatoes, parsley, paprika and salt to taste, replace the chops, cover and simmer gently for 1½–2 hours, or bake in a covered casserole in a warm oven (325°F., 170°C., mark 3) for 2 hours. Heat the soured cream (or yoghurt) in a saucepan and add a little of the stock, then pour the mixture back into the casserole dish, stir in well, re-season, and re-heat without boiling. (Serves 4)

Lamb Hot-pot

1½ lb. (*700 g*) scrag end of lamb	2 level tsps. (*10 ml*) dried lovage if available
2 large carrots	
2 medium-sized onions	½ pint (*300 ml*) stock and water
seasoned flour	2 large potatoes, thinly sliced
1 oz. (*25 g*) dripping	
salt and freshly ground pepper	chopped parsley to garnish
1 tbsp. (*15 ml*) pearl barley	

Oven temperature: 325°F., 170°C., mark 3
Trim the meat, removing the excess fat, and chop it into pieces. Slice the carrots and onions thinly. Dip the meat in the seasoned flour, brown it in the melted fat, then remove it and lightly brown the carrots and onions. Season and place in a casserole, arranging the meat on top, and sprinkle with the pearl barley and lovage (if used). Pour the liquid over and cover with a layer of sliced potatoes. Put on a tightly fitting lid and bake for 2¾ hours. Raise the heat to hot (425°F., 220°C., mark 7), remove the lid and brown the potatoes. Serve the hot-pot dusted with freshly ground pepper and chopped parsley. (Serves 4)

Finnish Cabbage and Lamb Hot-pot

2 lb. (*1 kg*) white cabbage	salt and pepper tomato paste to taste
1 lb. (*450 g*) best end of neck of lamb	

Wash the cabbage and chop it finely. Brown the meat on both sides in a saucepan without any extra fat, then add the cabbage, seasoning, tomato paste and a very little water, and simmer until the cabbage is quite transparent and the meat tender. (Serves 4)

Ragoût of Lamb

1½ lb. (*700 g*) best end of neck of lamb	oil stock or water
4–5 carrots	bouquet garni
2 onions	salt and pepper
2 turnips	3 eggs
½ lb. (*225 g*) tomatoes	

Trim the meat. Prepare the vegetables and cut into dice or straws, skin the tomatoes, remove the pips and cut up the flesh. Fry the meat in oil to brown it, then pour off the excess oil and add stock or water to half-cover the meat, with the tomatoes, bouquet garni and salt and pepper. Simmer gently for about 1½ hours. Add the vegetables to the meat and continue cooking until both are tender. To make a sauce, beat the eggs and add ½ pint (300 ml) of the liquor; add to the ragoût and heat, stirring continuously, until it thickens. (Serves 3–4)
As an alternative sauce, omit the eggs, turn the liquor into a saucepan and boil vigorously to reduce it.

Devonshire Squab Pie

½ lb. (*225 g*) cooking apples, peeled, cored and sliced	1 onion, skinned and sliced
4 small lamb chops	¼ pint (*150 ml*) water
salt and pepper	4 oz. (*100 g*) short-crust pastry

Oven temperature: 425°F., 220°C., mark 7
Put a layer of apples in a casserole or pie dish, then a layer of the lamb chops well seasoned with salt and pepper. Next add a layer of onion and apples. Pour on the water, cover with the pastry and bake for 10 minutes; then reduce to moderate (350°F., 180°C., mark 4) and cook for ¾ hour, or until the meat is done. Serve with baked or grilled tomatoes or other vegetables. (Serves 2)

Marinaded Lamb Kebabs

a thick slice of lamb taken from the leg (approx. 1 lb., *450 g*)
3 tbsps. (*45 ml*) olive oil
1 tbsp. (*15 ml*) lemon juice
salt and pepper
clove of garlic, skinned and crushed
4 small tomatoes, halved

8 rashers of streaky bacon, rolled up
8 button mushrooms, washed
few bay leaves (optional)
2 small onions, skinned and quartered (optional)
melted butter

This Eastern dish has become very popular in recent years.

Remove all the fat and gristle from the meat and cut it into 1-inch (2.5-cm) cubes. Marinade for 2 hours (or preferably overnight) in the olive oil, lemon juice, seasoning and crushed garlic. Thread 8 skewers alternately with meat cubes, halved tomatoes, bacon rolls and whole mushrooms. If liked, a bay leaf or an onion quarter may be placed on each side of the meat pieces, to give more flavour. Brush with melted butter and cook under a low grill for 10–15 minutes, turning the kebabs about 3 times until the meat is tender. Serve on plain boiled rice. (Serves 4)

Lambs' kidneys may also be used; allow $\frac{1}{4}$ kidney for each person. Remove the core, thread the pieces on to the skewers with the other ingredients and cook as above.

Roast Beef

Oven temperature: 425°F., 220°C., mark 7

Wipe the meat, trim if necessary, then weigh it and calculate the cooking time, allowing 20 minutes per lb. (40 mins/kg) plus 20 minutes if the meat is on the bone; 25 minutes per lb. (50 mins/kg) plus 25 minutes if rolled. Put the meat in a roasting tin so that the thickest layer of fat is uppermost and the cut sides are exposed to the heat. Add about 2 oz. (55 g) dripping if the meat is lean. Put the joint in the middle of the oven and cook uncovered for the calculated time, basting from time to time with the juices from the tin. Serve slightly rare, accompanied by Yorkshire Pudding, horseradish sauce, thin brown gravy and vegetables as desired.

To roast meat in a moderate oven (350°F., 180°C., mark 4), which tends to give a moister joint, prepare and cook as above, but allow 27 minutes per lb. (45 mins/kg) plus 27 minutes for joints on the bone; 33 minutes per lb. (70 mins/kg) plus 33 minutes for rolled joints.

Suitable Joints: Sirlion, ribs, rump, topside, aitch-bone.

Carpet-bag Steak

$1\frac{1}{2}$–2 lb. ($\frac{3}{4}$–1 kg) rump or fillet steak, cut in one piece at least 2 in. (*5 cm*) wide
12 raw oysters

2 oz. (*55 g*) mushrooms, sliced (optional)
salt and cayenne pepper
olive oil or butter

Choose a piece of the very best rump or fillet steak; slit through its thickness so that it opens like a book. Fill with the raw oysters, cover these with the mushrooms (if used) and sprinkle with a very little salt and some cayenne pepper. Sew up with fine white string, so that neither the filling nor the juices can escape. Rub the steak over on both sides with oil or melted butter, and cook under a high grill for 5–6 minutes on each side. When the meat has browned, finish cooking for a further 10 minutes or so, according to the degree of 'rareness' desired. (Serves 4)

Filet Mignon
(see picture right)

4 rashers of streaky bacon
2 5-oz. (*140-g*) pieces of fillet steak, cut 1 in. (*2.5 cm*) thick

salt and pepper
2 oz. (*55 g*) butter
8 oz. (*225 g*) mushrooms, sliced

Wrap a rasher round the edge of each steak, and secure with a cocktail stick. Season and grill under a moderate heat, turning once. In the meantime, melt the butter and sauté the mushrooms. Serve the steaks with the mushrooms piled on

Filet Mignon

top, and accompanied by tomatoes and green salad. (Serves 2)

Silverside

4-lb. (*1.75-kg*) piece of salt silverside	1 tbsp. (*15 ml*) vinegar
1 tbsp. (*15 ml*) golden syrup	1 lb. (*450 g*) small carrots, peeled

Place the silverside in cold water, bring to the boil and drain off the liquid. Cover with fresh water and add the syrup and vinegar; simmer gently for 2–2¼ hours. About ¾ hour before the end of the cooking time, add the carrots, and continue simmering. (Serves 8)

Salt Beef in Cider

4 lb. (*1.75 kg*) salt silverside	bouquet garni
flagon of dry cider	6–8 carrots
8 peppercorns	6 onions

Cover the meat with cold water, bring to the boil and drain. Add the cider and sufficient water to cover the meat, with the peppercorns and bouquet garni. Bring to the boil and simmer gently for 1½ hours. Add the carrots, cut lengthwise, and the onions. Continue to cook for a further 30–40 minutes. Serve the meat surrounded by the vegetables. (Serves 8)

Grilled Entrecôte Steak

Buy 4 entrecôte steaks each about 6 oz. (*170 g*) in weight and ¾ inch (2 cm) thick. Season and brush each side with oil. Quickly brown on both sides under a hot grill, then reduce the heat and continue to cook until tender—7–10 minutes according to the degree of 'rareness' desired. Place a pat of Roquefort butter (see below) on each steak and garnish with grilled mushroom and tomatoes and some watercress. Serve with salad. (Serves 4)

Roquefort Butter

2 oz. (*55 g*) Roquefort cheese	1 tbsp. (*15 ml*) chopped parsley
2 oz. (*55 g*) butter lemon juice	1 tbsp. (*15 ml*) minced onion

Cream the cheese and butter together and add a little lemon juice, parsley and onion. Roll into a long finger shape, wrap in greaseproof paper and place in the refrigerator to harden. When the meat is ready to serve, cut off slices of the butter and place one on each steak.

Grilled Steak with Onion Rings

Choose fillet or rump steak about 1–1½ inches (3–4 cm) thick; allow 6 oz. (*170 g*) per serving. Season with salt and pepper and a little garlic juice (optional). Place on a grill rack under a hot grill and cook for 2–3 minutes on each side, turning the meat carefully to avoid losing the juices. Continue cooking, turning frequently, until done. Meanwhile part-boil some sliced onions in a little lightly salted water and drain. Place in the meat drippings beneath the steak, and continue cooking until both steak and onions are tender.

Tournedos with Mushrooms

1½ lb. (*700 g*) fillet beef or rump steak	salt and pepper
lemon juice	6 oz. (*170 g*) mushrooms
oil	

Ask the butcher to cut the steaks about ¾–1 inch (2–3 cm) thick. Squeeze some lemon juice over the meat, brush over with a little oil and season with salt and pepper. Prepare the mushrooms and fry slowly in oil. Grill the fillets under a hot grill for 9–12 minutes, according to how well done you like the meat. Top the steak with mushrooms and serve with a savoury rice dish. (Serves 4)

Orange-Apple Steak

4 rump steaks 1 in. (*2.5 cm*) thick	1 orange
	1 cooking apple
4 tbsps. (*60 ml*) fresh breadcrumbs	1 oz. (*25 g*) butter
	1 egg yolk
2 tsps. (*10 ml*) coarsely chopped parsley	salt and pepper
	oil

Trim the steaks; using a sharp knife, slit each piece horizontally to within $\frac{1}{2}$ inch of the edge and open it out. Mix the crumbs, parsley, finely grated orange rind, grated unpeeled apple, melted butter and the egg yolk; season to taste. Spread this stuffing on one half of the steak, fold the other half over, brush with oil and grill for 3–7 minutes each side. Heat the orange juice and pour over the steaks. (Serves 4)

Beef and Mushrooms with Sweet-sour Sauce

1$\frac{1}{2}$ lb. (*700 g*) frying steak	6 tbsps. (*90 ml*) vinegar
2 cloves of garlic	1 tbsp. (*15 ml*) soy sauce
oil	
1 lb. (*450 g*) mushrooms, thinly sliced	1$\frac{1}{2}$ level tbsps. (*22.5 ml*) cornflour mixed with a little water
2 large green peppers, seeded and cut up	artificial sweetener
$\frac{1}{2}$ pint (*300 ml*) stock	boiled rice

Rub the meat with the garlic; cut it into very thin slices, about 1 by 2 inches (2.5 × 5 cm), and fry lightly in hot oil, then add the mushrooms. Meanwhile cook the peppers in boiling water for 5 minutes, drain thoroughly and add to the meat. To make the sauce, combine the stock and vinegar, add the soy sauce and the blended cornflour and boil, stirring well, for 2 minutes; add sweetener to taste. Serve

the beef and mushrooms with a border of rice, and cover with the sauce. (Serves 4)

Barbecued Steak

1 lb. (*450 g*) chuck steak	1 tbsp. (*15 ml*) vinegar
1 oz. (*25 g*) seasoned flour	1 tbsp. (*15 ml*) lemon juice
1 tbsp. (*15 ml*) oil	1 green pepper, seeded and chopped
$\frac{1}{4}$ pint (*150 ml*) stock	
1 tbsp. (*15 ml*) tomato ketchup	liquid artificial sweetener

Oven temperature: 350°F., 180°C., mark 4
Trim any excess fat from the meat and cut it into 6–8 portions. Toss in seasoned flour and brown in the hot oil. Add the stock, ketchup, vinegar, lemon juice and green pepper, cover, and bake for 1–1$\frac{1}{2}$ hours. Add 3–4 drops of artificial sweetener just before serving. (Serves 3)

Carbonade of Beef

1 lb. (*450 g*) chuck steak	1 lb. (*450 g*) onions, skinned and chopped
salt and pepper	
1 oz. (*25 g*) dripping	1 clove of garlic, skinned and chopped
1 oz. (*25 g*) lean bacon, chopped	
1 oz. (*25 g*) plain flour	bouquet garni
	2 tbsps. (*30 ml*) vinegar
$\frac{1}{4}$ pint (*150 ml*) beer	
$\frac{1}{4}$ pint (*150 ml*) stock or water	

Oven temperature: 300°F., 150°C., mark 2
Cut the meat up neatly, season and brown in the dripping; add the bacon and continue cooking for a few minutes. Remove the meat and bacon from the pan, stir in the flour and brown lightly over a very gentle heat. Gradually add the beer and stock, stirring continuously. Fill a casserole with layers of meat, bacon, onion and garlic, pour the sauce over and add the bouquet garni. Cook in the oven very gently for 3$\frac{1}{2}$–4 hours, adding a little more beer while cooking if necessary. Just before serving, remove the bouquet garni and stir in the vinegar. (Serves 2–3)

French Beef and Olive Casserole

(see picture below)

¾ lb. *(350 g)* rump steak	bunch of fresh herbs
2 tbsps. *(30 ml)* olive oil	1 clove of garlic, skinned and crushed
1 carrot, sliced	few peppercorns
1 onion, sliced	salt and pepper
2–3 sticks of celery, cut in 1-in. *(2.5-cm)* pieces	¼ lb. *(115 g)* bacon, diced
¼ pint *(150 ml)* red wine	¼ lb. *(115 g)* black and green olives
4 tbsps. *(60 ml)* wine vinegar	3–4 tomatoes

Oven temperature: 325°F., 170°C., mark 3
Wipe and trim the meat and cut into thick chunks. Make a marinade: heat the oil, add the vegetables and cook until brown. Add half the wine, the vinegar, herbs, garlic, peppercorns, salt and pepper, bring to the boil and simmer for 15 minutes, then leave to become quite cold. Cover the meat with the strained marinade and leave for 2 hours. Fry the bacon and remove from the pan, then fry the drained meat on both sides and put into an earthenware casserole. Add the marinade to the meat with the bacon diced and the wine and olives. Cover with greased greaseproof paper, then with the lid, and cook for 2½ hours. Shortly before serving, remove any excess fat and add the skinned and sliced tomatoes. Serve with noodles and grated cheese. (Serves 2–3)

Beef and Pineapple Casserole

1½ lb. *(700 g)* chuck steak	½ pint *(300 ml)* stock
1 oz. *(25 g)* seasoned flour	1 tbsp. *(15 ml)* soy sauce
2 tbsps. *(30 ml)* oil	4 tbsps. *(60 ml)* dry white wine
1 onion, skinned and chopped	8 oz. *(225 g)* fresh pineapple chunks

Oven temperature: 350°F., 180°C., mark 4
Remove any excess fat from the meat and cut into pieces. Toss it in seasoned flour. Heat the oil and lightly brown the meat. Add the onion, stock, soy sauce and wine, transfer to a casserole, cover and bake for 1 hour; add the pineapple and cook for a further 30 minutes. (Serves 4)

Burgundy Beef

2 tbsps. *(30 ml)* olive oil	2 level tbsps. *(30 ml)* tomato paste
1 large onion	salt and pepper
2 green peppers	1 pkt. frozen corn kernels
1½ lb. *(700 g)* chuck steak	
¼ pint *(150 ml)* Burgundy	

Heat the oil. Skin the onion, cut into rings and fry lightly. Cut the flesh of the peppers in thin strips and add to fried

French Beef and Olive Casserole

133

onion. Remove any gristle from the meat, cut into 1-inch (2.5-cm) cubes, add it to the vegetables and fry lightly. Stir in the Burgundy and tomato paste, and season. Simmer gently for 1½–2 hours, topping up with a little stock if necessary, then add the corn kernels and continue cooking for a further 10–15 minutes. (Serves 4) Alternatively, cook the mixture in a tightly lidded casserole, in a moderate oven (350°F., 180°C., mark 4) 1½–2 hours; add the corn and cook 15 minutes longer.

Malayan Curried Beef

1½ lb. (700 g) beef-steak	1 level tsp. (5 ml) ground cardamom
4 cloves of garlic, skinned	2 tbsps. (30 ml) oil
2 level tsps. (10 ml) powdered ginger	¼ pint (150 ml) stock or water
4 level tsps. (20 ml) ground coriander	1 lb. (450 g) onions, skinned and
2 level tsps. (10 ml) cumin powder	quartered
½ level tsp. (2.5 ml) ground cloves	½ pint (300 ml) milk juice of 1 lemon

Cut the meat into 4 pieces and wipe it. Pound or crush the garlic, add the spices and mix to a smooth paste with a little water. Rub well into the meat and leave for 20 minutes. Heat the oil in a saucepan, put in the meat and keep it moving for 2 minutes. Add stock, simmer for 10 minutes, then add the onions, turn the heat low, cover, and simmer for 15 minutes. Add the milk, soured by the addition of the lemon juice, and simmer till the meat is tender. If the gravy has not thickened at this stage, remove the meat, keep it hot, and boil the gravy until it is sufficiently reduced. (Serves 4)

Shepherd's Soufflé

1 tbsp. (15 ml) oil	½ a green pepper, seeded and chopped
1 onion, skinned and finely chopped	2 tomatoes, skinned and sliced
1 lb. (450 g) minced beef	2 eggs, separated
salt and pepper soy sauce	1 tbsp. (15 ml) water
4 oz. (115 g) mixed vegetables	

Oven temperature: 350°F., 180°C., mark 4
Heat the oil and sauté the onion until clear. Add the beef and brown thoroughly. Add salt, pepper and soy sauce to taste. Place the mixture in a small casserole and add all the vegetables. Beat the egg whites until stiff. Beat the yolks with water until thick and fluffy; fold into the whites and pour over the meat and vegetables. Bake for 30–40 minutes, until the egg topping is firm. (Serves 4)

Curried Mince

1 large onion, skinned and chopped	grated rind and juice of 1 lemon
1 clove of garlic, skinned and crushed	2 tsps. (10 ml) piquant table sauce
1 oz. (25 g) butter	1 tbsp. (15 ml) raisins
1 lb. (450 g) beef, minced	salt
2 apples, chopped	6 oz. (170 g) long grain rice
1 level tbsp. (15 ml) curry powder	

Fry the onion and garlic in the butter, add the meat and sauté lightly. Add the remaining ingredients (except the rice) and simmer until the meat is cooked. Cook the rice in boiling salted water for about ¼ hour, or until tender; rinse in hot water, drain well and dry off in a cool oven. Serve the curry on a bed of rice, with mango chutney, sliced banana and sliced tomato. (Serves 2–3)

Beef Olives

1 lb. (450 g) braising steak	2 onions, skinned and chopped
salt and pepper	2 level tbsps. (30 ml) tomato paste
clove of garlic (optional)	jellied stock
4 oz. (115 g) ham, chopped	a pinch of mixed herbs
2 carrots, grated	

Divide the steak into 4 thin pieces and flatten them; season and rub with garlic if liked. Mix the ham with a little of the carrot and onion, the tomato paste, a little stock, seasoning and herbs, and combine well. Put the rest of the carrot and onion into a casserole. Spread the filling over the 4 pieces of steak, roll them up and pin each with a skewer. Place the meat on the layer of vegetables, add about ½ pint (300 ml) of stock and some herbs, and simmer gently for 2–3 hours. (Serves 4)

As a variation, serve on a bed of spinach.

Beef Olives with Orange

¾ lb. (340 g) rump steak	*For the Filling:*
1 tbsp. (15 ml) oil	2 oz. (55 g) mush-
2 sticks of celery, diced	rooms, chopped
2 carrots, diced	grated rind of ½ an orange
¼ lb. (115 g) peas, shelled	2–3 tomatoes, chopped
stock	2 tbsps. (30 ml) bread-
2 level tsps. (10 ml) cornflour	crumbs (starch-reduced)
	salt and pepper

Oven temperature: 350°F., 180°C., mark 4

Trim the meat and beat until thin, then cut into 4 pieces. Prepare a filling by mixing all the ingredients together, adding seasoning to taste. Spread the filling on the strips of meat, roll them up and tie with cotton; fry lightly in the hot oil and place in an ovenproof dish. Add the celery, carrots and peas, half-cover with stock and bake for about 1½ hours. Remove the cottons, thicken the gravy with cornflour and serve with the beef olives. (Serves 4)

Uccelli Scappari

3 thin slices of topside	1 tbsp. (15 ml)
3 rashers of lean bacon	Worcestershire sauce
3 fresh sage leaves	¼ pint (150 ml) red wine
seasoned flour	3 tbsps. (45 ml) water
1 tbsp. (15 ml) oil	

Beat the topside until very thin and place a piece of bacon on each slice. Put a sage leaf on the bacon, roll up and secure with string or cocktail sticks. Dust with seasoned flour. Heat the oil and fry the rolls until evenly browned; place in a saucepan. Mix together the sauce, wine and water, pour over the rolls, cover and cook slowly, turning occasionally. When the meat is tender, place on a serving dish and remove the string or cocktail sticks. Boil the sauce rapidly to reduce, pour over the meat rolls and serve at once. (Serves 3)

Summer Casserole

2 lb. (1 kg) shin of beef	1 level tsp. (5 ml) celery salt
1 oz. (25 g) dripping	1 pint (600 ml) tomato juice
½ oz. (15 g) flour	salt
½ tsp. (2.5 ml) mustard	fresh vegetables, as available
2 chillies, chopped	

Oven temperature: 325°F., 170°C., mark 3

Wipe the beef, and remove any sinews and skin; cut into cubes, fry in the hot fat until golden-brown, drain and place in a casserole. Add the flour, flavourings, etc., to the fat in the pan, bring to the boil, add salt to taste and pour over the meat. Cover and cook in the oven for 1½ hours. Add the prepared vegetables to the casserole, then cook for a further ½–¾ hour, until they are tender. (Serves 4)

Bulgarian Hot-pot

1 large aubergine	1 oz. (25 g) butter or oil
salt and pepper	½ pint (300 ml) stock
3 potatoes	1–2 eggs
5 tomatoes	1 level tbsp. (15 ml) flour
4 oz. (115 g) French beans	juice of ½ a lemon
3 green peppers	
1½ lb. (700 g) braising beef	

Slice the aubergine, sprinkle with salt and allow to stand for 1 hour, then drain off the liquid. Prepare and cut up the other vegetables. Cut the meat into small pieces, put in a saucepan with the butter or oil, salt and pepper and fry gently until brown. Cover with stock and simmer for about ½ hour. Now add the vegetables, with more stock, stir, and simmer for ½–¾ hour, until the vegetables and meat are tender. Turn into a baking dish and put into a moderate oven (350°F., 180°C., mark 4). Beat up the eggs, add the flour, lemon juice and a little salt, and pour this mixture over the dish. Continue cooking for 20–30 minutes, until the egg topping is lightly set; serve at once. (Serves 4)

Swiss Steak

(see colour picture facing page 48)

1 tbsp. (*15 ml*) oil	1 oz. (*25 g*) flour
2 large onions, skinned and sliced	salt and pepper
	8 tomatoes, skinned
1½ lb. (*700 g*) chuck or blade steak	14-oz. (*396-g*) can of tomato juice

Oven temperature: 350°F., 180°C., mark 4
Heat the oil and sauté the onions until clear. Cut the steak into 8 portions, dredge with seasoned flour and brown in the oil. Add the tomatoes and tomato juice. Cover, and cook for 1½–2 hours. (Serves 4)

Russian Casseroled Beefsteak

1½ lb. (*700 g*) braising steak	6 small cabbage leaves
1 oz. (*25 g*) plain flour	2 carrots, sliced
oil for frying	6 peppercorns
2 raw potatoes, thinly sliced	3 tomatoes, sliced
	stock or water if required

Oven temperature: 350°F., 180°C., mark 4
Wipe the steak and beat well, then cut it up into 4-inch (10-cm) squares, coat with flour and fry in the oil until lightly browned. Put into a deep casserole layers of steak, potato, whole cabbage leaves and sliced carrot, with the peppercorns and sliced tomatoes. Add 1 tbsp. (15 ml) stock or water if necessary, but the juice from the meat and vegetables may give enough liquid—the casserole should be kept fairly dry. Cover and bake for about 2 hours. (Serves 4)

Austrian Beef Goulash

1 lb. (*450 g*) beef	salt
1 lb. (*450 g*) onions	2 tbsps. (*30 ml*) vinegar
1 tbsp. (*15 ml*) oil	
1 level tbsp. (*15 ml*) paprika	pinch of marjoram
¼ pint (*150 ml*) tomato paste	pinch of caraway seed

Cut the beef into neat cubes and slice the onions. Heat the oil in a pan and fry the onions, then add the paprika and 2 tbsps. water. Put the meat into the pan and stir well until all the liquor has disappeared, then add the tomato paste, salt, vinegar, marjoram and caraway seed. Cover the pan with a lid and simmer gently for 2 hours, or until the meat is quite tender; if the goulash gets very dry, add a little liquor. (Serves 3)

Goulash

1½ lb. (*700 g*) chuck steak	1 level tsp. (*5 ml*) tomato paste
seasoned flour	4 oz. (*115 g*) peas
2 tbsps. (*30 ml*) oil	2 level tsps. (*10 ml*) paprika
1 onion, skinned and thinly sliced	¼ level tsp. (*2.5 ml*) cayenne
¼ pint (*150 ml*) stock	2 tbsps. (*30 ml*) fat-free yoghurt
14-oz. (*396-g*) can of tomatoes	

Coat the meat with seasoned flour. Heat the oil and brown the meat quickly, then remove from the pan. Add the onion and sauté until clear. Return the meat, add the stock, tomatoes and paste, cover and simmer for 1¾ hours. Add the peas, paprika and cayenne and cook for 10 minutes. Remove from the heat, stir in the yoghurt and serve immediately. (Serves 4)

Hunter's Harvest Stew

1½ lb. (*700 g*) chuck steak	2 tsps. (*10 ml*) Worcestershire sauce
3 level tbsps. (*45 ml*) flour	⅓ pint (*200 ml*) stock or water
1 level tsp. (*5 ml*) salt	¾ lb. (*340 g*) carrots, sliced
½ level tsp. (*2.5 ml*) black pepper	12 shallots
1 oz. (*25 g*) butter	½ lb. (*225 g*) button mushrooms, quartered
15-oz. (*425-g*) can of tomatoes	

Remove any excess fat from the meat and cut it into 1-inch (2.5-cm) cubes. Mix together the flour, salt and pepper and toss the meat in it. Melt the fat in a pan and brown the meat all over; stir in the remaining flour. Add the tomatoes, sauce and liquid, cover and simmer gently for 1 hour. Add the carrots and shallots and simmer for a further 45 minutes. Add the mushrooms and continue to cook for 15 minutes. Adjust the seasoning before serving. (Serves 4)

Roast Loin of Veal

Oven temperature: 425°F., 220°C., mark 7
Bone and roll the joint, season well, cover with some strips of streaky bacon and weigh. Roast, allowing 30 minutes per lb. (65 mins/kg) plus 30 minutes. Serve cut in thick slices, accompanied by bacon rolls and veal forcemeat balls.

Veal Forcemeat Balls

4 oz. (*115 g*) lean veal	2–3 mushrooms, chopped
3 oz. (*85 g*) lean bacon	1 tsp. (*5 ml*) chopped parsley
½ oz. (*15 g*) butter	salt and pepper
1 onion, skinned and finely chopped	1 egg, beaten
2 oz. (*55 g*) fresh breadcrumbs	

Mince together the veal and bacon and mix well. Melt the butter and sauté the onion until clear. Add to the meat, with the remaining ingredients; mix well, form into small balls and cook alongside the roast. (Serves 4)
This mixture may also be used as an alternative stuffing for Colonial Goose (page 140) or for roast chicken.

Veal Cutlets

4 veal cutlets	1 small onion, skinned and chopped
salt and pepper	
1 tbsp. (*15 ml*) oil	
4 oz. (*115 g*) mush-rooms, chopped	¼ lb. (*115 g*) calf's liver, finely chopped

Oven temperature: 375°F., 190°C., mark 5
Trim the cutlets, season lightly and place each on a piece of greased foil. Heat the oil and sauté the mushrooms; add the onion and liver and cook for 2–3 minutes. Divide into 4 and spread evenly over each chop. Parcel up firmly, place on a baking tray and cook near the top of the oven until tender—25–30 minutes. (Serves 4)

French Veal Cutlets

1½ lb. (*700 g*) best end of neck of veal, or 4 cutlets	10 shallots, chopped
	1 clove of garlic, skinned and crushed
4 oz. (*115 g*) lean bacon, chopped	sprig of chervil
	salt and pepper

Divide the meat into cutlets and trim neatly. Gently heat the bacon until the fat runs, add shallots, garlic and chervil, season and fry for 5–7 minutes. Grill the cutlets on both sides under a hot grill. When cooked, arrange on a hot dish, with a spoonful of the savoury mixture on each. (Serves 4)

Escalopes Fines Herbes

(see picture below)

1 oz. (*25 g*) butter	½ level tsp. (*2.5 ml*) mixed herbs
2 escalopes of veal	
1 oz. (*25 g*) flour	3 tbsps. (*45 ml*) single cream
salt and pepper	
1 level tsp. (*5 ml*) tomato paste	8-oz. (*226-g*) can tomatoes
5 tbsps. (*75 ml*) red wine	artificial sweetener
	1 oz. (*25 g*) cheese, grated
2 oz. (*55 g*) mush-rooms, sliced	

Heat the butter in a frying pan. Roll the escalopes up tightly and secure each with a cocktail stick. Mix half the flour with some seasonings and toss the meat in this. Cook the escalopes gently in the fat for

Escalopes Fines Herbes

7–10 minutes, turning them frequently until evenly browned. Remove, drain and keep hot. Add the remaining flour to the pan, stir in the tomato paste and wine and bring slowly to the boil; add the mushrooms, herbs and lastly the cream, season as required and cook very gently for 5 minutes.

Heat the canned tomatoes with artificial sweetener to taste. Pour into a dish, put the meat on top, pour the sauce over, sprinkle with the cheese and brown under the grill. Garnish if desired with sliced tomato. (Serves 2)

Note: Fresh tomatoes may be used instead of canned; peel and chop them (discarding the seeds) and omit the sweetener.

Veal and Mushroom Rolls

2 veal escalopes, beaten	6-oz. (*170-g*) can condensed mushroom soup
2 oz. (*55 g*) mush-rooms, chopped	sliced hard-boiled egg and chopped parsley
2 oz. (*55 g*) ham, chopped	

Cover the escalopes with the mushrooms and ham. Roll up, secure with cocktail sticks and place in an ovenproof dish. Mix the condensed mushroom soup with water as directed on the can. Pour over the rolls, cover and bake for about 1½ hours. Serve garnished with hard-boiled egg and parsley. (Serves 2)

Note: If required for 4 people, the quantities may be doubled—use an 11-oz. (*312-g*) can of soup.

Veal Marengo

2 lb. (*1 kg*) veal	¼ pint (*150 ml*) stock or water
1 oz. (*25 g*) butter	
2 onions, skinned and sliced	4 tbsps. (*60 ml*) tomato paste
1 clove of garlic, skinned and crushed	bouquet garni
¼ pint (*150 ml*) dry white wine	½ lb. (*225 g*) mush-rooms, sliced

Oven temperature: 350°F., 180°C., mark 4

Wipe the meat and cut into cubes. Melt the butter and sauté the onions and garlic. Add the veal and brown it. Add all the ingredients except the mushrooms, cover and cook in the oven for 1 hour. Add the mushrooms and cook for a further 15 minutes. (Serves 4–6)

Veal, Ham and Mushroom Fricassee

4 oz. (*115 g*) stewing veal	salt and pepper
¼ pint (*150 ml*) stock or water	1 slice of ham, ¼ in. (*0.5 cm*) thick
1 small onion	2 oz. (*55 g*) mush-rooms, sliced
bouquet garni	juice of ½ a lemon
milk	1 egg yolk
½ oz. (*15 g*) butter	bacon rolls and parsley
½ oz. (*15 g*) flour	

Dice the veal and simmer in the stock with the onion and bouquet garni for ½ hour, or until tender, then remove from the heat. Strain off the stock, make up to ½ pint with milk and use to make a sauce with the butter and flour. Add the veal, seasoning, diced ham, mushrooms and lemon juice and cook for a further 10 minutes. Add the egg yolk and re-heat gently. Serve accompanied by bacon rolls and garnished with parsley sprigs. (Serves 1)

Italian Veal Casserole

1 lb. (*450 g*) pie veal	¼ lb. (*115 g*) tomatoes, skinned and chopped
2 cloves of garlic, skinned and chopped	
2 tbsps. (*30 ml*) oil	2 level tsps. (*10 ml*) tomato paste
salt and pepper	2 sprigs of rosemary
¼ pint (*150 ml*) white wine	strip of lemon rind

Oven temperature: 350°F., 180°C., mark 4

Slice the meat or cut it into small pieces. Fry the chopped garlic in the oil until it is golden-brown—about 1 minute. Add the meat, salt and pepper and continue cooking until the meat is golden-brown—about 8–10 minutes. Stir in the wine, tomatoes, tomato paste, rosemary and lemon rind, and just enough water to cover. Pour into a casserole, cover tightly and cook in the centre of the oven for about 1 hour, or until the meat is tender. Remove the lemon rind. (Serves 3)

Veal Goulash with Sauerkraut

(see picture right)

1½ lb. (700 g) veal	¼ pint (141 g) soured
2 tbsps. (30 ml) oil	cream
4 onions	2 level tsps. (10 ml)
1 clove of garlic,	paprika
crushed	1 level tsp. (5 ml)
1 level tsp. (5 ml) salt	caraway seeds
pepper	1 large can of
6 medium-sized	sauerkraut (about
tomatoes	2 lb. or 1 kg)
stock	chopped parsley

Veal Goulash with Sauerkraut

Cut the meat into 1½-inch (3–4-cm) cubes and sauté in the hot oil until they are lightly browned. Skin, slice and fry the onions, add the garlic, seasoning and the skinned and sliced tomatoes. Pour on just enough stock to cover the meat and vegetables, bring to the boil and simmer gently for 1½ hours (or until the meat is tender), stirring occasionally. Remove the meat, keeping it hot, and reduce the sauce to half; add the soured cream, paprika and caraway seeds and simmer very gently for 30 minutes. Meanwhile heat the sauerkraut, and when it is quite hot, arrange it on a hot dish with the meat and sauce. Serve sprinkled with parsley. (Serves 4)

Swiss Veal

(see colour picture facing page 209)

2 tbsps. (30 ml) oil	½ pint (300 ml) stock
4 lb. (2 kg) pie veal	¼ pint (150 ml) dry
seasoned flour	white wine
8 oz. (225 g) carrots,	bouquet garni
peeled and diced	4 egg yolks
8 oz. (225 g) shallots,	½ pint (300 ml) fat-
peeled	free yoghurt
1 tbsps. (15 ml) lemon	salt and pepper
juice	chopped parsley

Heat the oil. Dust the veal with seasoned flour and lightly brown in the oil. Add the carrots, shallots, lemon juice, stock, wine and bouquet garni and simmer gently until the meat is tender. (Altern-atively, turn the mixture into a casserole dish and cook in a moderate oven—350°F., 180°C., mark 4—for about 1½ hours.) Beat the egg yolks and blend with the yoghurt; add a little of the hot stock, then stir into the meat mixture and ad-just the seasoning. Re-heat gently with-out boiling, and serve sprinkled with chopped parsley. (Serves 8)

Veal and Sausage Casserole

3–4 chipolata	3 oz. (85 g) long-
sausages	grain rice
3–4 thin slices of veal,	14-oz. (396-g) can of
beaten	tomatoes
1 level tbsp. (15 ml)	1 tsp. (5 ml) piquant
seasoned flour	sauce
1 tbsp. (15 ml) oil	salt and pepper
1 onion, skinned and	chopped parsley
sliced	

Oven temperature: 350°F., 180°C., mark 4
Boil the sausages for 5 minutes and drain. Wrap a slice of veal around each sausage and secure with a cocktail stick, then roll them in seasoned flour. Heat the oil, lightly brown the rolls and place in a casserole dish. Add the onion, rice, tomatoes and seasonings, cover and cook for about 45 minutes. Serve sprinkled with chopped parsley. (Serves 3–4)

139

Veal and Ham Pie

Veal and Ham Pie

(*see picture above*)

12 oz. (*350 g*) plain flour	½ lb. (*225 g*) ham or bacon
½ level tsp. (*2.5 ml*) salt	1–2 hard-boiled eggs
3 oz. (*85 g*) lard	salt and pepper
¼ pint (*150 ml*) water	meat stock
1 lb. (*450 g*) pie veal	egg for glazing
	aspic jelly to fill up

Oven temperature: 400°F., 200°C., mark 6
Sift the flour and salt and make a well in the centre. Heat the fat and water to boiling point, pour into the dry ingredients and mix with a wooden spoon, then knead the dough well until smooth. Set aside a quarter of the pastry to make the lid, and keep this warm. Mould the rest into a pie shape. Cut the veal and ham into small dice and mix with the finely chopped eggs. Fill the pastry case with this mixture, adding seasoning as required and a little meat stock. Make a lid from the remaining pastry and place on the pie, making a hole in the top of it for steam to escape. Glaze with beaten egg and decorate as desired. Bake for about ½ hour, then reduce the heat to 350°F., 180°C., mark 4, and cook for a further 1½ hours; cover the pastry with a double sheet of greaseproof paper when it is sufficiently brown. Fill up the pie with some aspic jelly (made as directed with powdered aspic) and leave until cold. (Serves 4–6)

Carbonade of Pork

3 lb. (*1½ kg*) leg of pork	1 onion, 2 carrots and 1 turnip, sliced
1½ pints (*1 litre*) water	1 bay leaf
cloves	salt and pepper
½ pint (*300 ml*) lager	

Put the joint in a saucepan with the water, bring to the boil and boil for 20 minutes. Drain, skin, stud with cloves, return it to the pan, add the lager and remaining ingredients and simmer until tender—1½–2 hours. Remove the joint and keep it warm. Rapidly boil the liquid to reduce it, remove the bay leaf and adjust the seasoning. Serve the joint cut in slices, with the sauce poured over. (Serves 6)

Smothered Pork Chops

2 lean pork chops	1 small onion, sliced
salt and pepper	1 tomato, sliced
½ oz. (*25 g*) butter	1 slice of lemon
½ a green pepper	2 tbsps. (*30 ml*) water

Sprinkle the chops with salt and pepper on both sides, then fry in the butter until browned. Add the sliced vegetables, lemon, water and more seasoning, cover and simmer for 20 minutes. (Serves 2)

Stuffed Pork Fillets

(*see picture opposite*)

2 pork fillets	1 onion, finely chopped
2 rashers of lean bacon	grated orange rind
4 oz. (*115 g*) mush-rooms, chopped	¼ pint (*150 ml*) orange juice

Oven temperature: 350°F., 180°C., mark 4
Slit each fillet through the middle, leaving a 'hinge', and beat it flat. Lay a bacon rasher on each and divide the

mushrooms and onion between the fillets, spreading evenly. Close the fillets and secure with string. Put in a lightly greased baking dish with the orange rind and juice and bake for 40 minutes, basting frequently with orange juice. Remove the string before serving. (Serves 4)

Pork Chops with Creamed Cabbage

2 lb. (*1 kg*) cabbage	2 tbsps. (*30 ml*) dry
salt and pepper	white wine
4 pork chops	(optional)
oil	1 oz. (*25 g*) cheese,
½ pint (*300 ml*) low-	grated
fat yoghurt	paprika to garnish
a little sage	

Oven temperature: 350°F., 180°C., mark 4
Shred the cabbage finely, blanch in boiling water and drain. Put half into a casserole with a little pepper. Trim the chops, brush with oil and grill until golden brown, turning them over once; sprinkle with seasoning and keep warm. Add the yoghurt, sage and wine to the grill pan, stir to loosen any meat pieces, then add to the casserole. Place the chops on top, and cover with the remaining cabbage. Cook in the oven for ¾ hour; just before the dish is cooked, sprinkle with the cheese. Garnish with paprika. (Serves 4)

Tipsy Chops

Oven temperature: 350°F., 180°C., mark 4
Trim 4 4-oz. (115-g) pork chops, then brown them quickly under the grill. Place in a shallow casserole dish. Add 2 large cooking apples, peeled and sliced, and ¼ pint (150 ml) dry cider. Cover and bake for 1 hour. (Serves 4)

Orange-Braised Pork Chops
(see colour picture between pages 48, 49)

4 pork chump chops	¼ pint (*150 ml*) dry
1 clove of garlic	white wine
(optional)	¼ pint (*150 ml*)
salt and pepper	orange juice
1 onion, skinned and	2 large oranges
finely sliced	
2 level tsps. (*10 ml*)	
cornflour	

Stuffed Pork Fillets

Oven temperature: 350°F., 180°C., mark 4

Trim the fat from the chops, rub with garlic and season with salt and pepper. Grill under a moderate heat until lightly browned on both sides, and place in a shallow casserole dish. Scatter the onion rings over the chops. Mix the cornflour to a smooth paste with a little wine, add the remaining wine and orange juice and slowly bring to the boil. Pour over the chops, cover tightly and cook for 1–1¼ hours.

Peel the oranges and remove all the pith. Slice, discard the pips and cut each slice in half; arrange over the onion and cook for a further 15 minutes, basting occasionally. Adjust the seasoning, and serve garnished with watercress. (Serves 4)

Pork and Pineapple Curry

1 lb. (*450 g*) pork	1 tbsp. (*15 ml*) grated
1 tbsp. (*15 ml*) oil	lemon rind
1 clove of garlic,	1 level tsp. (*5 ml*)
skinned and crushed	coriander powder
1 medium-sized	2 oz. (*55 g*) blanched
onion, skinned and	almonds, chopped
chopped	½ pint (*300 ml*) stock
2 red peppers, seeded	or water
and sliced	12-oz. (*340-g*) can of
1 tbsp. (*15 ml*) shrimp	pineapple chunks,
or anchovy paste	drained
1½ oz. (*40 g*) fresh	¼ level tsp (*1.25 ml*)
ginger, chopped	saffron

Cut the pork into small pieces and sauté in the oil with the garlic, onion and peppers. Mix together the fish paste, ginger, lemon rind, coriander powder and almonds; add this to the pork mixture and continue frying gently for a few minutes. Add the liquid and cook until the meat is tender. Finally, add the pineapple chunks and saffron and cook for a few minutes longer. Serve very hot. (Serves 3)

Note: If you cannot obtain the fresh ginger (also called 'green' ginger) or the coriander powder, use root ginger and ¼ oz. (7 g) coriander seed; tie them in a muslin bag and remove when the curry is cooked.

Sweet and Sour Pork

(see colour picture facing page 176)

1½ lb. (*700 g*) pork	8 oz. (*225 g*) pine-
fillet	apple, cubed
2 tbsps. (*30 ml*) oil	1 level tbsp. (*15 ml*)
¾ pint (*375 ml*)	cornflour
chicken stock	1 tbsp. (*15 ml*) soy
bouquet garni	sauce
salt and pepper	¼ pint (*150 ml*)
1 green pepper,	vinegar
seeded and sliced	artificial sweetener
1 red pepper, seeded	
and sliced	

Oven temperature: 350°F., 180°C., mark 4

Cut the pork into 1-inch (2.5-cm) cubes. Heat the oil and lightly brown the meat; drain on absorbent paper and place in a casserole dish. Pour the chicken stock over, add the bouquet garni, salt and pepper. Cover and cook for 30–45 minutes. Drain off the stock into a pot, add the peppers, and pineapple and simmer for 5–7 minutes. Mix the cornflour with the soy sauce and vinegar, then add this to the stock mixture, stirring continuously until it thickens and becomes transparent. Sweeten to taste, add the meat and heat gently. Serve in a ring of rice. (Serves 4)

Pork Chops with Apple

1 tbsp. (*15 ml*) onion,	fresh breadcrumbs
finely chopped	(starch-reduced)
1 tbsp. (*15 ml*)	1 lb. (*450 g*) apples
chopped parsley	¼ oz. (*10 g*) butter
1 tsp. (*5 ml*) chopped	juice of 1 lemon
sage	3 tbsps. (*45 ml*) dry
salt and pepper	white wine
1 egg	artificial sweetener
4 pork chops	

Oven temperature: 375°F., 190°C., mark 5

Mix together the onion, parsley, sage, seasoning and egg, beat lightly and put in a shallow dish. Put the trimmed chops into this mixture for about 15 minutes, turning them occasionally. Drain, and dip into the breadcrumbs, then place on a lightly greased baking dish and bake for 30–40 minutes.

Meanwhile, peel and slice the apples and put into a pan with the butter, lemon juice and some wine. Simmer gently until tender. Adjust the sweetening. Serve the chops on a platter and spoon the apple mixture over them. (Serves 4)

Grilled Ham with Pineapple

4 small ham steaks	1 oz. (25 g) flour
4 rashers of bacon	¾ pint (375 ml) stock
2 small onions, cut up	salt and pepper
4 tomatoes, cut up	4 rings of pineapple

Slash the rind of the ham, to prevent it from curling. Make the sauce: cut up the bacon and fry it until the fat runs, then add the cut-up onions and tomatoes and continue to fry for a minute or two. Add the flour, cook for ½ a minute, then pour in the stock. Stir well, bring to the boil and season with salt and pepper. Allow to simmer gently for 15 minutes, sieve and re-heat.

Grill the ham for about 3 minutes on each side, then brush the pineapple rings with the fat that has dripped out of the ham and grill until they are just turning brown. Arrange on a dish with the ham, and serve with the sauce. (Serves 4)

Ham Montmorency

1 rasher of bacon, rinded and chopped	1 level tbsp. (15 ml) tomato paste
1 small onion, skinned and chopped	bouquet garni
	1 tbsp. (15 ml) dry cider
1 carrot, sliced	12 fresh cherries
1 oz. (25 g) flour	2 thick gammon rashers
1 tsp. (5 ml) soy sauce	
½ pint (300 ml) stock	

Heat the bacon until the fat runs, add the onion and carrot and sauté until the onion is transparent. Stir in the flour. Gradually stir in the soy sauce and stock and add the tomato paste, bouquet garni and cider. Bring to the boil and simmer for 30 minutes, stirring occasionally.

Stone the cherries and trim the gammon rashers, snipping their edges to prevent curling. Fifteen minutes before serving the meal, grill the rashers for 7 minutes on each side. Strain the sauce, add the cherries and serve poured over the rashers. (Serves 2)

Gammon and Mushroom Bake

4 thick gammon rashers	pepper
¾ lb. (340 g) mushrooms, sliced	1 level tsp. (5 ml) tomato paste
3 medium-sized courgettes, sliced	¼ pint (150 ml) stock
salt	¼ pint (150 ml) dry cider

Oven temperature: 375°F., 190°C., mark 5
Grill the gammon quickly on both sides to seal it; place in an ovenproof dish, add the mushrooms and courgettes and season. Mix the tomato paste with the stock and cider and pour into the dish. Cover with a lid and cook for about 45 minutes. (Serves 4)

Ham Casserole

3¼-lb. (1.5-kg) piece of gammon, boned	freshly ground pepper
½ pint (300 ml) dry cider	1 lb. (450 g) carrots, peeled
2 bay leaves	1 lb. (450 g) leeks, prepared
½ level tsp. (2.5 ml) ground ginger	1 lb. (450 g) courgettes, sliced

Oven temperature: 350°F., 180°C., mark 4
Soak the gammon for several hours, drain and place in a casserole dish with the cider, ginger, bay leaves, pepper and carrots. Cover and cook in the oven for 1¾ hours. Add the leeks and courgettes and cook for a further 20 minutes. When the gammon is cooked, remove it, strip off the skin, score with a knife and place under a hot grill to brown the scored surface quickly. Serve on a large platter, with the vegetables. (Serves 6–8)

Ham and Mushroom Patties

1 small onion, skinned and chopped	½ level tsp. (2.5 ml) dried sage
1 oz. (25 g) butter	½ lb. (225 g) cooked ham, chopped
4 oz. (115 g) mushrooms, chopped	2 tbsps. (30 ml) piquant table sauce
2 oz. (55 g) fresh white breadcrumbs	salt and pepper
pinch of garlic powder	8 oz. (225 g) short-crust pastry
	beaten egg to glaze

Oven temperature: 400°F., 200°C., mark 6
Fry the onion in the melted butter until

soft but not coloured, add the mushrooms and cook for a few minutes longer. Stir in the breadcrumbs, garlic, sage, ham and sauce; adjust the seasoning. Roll out the pastry, reserving some for the lids; use to line 4 individual 4-inch (10-cm) fluted, loose-bottomed flan tins. Divide the ham and mushroom mixture and fill the tins; brush the edges with beaten egg, top with the pastry lids and seal the edges. Decorate with the pastry trimmings and brush these with egg. Bake for about 30 minutes and serve warm. (Serves 4)

Mixed Grill

The ingredients can be varied to suit individual taste and circumstances, but a typical mixed grill includes a chop or a piece of steak, a piece of kidney or liver, bacon, a sausage, tomato and mushroom. Prepare the various ingredients according to type and brush them all over with melted fat or oil. Heat the grill thoroughly and begin by cooking the ingredients that require the longest time. Keep everything very hot and serve attractively, garnished with watercress, putting a pat of maître d'hôtel butter on each chop or piece of steak. Pineapple rings may be served instead of a vegetable.
The following are the approximate grilling times:

Pork chops	15–20 minutes
Sausages: Thick	15 minutes
Thin	10 minutes
Steak	10–15 minutes
Lamb chops	10–15 minutes
Kidneys	10 minutes
Liver	5–10 minutes
Tomatoes	5 minutes
Mushrooms	5 minutes

Stuffed Cabbage Leaves

½–¾ lb. (225–340 g) minced raw meat	salt and pepper stock
1 onion, skinned and chopped	2 tbsps. (30 ml) cooked rice
1 tbsp. (15 ml) oil	8–12 medium sized cabbage leaves
2 tsps. (10 ml) chopped parsley	

144

Oven temperature: 350°F., 180°C., mark 4
Cook the minced meat and chopped onion in the hot oil, turning the mixture frequently. Add parsley, salt and a little stock, and simmer for 10 minutes, then stir in the rice. Break off the cabbage leaves, remove the hard white spine, blanch the leaves in boiling water for 2 minutes and drain them. Place 1 tbsp. of the meat mixture on each leaf and fold it over the filling to make a neat 'parcel'. Put close together in a casserole, almost cover with stock and cook in the oven for about ¾ hour. Serve with sliced tomatoes and watercress. (Serves 4)

Greek Moussaka
(see picture opposite)

2 aubergines	4 tomatoes, skinned
2 tbsps. (30 ml) oil	¼ pint (150 ml) stock
4–5 medium-sized onions, skinned and sliced	¼ pint (150 ml) tomato purée
	2 eggs
1 lb. (450 g) minced beef or lamb, cooked	4 tbsps. (60 ml) milk salt and pepper

Oven temperature: 350°F., 180°C., mark 4
Slice the aubergines and fry in some of the oil, then arrange them in the bottom of an ovenproof dish. Cover with layers of onion and minced meat and lastly add slices of tomato. Pour in the stock and tomato purée, and bake for about 30 minutes. Beat together the eggs and milk, add salt and pepper and pour this mixture into the casserole. Return to the oven for 15–20 minutes, until the sauce is set, firm and golden-brown. (Serves 4)

Mushroom-stuffed Meat Loaf

½ lb. (225 g) mushrooms	¼ tsp. (1.25 ml) dried thyme
1 oz. (25 g) butter	1 egg
1 tsp. (5 ml) lemon juice	1½ lb. (700 g) minced beef
1 small onion, minced	
2 oz. (55 g) breadcrumbs (starch-reduced)	2 tbsps. (30 ml) milk
	3 tbsps. (45 ml) tomato sauce or paste
salt and pepper	
2 tbsps. (30 ml) chopped parsley	1 level tsp. (5 ml) dry mustard

Mushroom Bouillon (see page 106), Grilled Lamb Cutlets (see page 127), Cheese-board

Oven temperature: 400°F., 200°C., mark 6
Put aside 5 whole mushrooms and slice the remainder; sauté the slices in the butter, adding the lemon juice and onion. Stir in the breadcrumbs, ½ level tsp. (2.5 ml) salt, pinch pepper, the parsley and thyme. Beat the egg and mix it into the minced beef; add 2 level tsps. (10 ml) salt, pinch pepper, the milk, tomato sauce and mustard. Pack half the meat mixture into a greased loaf tin, spread the herb stuffing over the top, then add the remainder. Press the 5 whole mushrooms on top. Refrigerate or leave in a cold place for 1–2 hours, then bake for ¾–1 hour. (Serves 6)

Pork and Liver Loaf

1 lb. (*450 g*) lean pork	1 level tsp. (*5 ml*) dried thyme
½ lb. (*225 g*) lambs' liver	1 egg, lightly beaten
1 onion	salt and pepper
2 oz. (*55 g*) soft breadcrumbs	

Oven temperature: 350°F., 180°C., mark 4
Mince together the pork, liver and onion, blend in the breadcrumbs and thyme and bind with seasoned egg. Shape into an oblong and wrap firmly in foil. Place in a greased baking dish and bake for 1½ hours. Serve with apple sauce. (Serves 4)

Bacon and Beef Loaf

1 lb. (*450 g*) steak	2 eggs, lightly beaten
1-lb. (*450-g*) bacon joint, cooked	salt and pepper
1 medium-sized onion	1 level tsp. (*5 ml*) dry mustard
¼ pint (*150 ml*) tomato purée	

Oven temperature: 350°F., 180°C., mark 4
Finely mince the steak, bacon and onion. Add the tomato purée, eggs and seasoning, press firmly into a greased loaf tin and bake for about 2 hours. Pour off any accumulated fat, turn the loaf out onto a platter and serve with cheesy mustard sauce—see below. (Serves 6–8)

Cheesy Mustard Sauce

2 tbsps. (*30 ml*) milk	1 level tsp. (*5 ml*) dry mustard
4 oz. (*115 g*) mature Cheddar cheese, finely grated	freshly ground pepper

Heat all the ingredients together over a low heat, stirring constantly, but avoid

Greek Moussaka

145

Colonial Goose (see page 127), Apricot Sponge (see page 194)

boiling. Season with freshly ground
pepper and serve immediately.

Continental Meat Loaf

½ lb. (*225 g*) beef, minced	1 egg, lightly beaten
½ lb. (*225 g*) veal, minced	1 oz. (*25 g*) bread-crumbs (starch-reduced)
½ lb. (*225 g*) pork, minced	6 tomatoes, sliced
1 onion, grated	2 onions, finely sliced
salt and pepper	4 oz. (*115 g*) cheese, grated

Oven temperature: 350°F., 180°C., mark 4
Mix the beef, veal, pork, grated onions,
seasoning, egg and crumbs. Place half the
mixture in the bottom of a lightly
greased loaf tin, add a layer of tomatoes
and sliced onion and cover with the
remaining meat. Top with the rest of the
tomato and onion and sprinkle the cheese
over. Bake for 1–1¼ hours. (Serves 6)

Chilled Meat Loaf
(*see colour picture facing page 193*)

¼ lb. (*115 g*) bacon, finely chopped	2 pints (*1 litre*) aspic jelly
¼ lb. (*115 g*) sausage-meat	few slices of cucumber and radish
½ lb. (*225 g*) beef, finely minced	1 tbsp. (*15 ml*) mush-room ketchup
1 large onion, skinned and finely chopped	salt and pepper
bouquet garni	lettuce, radish roses and tomato lilies
½ pint (*300 ml*) stock or water	

Cook the bacon, sausage-meat, minced
beef and onion with the bouquet garni
in the liquid for ½ hour, then strain off
the liquid and use this to make up the
aspic jelly as directed on the packet.
Pour a little jelly into the bottom of a
wetted loaf tin (about 9 by 5 inches, 23 × 13
cm), add cucumber and radish and leave
to set. Combine remaining jelly, ketchup,
salt and pepper with the meat mixture and
put in the tin. Place in the refrigerator
for 3–4 hours, until set. Turn out and
garnish. (Serves 6)

Shish Kebabs
(*see colour picture between pages 48, 49*)

1 lb. (*450 g*) minced beef	8 lean rashers, halved
1 medium-sized onion, grated	4 slices of fresh pine-apple, cored
1 egg, lightly beaten	1 large green pepper, seeded
salt	4 tomatoes, quartered
freshly ground pepper	8 stuffed green olives
1 level tsp. (*5 ml*) marjoram	

Oven temperature: 350°F., 180°C., mark 4
Mix together the beef, onion, egg,
seasoning and marjoram. Form into 16
small balls and bake in a shallow dish for
20–30 minutes. Allow to cool.
Wrap each meat ball in a half-rasher of
bacon. Cut the pineapple and pepper
into small chunks. Alternate the meat
balls, tomatoes, pepper and pineapple on
8 kebab skewers. Top each with an olive
and bake (or rotate under a moderate
grill) for 15–20 minutes. (Serves 4)

Hamburger Steaks
(*see picture below*)

1 lb. (*450 g*) minced beef	salt and pepper
1 onion, finely grated	1 egg, lightly beaten
1 tbsp. (*15 ml*) curry powder	4 rashers of streaky bacon

Oven temperature: 350°F., 180°C., mark 4
Mix together the beef, onion, seasoning
and curry powder, and add the egg to

Hamburger Steaks

blend. Form into 4 rounds, wrap a rasher of bacon around each and secure with a cocktail stick. Place in a baking dish and cook for 1 hour. (Serves 4)

Chilli-burgers

1½ lb. (700 g) minced beef	½ level tsp. (2.5 ml) chilli powder
salt and pepper	1 egg
2 tbsps. (30 ml) chopped chives	

Oven temperature: 350°F., 180°C., mark 4
Mix all the ingredients together. Form into 8 balls, flatten, put into a small baking dish and bake for ½–¾ hour. (Serves 4)

Beef Potato Bake

2 oz. (55 g) bacon rashers, rinded and chopped	2 tbsps. (30 ml) piquant sauce
1 small onion, skinned and finely chopped	1 tbsp. (15 ml) red wine or water
¾ lb. (340 g) lean raw beef, minced	1 clove of garlic, skinned and crushed
½ level tbsp. (7.5 ml) flour	salt and pepper
	2 tomatoes, sliced
	½ lb. (225 g) potatoes, cooked and creamed

Oven temperature: 375°F., 190°C., mark 5
Lightly fry the bacon until the fat runs, add the onion and fry until soft. Stir in the minced beef and brown evenly, then blend in the flour and cook for 2–3 minutes. Stir in the sauce, wine and garlic and adjust the seasoning. Divide between 4 individual ovenproof dishes, cover with the sliced tomatoes and top with potato. Bake for about 20 minutes. (Serves 2)

Hungarian Steaks

2½ oz. (70 g) salami	1 level tbsp. (15 ml) tomato paste
4 onions	
2 tomatoes, skinned	salt, pepper and dry mustard
2 small green peppers	
¾ lb. (340 g) beef, finely minced	1 level tbsp. (15 ml) flour
1 tbsp. (15 ml) lemon juice	

Oven temperature: 350°F., 180°C., mark 4
Finely mince the salami, 1 onion and the tomatoes with the flesh of the green peppers; mix these with the beef. Add the lemon juice, tomato paste, seasoning and flour. Shape into 4 rounds and place on a lightly greased baking dish. Slice the remaining onions and add to the steaks. Bake for 1–1½ hours, until the onions are clear and tender. Pipe some mashed potato round the edge of a dish and brown lightly under the grill. Place the steaks in the dish and put the onion rings on top. (Serves 3–4)

Cheesy Beef Patties

8 oz. (225 g) short-crust pastry flavoured with 4 oz. (115 g) grated cheese	2 level tsps. (10 ml) tomato paste
	½ an onion, skinned and chopped very finely
8 oz. (225 g) steak, minced	salt and pepper
2 tomatoes, skinned and chopped	dry mustard
	egg to glaze
3 rashers of short back bacon, diced	

Oven temperature: 400°F., 200°C., mark 6
Roll out the pastry ⅛ inch (0.3 cm) thick and cut into 6-inch (15-cm) squares. Mix the remaining ingredients and divide equally between the pastry squares; fold the pastry over to form a triangle, damp the edges and seal. Glaze, place on greased trays and bake for 20 minutes, then lower the temperature to 350°F., 180°C., mark 4 and cook until the meat is tender—30–40 minutes. (Serves 4)

Savoury Meatballs in Casserole

1 lb. (450 g) minced steak	salt and pepper
1 egg, beaten	½ lb. (225 g) carrots, cut into matchstick pieces
½ level tsp. (2.5 ml) marjoram	½ lb. (225 g) mush-rooms, sliced
1 tsp. (5 ml) piquant sauce	¼ pint (150 ml) stock
½ lb. (225 g) onions, sliced	nutmeg

Oven temperature: 350°F., 180°C., mark 4
Combine the mince, egg, herbs and seasoning. Form into small balls (approxi-

mately 16), place in a shallow baking dish and bake for 30 minutes. Transfer to a deep casserole dish and add the onion, carrots, mushrooms and stock, with a little salt and grated nutmeg. Cover and cook for 30 minutes. (Serves 3–4)

Stuffed Peppers

4 medium-sized green peppers	8 oz. (*225 g*) mushrooms, sliced
8 oz. (*225 g*) lean bacon, chopped	1 tbsp. (*15 ml*) soy sauce
4 oz. (*115 g*) onion, skinned and chopped	¼ pint (*150 ml*) tomato juice
4 oz. (*115 g*) celery, chopped	

Oven temperature: 350°F., 180°C., mark 4
Cut off the stalk of each pepper to form a 'lid' and remove all the seeds. Pour boiling water over the pepper cases and allow them to stand for ½ hour. Heat the bacon until the fat runs; add the onion, celery, mushrooms and soy sauce and simmer for 5 minutes. Fill the drained peppers with the mixture. Place in a shallow casserole, pour the tomato juice over and bake for ¾–1 hour. (Serves 4)

Vegetable Platter with Beef Balls

(*see picture right*)

1½ lb. (*700 g*) potatoes, peeled	½ level tsp. (*2.5 ml*) chilli powder
salt and pepper	a little flour
1 lb. (*450 g*) minced beef	¼ pint (*150 ml*) stock
dripping	a little beaten egg
1 small onion	1 lb. (*450 g*) baked onions
1 egg, lightly beaten	½ lb. (*225 g*) carrots, cooked
2 oz. (*55 g*) breadcrumbs	1 lb. (*450 g*) green beans, or peas, cooked
1 level tbsp. (*15 ml*) tomato paste	

Oven temperature: 350°F., 180°C., mark 4
Cook the potatoes in salted water. Finely mince the meat twice. Melt a little fat and add the chopped onion, combine with the meat and work in the egg, bread-

crumbs, flavourings and seasoning. Form into small balls, using a little flour to prevent them from sticking, and bake for ½ hour. Add the stock and cook gently for 10–15 minutes. Meanwhile, cream the potatoes and pipe on to a heatproof platter, making a border and marking out into 4 portions. Brush with beaten egg and brown in the oven. Fill the sections with the meatballs, onions, and cooked carrots and beans (or peas) each tossed in a little melted butter. (Serves 4)

Meatballs Sweet and Sour

1 lb. (*450 g*) minced beef	4 sticks of celery, chopped
1 onion, finely minced	15-oz. (*425-g*) can of pineapple chunks, drained
1 tbsp. (*15 ml*) chopped parsley	2 level tbsps. (*30 ml*) cornflour
salt and pepper	5 tbsps. (*75 ml*) vinegar
1 egg, lightly beaten	
1 pint (*600 ml*) chicken stock	2 tbsps. (*30 ml*) soy sauce
1 red pepper, seeded and sliced	artificial sweetener

Oven temperature: 350°F., 180°C., mark 4
Mix together the beef, onion, parsley, salt and pepper. Bind with egg and form into small balls. Bake in a shallow dish for 30 minutes. Bring the stock to the boil, add the pepper, celery and pine-apple, and simmer for 5 minutes. Blend

Vegetable Platter with Beef Balls

148

the cornflour to a smooth paste with the vinegar and soy sauce, stir into the stock and return the mixture to the boil. Add the cooked meatballs and leave over a low heat to heat through thoroughly. Adjust the flavour by adding a little artificial sweetener. (Serves 4)

Kofta

6 small onions	1 clove of garlic
1 lb. (450 g) fresh minced meat	2 oz. (55 g) butter salt
2 level tbsps. (30 ml) curry powder	1 lb. (450 g) tomatoes ½ pint (300 ml) stock

Mince 3 of the onions and add to the meat, together with half the curry powder; knead, divide into small portions and roll into balls. Slice the rest of the onions, chop the garlic and fry in the butter until just turning golden-brown. Add the remaining curry powder, some salt, the quartered tomatoes and the stock, and leave to cook for a minute or two. Carefully add the meatballs, cover with a lid and cook very gently for 20–30 minutes, taking care not to break up the balls. (Serves 4)

Chop Suey

1 tbsp. (15 ml) oil	pepper
½ an onion, finely chopped	2 oz. (55 g) green beans, sliced
4 oz. (115 g) pork, cut into strips	2 oz. (55 g) cabbage, shredded
2 tbsps. (30 ml) diced celery	1 level tsp. (5 ml) cornflour
¼ pint (150 ml) water	1 tbsp. (15 ml) soy
½ level tsp. (2.5 ml) salt	sauce

Heat the oil and sauté the onion and pork for 3 minutes. Add the celery, water, salt and pepper, and cook for 7 minutes, then add the beans and cabbage and cook for a further 3 minutes. Combine the cornflour and soy sauce with sufficient water to give a smooth paste, add to the meat mixture, stir lightly and cook for 1 minute. Serve with noodles. (Serves 1)

Risotto

1 tbsp. (15 ml) oil	1 green pepper, seeded and chopped
3 oz. (85 g) long grain rice	1 red pepper, seeded and chopped
1 lb. (450 g) minced beef	1 tbsp. (15 ml) soy sauce
½ level tsp. (2.5 ml) salt	½ pint (300 ml) stock
¼ level tsp. (1.25 ml) chilli powder	

Heat the oil in a frying pan and fry the rice without browning. Add the mince and brown, then add the salt, chilli powder, peppers, soy sauce and stock. Cook over a moderate heat until all the liquid is absorbed—about 20–30 minutes. (Serves 4)

Salt Beef Omelette

1 egg, separated	freshly ground pepper
¼ level tsp. (1.25 ml) salt	1 oz. (25 g) salt beef, finely minced
1 tbsp. (15 ml) water	

Beat the egg white to a foam, add the salt and continue beating until stiff. Add the water and some pepper to the egg yolk, and beat until thick and creamy. Fold in the egg white, blending thoroughly without over-mixing. Turn the mixture into a small non-stick pan and cook over a low heat until it is almost set. Sprinkle the beef over the omelette, then place under a moderate grill to finish cooking. Crease the omelette at right angles to the handle of the pan, fold it over and turn out on to a hot plate. Serve immediately. (Serves 1)

Dutch Hussar's Salad

12 oz. (340 g) cold meat	cheese dressing (see page 192)
1 small cucumber	1 lettuce
3 tomatoes, skinned and de-seeded	2 eggs, hard-boiled and sliced
3 eating apples, cored but not peeled	1 beetroot, sliced pickled onions and gherkins (optional)
2 cold cooked potatoes	

Dice the meat and cube the cucumber, tomatoes, apples and potatoes, then add the cheese dressing. Press this mixture into a basin, making it quite firm; chill. Arrange some lettuce leaves on a dish and turn the salad out on to this. Decorate with sliced hard-boiled egg and beetroot, and pickled onions and gherkins, if used. (Serves 4)

Liver Piquant

¾ lb. (*340 g*) lamb's or calf's liver
¼ pint (*150 ml*) vinegar
1 clove of garlic
pepper
2 large onions
1 oz. (*25 g*) butter
boiled rice

Slice the liver thinly and marinade it overnight in the vinegar with the garlic and pepper. Slice the onions and sauté in the hot butter until brown; remove and keep hot while the liver is fried on both sides. Take out the liver and pour the strained vinegar into the pan; when this is almost boiling, add the onion and liver and simmer gently until the liver is tender. Serve on a bed of rice with the cooked onions, and pour the sauce over. (Serves 2)

Liver Hot-pot

½ lb (*225 g*) liver
seasoned flour
1 small onion
1 oz. (*25 g*) mush-rooms
2 tomatoes, skinned
½ tsp. (*2.5 ml*) mixed herbs
salt and pepper
½ lb. (*225 g*) potatoes, peeled
stock

Oven temperature: 350°F., 180°C., mark 4
Wash and trim the liver, toss it in the seasoned flour and place in an ovenproof dish. Dice the onion; thinly slice the mushrooms and tomatoes. Cover the meat with these vegetables and add the herbs and seasoning; add the thinly sliced potatoes, half-cover the hot-pot with stock and bake for 1–1½ hours. (Serves 2)

Baked Stuffed Liver

1 lb. (*450 g*) liver
a little seasoned flour
forcemeat stuffing
6–8 small pieces of streaky bacon
½ pint (*300 ml*) stock

Oven temperature: 375°F., 190°C., mark 5
Wash and dry the liver, cut it into 6–8 slices, dip into seasoned flour and lay them in a greased baking tin. Put a little stuffing on each slice of liver and lay a piece of bacon on top. Pour the stock round, cover the baking tin with a lid or with greased paper, and bake until the liver is tender—about 40 minutes. Serve on a hot dish and pour the stock over. Garnish with parsley. (Serves 4)

Liver Française

1 lb. (*450 g*) calf's liver
3 oz. (*85 g*) bread-crumbs
1½ oz. (*40 g*) suet, chopped
2 tsps. (*10 ml*) finely chopped parsley
a pinch of dried herbs
salt and pepper
beaten egg
bacon rashers

Oven temperature: 400°F., 200°C., mark 6
Grease a shallow ovenproof dish and arrange the sliced liver over the base of it. Mix together the breadcrumbs, suet, parsley, herbs and seasoning, and bind with egg, adding a little milk if necessary. Spread this mixture evenly over each slice of liver, then cover with a piece of bacon from which the rind has been removed. Cover the dish loosely with aluminium foil and cook in the oven for ¾–1 hour. (Serves 3–4)

Braised Liver

1 lb. (*450 g*) liver
1 oz. (*25 g*) seasoned flour
4 rashers of lean bacon, chopped
4 onions, sliced
14-oz. (*396-g*) can of tomatoes
1 tbsp. (*15 ml*) Worcestershire sauce

Oven temperature: 350°F., 180°C., mark 4
Wipe the liver and remove any skin or tubes; cut into even-sized pieces and coat with seasoned flour. Heat the bacon until the fat runs, add the onions and sauté; fry the liver, browning it lightly. Transfer the liver, onions and bacon to a casserole dish, add the tomatoes and Worcestershire sauce, cover and cook for 1¼ hours. (Serves 4)

Braised Liver in Wine

1½ lb. (*700 g*) lamb's or ox liver, sliced
2 level tbsps. (*30 ml*) flour
½ level tsp. (*2.5 ml*) salt
pepper
1 oz. (*25 g*) butter
2 onions, skinned and chopped
1 tbsp. (*15 ml*) chopped parsley
5 tbsps. (*75 ml*) red wine
½ pint (*300 ml*) beef stock

Toss the liver in seasoned flour. Melt the butter and sauté the onions and parsley. Add the liver and brown lightly. Add the red wine and stock, cover and simmer gently for 15–20 minutes. (Serves 4)

Leek and Liver Casserole

1 tbsp. (*15 ml*) oil
1 lb. (*450 g*) lamb's liver
4 leeks
1 pint (*600 ml*) stock
1 level tbsp. (*15 ml*) tomato paste
salt and pepper

Oven temperature: 350°F., 180°C., mark 4
Heat the oil in a flameproof casserole, toss the liver in it and cook lightly. Cut the leeks into small pieces about ¼ inch (0.5 cm) thick and add to the liver, then add the stock, tomato paste and seasoning. Cover and cook in the oven for about 45 minutes, or simmer over a low heat for 30 minutes. (Serves 4)
Note: For 1 serving, use 1 tsp. (5 ml) oil, 4–6 oz. (115–170 g) liver, 1 leek, ¼ pint (150 ml) stock, 1 tsp. (5 ml) tomato paste; season to taste.

Liver and Bacon Casserole

1 lb. (*450 g*) liver
seasoned flour
a little dripping
1 onion, cut up
1 carrot, cut up
1–2 tomatoes, cut up
3–4 bacon rashers, cut up into short lengths

Oven temperature: 350°F., 180°C., mark 4
Cut the liver into small chunks, toss in the seasoned flour and fry in the hot dripping. Add the onion, carrot and tomatoes, and barely cover with water, then bring to the boil, stirring. Put into a casserole and cook in the oven until tender—about ¾ hour. Cover the top with the cut-up bacon rashers, and replace in the oven until the bacon is browned—about 20 minutes. (Serves 4)

Liver Rolls

6 rashers of back bacon
6 slices of ox liver
salt and pepper
1 tbsp. (*15 ml*) oil
¼ pint (*150 ml*) stock
2 level tbsps. (*30 ml*) tomato paste
1 egg yolk
¼ pint (*140 g*) low-fat yoghurt
parsley to garnish

Place each bacon rasher on a slice of liver, season, roll up tightly and secure with a cocktail stick. Heat the oil and lightly brown the rolls, then add the stock and tomato paste. Cover and cook over a low heat for 20–30 minutes. Lightly beat the egg yolk and blend in the yoghurt and a little liquor from the pan. Place the rolls on a serving dish. Blend the yoghurt mixture with the remaining liquor and heat without boiling. Pour over the rolls, and serve sprinkled with parsley. (Serves 3)

Liver and Bacon Kebabs

¾ lb. (*340 g*) calf's or lamb's liver
4 rashers of bacon, rolled
4 medium-sized mushrooms
oil
salt and pepper
2 medium-sized tomatoes
3 tbsps. (*45 ml*) stock or water
a squeeze of lemon juice

Cut the liver into thick chunks and arrange on long skewers alternately with the bacon rolls and mushrooms; brush with oil and season lightly. Quarter the tomatoes, sprinkle with a little salt and pepper, brush with oil and grill; arrange on a dish and keep hot. Now grill the kebabs, allowing 5 minutes on each side, and place on the dish. Add the stock to the juices in the grill pan, season, add the lemon juice, re-heat, then pour over the kebabs. (Serves 4)

Casserole of Kidney, Tomato and Bacon

6 lamb's kidneys
4 large tomatoes
4 lean bacon rashers
salt and pepper

Oven temperature: 350°F., 180°C., mark 4
Skin and core the kidneys and cut into even-sized pieces. Slice the tomatoes. Rind the bacon and fry the rinds to extract the fat, then fry the kidneys lightly for about 5 minutes (it may be necessary to add a little fat). Put in a casserole, lay the tomato slices on top, season well and add the rashers. Bake for ½ hour, until well cooked. (Serves 4)

Homestead Fry

1 lb. (*450 g*) raw potato, thinly sliced	2 rashers of lean bacon, chopped
1 lb. (*450 g*) lamb's liver	15-oz. (*425-g*) can of concentrated
seasoned flour	vegetable soup
butter	¼ pint (*150 ml*) water
1 onion, skinned and finely chopped	

Oven temperature: 350°F., 180°C., mark 4
Line the base and sides of a casserole dish measuring about 9½ by 6½ inches by 2½ inches deep (23 × 16 × 6 cm) with slices of raw potato. Cut the liver into ½-inch (1.25-cm) slices, dust with seasoned flour, brown in melted butter and place in the casserole; add the onion and bacon. Mix the vegetable soup with the water and pour over the casserole. Cover and bake for 1¼–1½ hours. (Serves 4)

Kidneys in Red Wine

1 oz. (*25 g*) butter	¼ pint (*150 ml*) stock
1 onion, skinned and chopped	bouquet garni
6 sheep's kidneys	1 level tbsp. (*15 ml*) tomato paste
½ oz. (*15 g*) flour	salt and pepper
¼ pint (*150 ml*) red wine	6 oz. (*170 g*) mushrooms, sliced

Melt the butter and fry the onion until golden. Skin and core the kidneys, cut them into small pieces, add to the pan and cook for 5 minutes, stirring occasionally. Stir in the flour, pour in the wine and stock and bring slowly to the boil, then add the bouquet garni, tomato paste and some salt and pepper. Simmer for 5 minutes, then add the mushrooms and simmer for a further few minutes.

Remove the bouquet garni before serving, and check the seasoning. (Serves 4)

Braised Kidneys with Ham

6 sheep's kidneys	1 tbsp. (*15 ml*) dry sherry
1 oz. (*25 g*) butter	salt and pepper
1 tbsp. (*15 ml*) olive oil	6 oz. (*170 g*) lean cooked ham, cut in 1 thick slice
2 shallots, finely chopped	
⅓ pint (*200 ml*) stock	cooked peas
2 level tbsps. (*30 ml*) tomato paste	cress to garnish

Skin the kidneys and cut in small squares, removing any fat. Heat the butter and oil in a pan, fry the kidney lightly, then stir in the shallots and continue frying until just coloured. Pour off the oil, and add the stock, tomato paste, sherry and seasoning. Cover and cook gently for about 10 minutes. Cut the ham in cubes and add to the kidneys. Arrange the hot peas in a border around the dish, pour the kidney mixture into the centre and garnish with cress. (Serves 4)

Braised Kidneys with Tomatoes and Mushrooms

6 sheep's kidneys	small can tomato paste
¼ lb. (*115 g*) skinless sausages	salt and pepper
2 oz. (*55 g*) fat	bouquet garni
2 onions, sliced	little flour
4 oz. (*115 g*) button mushrooms	½ lb. (*225 g*) tomatoes and some watercress
½ pint (*300 ml*) meat stock or water	

Skin and halve the kidneys and remove the cores; cut the sausages into 2 or 3 pieces. Melt the fat in a heatproof casserole or saucepan and cook the kidneys and sausages slowly until brown. Remove, then fry the onions and mushrooms lightly. Pour off any excess fat. Add the stock and tomato paste and slowly bring to the boil, then return the kidneys and sausages to the casserole, season, add the bouquet garni and simmer for 25–30 minutes. Remove the bouquet garni, thicken the gravy with

the flour blended with a little water and cook for a few more minutes. Garnish with tomatoes and watercress. (Serves 4)
Note: To make 1 serving, use 1 kidney, 1 sausage, 1 small onion, 1 oz. (30 g) mushrooms, 2 tbsps. (30 ml) tomato paste and 4 tbsps. (60 ml) stock; reduce the amount of fat as necessary; garnish with salad ingredients as available.

Heart Hot-pot

4 lambs' hearts	2 tbsps. (*30 ml*)
1 onion	breadcrumbs
4 sticks of celery	1 oz. (*25 g*) seasoned
4 tomatoes	flour
8 oz. (*225 g*) mush-	1 oz. (*25 g*) fat
rooms	4 tbsps. (*60 ml*) cider

Oven temperature: 350°F., 180°C., mark 4
Cut the central membrane of the hearts and trim away any gristle or inedible parts; wash very thoroughly. Prepare and dice the onion and celery, and chop the tomatoes and mushrooms. Mix together the mushrooms and breadcrumbs, stuff the hearts, sew the edges together and roll them in the seasoned flour. Fry in the hot fat until well browned and drain on absorbent paper. Place the hearts in a casserole with the diced vegetables. Add the remaining flour to the fat and when well browned, stir in enough water to make a thick, brown gravy; pour with the cider over the hearts, adding sufficient water to half-cover the meat and vegetables. Cover the dish and cook in the oven for 2 hours. (Serves 4)

Stewed Heart

1–2 calves' hearts	salt and pepper
stock	finely chopped
carrot, onion, turnip	parsley to garnish
and celery, diced	

Prepare the heart (see previous recipe), cover with the stock, add the diced vegetables and seasoning and simmer gently for 1½–2 hours. Cut the heart into pieces and dish up with the vegetables in the stock; just before serving, sprinkle with chopped parsley. (Serves 4)

Boiled Ox Tongue

Before cooking a pickled tongue, soak it in cold water for several hours (overnight if the tongue has been smoked). Skewer the tongue into a convenient shape if very large, put it into a pan with water to cover, bring gradually to the boil and drain. Add flavouring ingredients such as peeled and sliced carrot, onion, turnip, a few peppercorns and a bouquet garni, cover with fresh cold water, bring to the boil and simmer until tender—2½–3 hours if pickled, 4½–6 hours if fresh; skim occasionally. Plunge it into cold water, then skin it, removing any bones or pieces of gristle. Place in a convenient-sized cake tin; a 7-inch (17.5-cm) one is required for a 6-lb. (3-kg) tongue. Fill up with a little of the stock, put a plate on top, weight down with a heavy object and leave to set. Turn out and sprinkle with parsley.

Devilled Tongue

1 lb. (*450 g*) cooked	¼ level tsp. (*1.25 ml*)
tongue, cubed	curry powder
1 level tbsp. (*15 ml*)	¼ level tsp. (*1.25 ml*)
flour	dry mustard
1 tbsp. (*15 ml*)	¼ level tsp. (*1.25 ml*)
vinegar	mixed spice
1 tbsp. (*15 ml*) tomato	salt and pepper
sauce	½ pint (*300 ml*) stock
¼ level tsp. (*1.25 ml*)	
ground ginger	

Oven temperature: 350°F., 180°C., mark 4
Place the cut-up tongue in a casserole dish. Mix together the remaining ingredients and pour over the tongue. Cover and bake for ½–¾ hour. (Serves 3)

Crumbed Brains

6 pairs of lamb's	½ level tsp. (*2.5 ml*)
brains	salt
1 tbsp. (*15 ml*)	2 oz. (*55 g*) toasted
vinegar	breadcrumbs
1 egg, lightly beaten	parsley and lemon

Oven temperature: 350°F., 180°C., mark 4
Wash the brains and soak for an hour in cold water. Remove as much of the skin and membrane as possible and place in a pan with the vinegar, salt and sufficient

water to cover. Bring to simmering point and cook gently for 15 minutes, put into cold water and then drain thoroughly. Dip into the egg, then coat with bread-crumbs. Place in a lightly greased baking dish and cook for 20 minutes. Serve sprinkled with parsley and garnished with lemon wedges. (Serves 4)

Belted Sausage Casserole
(*see picture below*)

2 rashers of streaky bacon	⅛ pint (*75 ml*) stock
¼ lb. (*115 g*) chipolata sausages	1 level tsp. (*5 ml*) tomato paste
1 small onion, skinned and finely sliced	¼ tsp. (*1.25 ml*) meat or vegetable extract
½ a green pepper, seeded and sliced	salt pepper

Oven temperature: 400°F., 200°C., mark 6

Halve the rashers of bacon and wrap each half round a sausage. Put the bacon-wrapped sausages in the bottom of a casserole and sprinkle the onion and green pepper over them. Mix the stock, tomato paste and meat or vegetable

Belted Sausage Casserole

extract and pour over the sausages; season with a little salt and some pepper. Bake for about 25 minutes. (Serves 2)

Open Sandwich
(*see colour pictures facing pages 192 and 193*)

Lightly spread a thin slice of pumper-nickel with butter or low-fat spread. Top with lettuce and sliced meat loaf, sliced cucumber and tomato; garnish with sieved hard-boiled egg.

As the second colour picture suggests, open sandwiches—provided they are carefully packed—also make delicious and decorative picnic fare.

Sausage and Cheese Salad

6 oz. (*170 g*) garlic sausage, diced	1 red pepper, seeded and diced
4 oz. (*115 g*) cheese, diced	lemon chive dressing (see page 192)
2 sticks of celery, chopped	lettuce

Toss together the sausage, cheese, celery and pepper, with a little lemon chive dressing. Pile into lettuce cups and if wished sprinkle with parsley.

Ham Salad

8 oz. (*225 g*) ham, diced	1 green pepper, seeded and chopped
3 sticks of celery, chopped	French dressing lettuce
1 red-skinned apple, diced	6 ripe olives

Mix together the ham, celery, apple and pepper. Toss in a little dressing, place in lettuce cups and garnish with olives.

Basic Brown Sauce

1 small carrot	½ oz. (*15 g*) flour
1 small onion	½ pint (*300 ml*) stock
2 mushrooms	salt and pepper
½ oz. (*15 g*) dripping	

Chop the carrot, onion and mushrooms. Melt the dripping and sauté the vege-tables for 5 minutes. Add the flour, stir well and cook for 1 minute, then remove from the heat. Blend in the stock, season, return the pan to the heat, and boil the sauce until it thickens, then cook for a further 3 minutes. Strain before using (e.g., in making Espagnole Sauce).

Barbecue Sauce

8-oz. (*226-g*) can tomatoes
2 medium-sized onions, skinned and sliced
1 tbsp. (*15 ml*) dry cider
½ level tsp. (*2.5 ml*) basil
salt and pepper
1 clove of garlic, crushed (optional)

Boil all the ingredients together to reduce the volume, until thick and pulpy. Sieve or blend well; adjust the seasoning. This spicy tomato sauce can be served with grilled chops, steaks and barbecues, or with savoury meatballs or patties.

Devil's Sauce

¼ pint (*150 ml*) cider vinegar
4 tbsps. (*60 ml*) Worcestershire sauce
5 tbsps. (*75 ml*) chilli sauce
½ level tsp. (*2.5 ml*) dry mustard
artificial sweetener to taste

Mix together the vinegar, sauces and mustard. Cook, stirring occasionally, for about 15 minutes, until reduced and slightly thickened. Add sweetener to taste. Serve with grills and barbecues.

Caper Sauce

Make some white sauce in the usual way, but use half meat liquor and half milk. Add about 1½ tbsps. (*23 ml*) coarsely chopped capers to ½ pint (*300 ml*) sauce. Serve with boiled mutton (or with poached fish).

Savoury Orange Sauce

1 orange
½ pint (*300 ml*) chicken stock
2 level tsps. (*10 ml*) cornflour
soy sauce

Squeeze the juice from the orange and finely slice half the peel. Add the sliced peel to the stock, bring to the boil and simmer gently until tender; add the orange juice. Mix the cornflour to a smooth paste with 1 tsp. (*5 ml*) soy sauce and a little water, pour into the orange mixture and return to the boil, stirring until clear. Serve with pork chops.

Quick Créole Sauce

¼ pint (*150 ml*) tomato juice
1 tsp. (*5 ml*) Worcestershire sauce
1 bay leaf
1 tbsp. (*15 ml*) butter
1 level tbsp. (*15 ml*) flour
1 level tsp. (*5 ml*) paprika
2 drops of Tabasco
¼ level tsp. (*1.25 ml*) salt

Simmer the tomato juice, Worcestershire sauce and bay leaf for 5 minutes. Melt the butter, blend in the flour and paprika and cook for 1–2 minutes. Add the tomato mixture, removing the bay leaf. Add the remaining seasonings and re-heat, stirring. Serve with grills.

Poultry and Game

Poultry, game (including venison) and rabbits are all important for their nutritive value—roughly equal to that of meat—and are therefore an excellent source of protein.

Chickens are now available fresh, chilled and deep frozen, whole, in halves, or in various portions; whatever the form, the flesh should be plump and compact, with clear, unbroken, unbruised skin—broken skin affects the keeping quality. A fresh bird has a soft, elastic skin, while that of the not-so-fresh is harder, stiff and yet flabby. The age of the bird can be determined by the texture of the skin and the firmness of the breast-bone. The young bird has a smooth, thin skin, flesh that is soft to the touch, and a flexible breastbone, whereas older fowls have a coarse, thick skin and a brittle breastbone. The younger birds are suitable for dry cooking methods such as roasting and grilling, and the older birds for moist heat methods such as stewing and casseroling.

Classification of Chickens

Poussins —very small chicken, 1–2 lb. (450–900 g), 6–8 weeks old. One serves 1–2 people.

Broilers —$2\frac{1}{2}$–$3\frac{1}{2}$ lb. (1–1.5 kg), 12 weeks old. One serves 3–4 people. (Frozen chickens are usually broilers.)

Large Roasters—Generally young cockerels or hens, but may be capons. 'Young roasters' are 4–5 lb. (about 2 kg), and one serves 5–6 people. Capons weigh up to 8 lb. (3–$3\frac{1}{2}$ kg) and serve 6–10.

Boiling Fowls —Older, tougher birds, 4–7 lb. (2–3 kg). Usually 18 months old, but may be older. Used for casseroles. Allow 3–4 oz. (85–115 g) meat per person.

Frozen Poultry

This should be allowed to thaw at room temperature, the time required depending on the size of the joint or bird. Single joints take from about 1–2 hours, large turkeys 48–72 hours. If you must hasten the defrosting process, hold the bird under cold (not hot) running water. The giblets are usually wrapped in polythene and placed inside the body cavity; remove them before cooking the bird. Frozen birds are usually sold trussed, ready for stuffing.

156

Buying Game and 'Protected' Birds

Try to choose a young bird. The plumage is a guide, as all young birds have soft, even feathers. With pheasants and partridge, the long wing feathers are V-shaped in a young bird, as distinct from the rounded ones of an older bird. Smooth, pliable legs, short spurs and a firm, plump breast are other points to look for. Ask whether the bird has been hung (overleaf), as some poulterers do this.

Hanging, Preparation and Cooking of Game Birds

All game birds need to be hung up by the legs, without being plucked or drawn, before being cooked, or the flesh will be tough and tasteless. The time for hanging depends on the weather and on your taste, varying from a week in 'muggy' weather to 2–3 weeks in frosty weather.

Keep the bird in a cold, dry, airy place and examine it from time to time, especially any that has been shattered when shot, or has got wet, or has been packed up for any length of time before hanging, as such birds do not keep so well. For most people the bird is sufficiently mature when the tail or breast feathers will pluck out easily. With a pheasant, the flesh on the breast begins to change colour and the bird smells 'gamey'.

Pluck, draw and truss the bird as for poultry, but leave the feet on and don't draw the sinews from the legs. Some birds, such as snipe, have the head left on and are not drawn before being roasted. The larger birds may be jointed like a chicken before being cooked.

Generally speaking, the more simply the game is cooked, the better. For a young bird, there is no better way than roasting, but for older birds, which are likely to be tough if plainly roasted, braising or casseroling is a better method.

Game birds lack fat, so it is usual to cover the breast before roasting with pieces of fat bacon (this is called 'barding') and to baste frequently with butter or margarine during the cooking. When the bird is nearly cooked, the bacon can be removed; the breast is then dredged with flour and basted (this is called 'frothing') in order to brown it. Sometimes a knob of butter or a piece of juicy steak is put inside the bird before roasting.

Hare and Rabbit

A *hare* should be hung by the feet for 7–10 days, to improve its flavour; it is usually sold ready hung.

Rabbit: Both the fresh and the frozen ones are usually sold cleaned and skinned. Only young rabbits should be roasted or fried. In general they can be fricasseed, braised or made into a pie. To make the flavour of a rabbit less strong, wash it and soak in water for 1–2 hours before cooking.

Venison

This tends to be tough, therefore should be hung for 1–2 weeks in a cool, airy place. Wipe it occasionally with a cloth to remove moisture and test it at intervals by running a skewer through the haunch—as soon as a slight 'high' smell is noticeable, the venison is ready for cooking. Best joints are the saddle, haunch and shoulder. Before cooking, marinade the meat in a mixture such as that given below.

Roasting Venison: Brush the marinaded joint with melted fat or oil and wrap loosely in foil. Roast in a warm oven (325°F., 170°C., mark 3), allowing 25 minutes per lb. (60 mins/kg). Remove the foil 20 minutes before the cooking time is complete.

Marinade for Venison

2 carrots, chopped	6 peppercorns
2 onions (cut up if large)	parsley
1 stick of celery, chopped	1 bay leaf
	a little mace
	red wine to half-cover

Mix all the ingredients together and pour over the venison. Leave to soak for 12 hours, turning it at regular intervals.

French-style Roast Chicken

2½–3-lb. (1–1½-kg) roasting chicken	¼ pint (*150 ml*) chicken stock
5–6 sprigs of tarragon or parsley	¼ pint (*150 ml*) dry white wine
½ oz. (*15 g*) butter	watercress to garnish
pepper and salt	1 oz. (*25 g*) flour
2 rashers of bacon	

Oven temperature: 375°F., 190°C., mark 5
Wipe the interior of the chicken, then put the sprigs of tarragon or parsley inside it, with the butter and some pepper. Cover the breast of the bird with rashers of bacon, place in a roasting tin, add the stock and wine and bake for 45–50 minutes, basting every 15 minutes with the stock. Remove the bacon during the last ¼ hour, to let the breast brown. Place the chicken on a serving dish and garnish with watercress. Thicken the liquor with the flour and season to taste; serve separately. (Serves 4)

Continental Chicken Casserole

3-lb. (*1½-kg*) oven-ready chicken	¾ pint (*375 ml*) giblet stock
2 tbsps. (*30 ml*) oil	salt and pepper
4 bacon rashers, cut up	1 level tbsp. (*15 ml*) tomato paste
1 small onion, skinned and chopped	2 oz. (*55 g*) mush-rooms, sliced
1 level tbsp. (*15 ml* flour	parsley to garnish

Cut the chicken into joints and fry in the olive oil, with the bacon and onion, until lightly browned. Remove from the saucepan, add the flour and cook for 1–2 minutes, then add the giblet stock and bring to the boil. Season well and add the tomato paste and the mushrooms. Return the chicken, bacon and onion to the sauce and allow to simmer gently for about 1 hour, until the chicken is tender. Serve garnished with chopped parsley. (Serves 4)

Chicken and Wine Casserole

3-lb. (*1½-kg*) oven-ready chicken	8 tomatoes, skinned
1 onion, skinned and sliced	1 level tsp. (*5 ml*) salt
1 clove of garlic, skinned and crushed	¼ level tsp. (*1.25 ml*) pepper
	¼ pint (*150 ml*) dry white wine

Oven temperature: 350°F., 180°C., mark 4
Place the chicken in a deep casserole dish and add all the remaining ingredients. Cover tightly and bake until the chicken is tender and the sauce is reduced—about 1½ hours. (Serves 4)

Casseroled Chicken
(see picture opposite)

3-lb. (*1½-kg*) oven-ready chicken	2 carrots, diced
2 rashers of lean bacon, rinded and chopped	1 swede, diced
	1 pint (*600 ml*) stock
	salt and pepper
2 sticks of celery, sliced	1 tomato
2 onions, skinned and sliced	2 rashers of bacon, rolled and grilled

Casseroled Chicken

Oven temperature: 350°F., 180°C., mark 4
Place the chicken in a large casserole dish with the chopped bacon and prepared vegetables. Add the stock, salt and pepper and cook in the oven for 1½ hours. Serve on a platter, surrounded by the vegetables and garnished with tomato wedges and bacon rolls. (Serves 4)
Alternatively, joint the chicken before cooking and reduce the cooking time to about 1 hour.

Chicken Rice Pimiento

(see picture right)

3-lb. (*1.5-kg*) oven-ready chicken	1 lb. (*450 g*) tomatoes, skinned
salt and pepper	2 red peppers, diced
1 pint (*600 ml*) stock	rind of 1 orange, finely shredded
2 oz. (*55 g*) long-grain rice	1 clove of garlic
1 oz. (*25 g*) butter	watercress to garnish
2 onions, skinned and chopped	

Oven temperature: 400°F., 200°C., mark 6
Sprinkle the chicken with salt and pepper, place on a rack in a baking dish and bake for about ¾–1 hour. Bring the stock to the boil, add the rice and cook until all the liquid is absorbed. Melt the butter and sauté the onions until clear. Add the tomatoes, peppers, orange rind, crushed garlic and seasoning. Simmer for 10–15 minutes. Place the cooked rice on a serving dish, carve the chicken and arrange on the rice. Pour the sauce over, and garnish with watercress. (Serves 4)

Poulet Chasseur

4 chicken joints	¾ pint (*375 ml*) stock
1 or 2 carrots	2 tomatoes
½ a turnip	salt and pepper
½ a swede	1 tbsp. (*15 ml*) sherry
1 small onion	4 oz. (*115 g*) mush-rooms, grilled
1 stick of celery	8 bacon rolls, grilled
oil or dripping for frying	

Wipe the chicken joints. Chop the vegetables and fry lightly in a saucepan in a little oil or dripping. Grill the joints of chicken on both sides, then place on the bed of vegetable. Add the stock, cut-up tomatoes and seasoning and simmer slowly for 1 hour. Remove the chicken and strain the sauce, keeping the vegetables hot; thicken the liquor by boiling to reduce it, and lastly add the sherry, and season to taste. Mound the vegetables in a dish and place the chicken portions on top. Pour a little sauce over and garnish with grilled mushrooms and bacon rolls. Serve the remainder of the sauce separately. (Serves 4)

Chicken Marengo

3-lb. (*1½-kg*) chicken, jointed	4 oz. (*115 g*) onions, skinned and chopped
4 oz. (*115 g*) carrots, sliced	¾ pint (*375 ml*) stock
4 oz. (*115 g*) mush-rooms, sliced	salt and pepper
	1 tbsp. (*15 ml*) white wine

Chicken Rice Pimiento

159

Oven temperature: 350°F., 180°C., mark 4
Brown the jointed chicken in a lightly greased frying pan, and place in a casserole dish. Add the carrots, mushrooms and onions, pour the stock over and season with salt and pepper. Cover and bake for 1¼ hours. Place the chicken on a serving dish and keep warm. Add the wine to the liquid, boil rapidly to reduce the volume, then pour over the chicken. (Serves 4)

Coq au Vin

2 oz. (*55 g*) bacon, chopped	3 chicken joints
4 oz. (*115 g*) mushrooms, sliced	½ pint (*300 ml*) red wine
	1 level tbsp. (*15 ml*) cornflour
12 button onions (or 3 medium-sized onions, sliced)	a pinch of grated nutmeg
½ oz. (*15 g*) butter	salt and pepper
1 tbsp. (*15 ml*) oil	a bouquet garni

Oven temperature: 350°F., 180°C., mark 4
Sauté the bacon, mushrooms and onions in the butter and oil until they are golden-brown. Remove from the pan, drain carefully, and place half of the mixture in a 3-pint (1.7-litre) casserole. Then sauté the chicken joints until golden-brown; remove from the pan, drain and place in the casserole, followed by the remaining bacon, mushrooms and onions. Blend the wine and cornflour together, then stir them gradually into the drippings in the pan; bring to the boil and allow to cook for 1–2 minutes. Finally add the nutmeg, salt, pepper and bouquet garni and bake for ¾ hour, or until the chicken is tender. Remove the bouquet garni before serving. (Serves 3)

Barbecued Chicken Casserole

3–3½-lb. (*1½-kg*) roasting chicken	2 green peppers, seeded and sliced
2 oz. (*55 g*) seasoned flour	¾ pint (*375 ml*) stock
2 tbsps. (*30 ml*) oil	2 tbsps. (*30 ml*) tomato sauce
1 onion, skinned and sliced	2 tbsps. (*30 ml*) chutney
small head of celery	salt and pepper

Divide the chicken into joints and coat these in seasoned flour. Fry in hot oil until golden-brown, in either a casserole or a frying pan. Add the onion and sauté it until golden-brown, then add all the other ingredients and bring slowly to the boil. Cover, and cook in a moderate oven for about 1½–2 hours, or until tender. (Serves 4)

Chicken Catalonian Style

3½-lb. (*1½-kg*) oven-ready chicken	2 level tsps. (*10 ml*) tomato paste
1 oz. (*25 g*) butter	salt and pepper
1 tbsp. (*15 ml*) olive oil	6 whole chestnuts
12 small onions	stock to cook chestnuts
1 tbsp. (*15 ml*) flour	½ lb. (*225 g*) chipolata sausages
½ pint (*300 ml*) good stock	
¼ pint (*150 ml*) white wine	

Oven temperature: 350°F., 180°C., mark 4
Cut the chicken into 8 pieces—wings, thighs, drumsticks and breasts. Heat the butter and oil in a pan and fry the chicken and the onions until lightly browned all over, then arrange them in a casserole. Sprinkle the flour into the fat left in the pan, stir in the stock, wine and tomato paste, season, bring to the boil and pour over the chicken. (The liquid should barely cover the joints.) Cover and cook gently in the oven for

Oriental Chicken

about 1 hour, or until the chicken is really tender when tested with a fork. Meanwhile, prepare the chestnuts by cutting a small piece from the tip of each, then boil for 10 minutes, drain, and peel off the shells; cook gently in stock until tender. Grill the chipolatas until they are nicely browned. A quarter of an hour before serving, add the cooked chestnuts and the chipolatas to the contents of the casserole. To serve, pile the chicken, etc., on to a hot dish. Re-season the gravy, which should be of a thin glazing consistency, and pour it over the chicken. (Serves 6)

Bengal Chicken Curry

(see colour picture facing page 80)

1 tbsp. (*15 ml*) oil	1 level tsp. (*5 ml*)
2 onions, skinned and	curry powder
chopped	4 chicken joints
1 clove of garlic	½ pint (*300 ml*)
1 level tsp. (*5 ml*) dry	chicken stock
mustard	2 level tbsps. (*30 ml*)
salt and pepper	tomato paste

Oven temperature: 350°F., 180°C., mark 4
Heat the oil and sauté the onions and garlic. Mix together the mustard and curry powder and rub into the chicken joints. Add the joints to the pan and brown lightly. Mix together the stock and tomato paste, pour over the chicken and add a little salt and pepper. Cover and bake for 1 hour. Garnish with shredded lettuce. (Serves 4)

Oriental Chicken

(see picture opposite)

3 chicken joints	3 level tsps. (*15 ml*)
juice of ½ a lemon	cornflour
salt and pepper	8 oz. (*225 g*) pine-
1 tbsp. (*15 ml*) soy	apple pieces
sauce	½ oz. (*15 g*) blanched
½ pint (*300 ml*)	almonds, toasted
chicken stock	

Sprinkle the chicken joints with the lemon juice and season with salt and pepper. Grill until golden brown and tender. Add the soy sauce to the stock and heat to boiling point. Mix the corn-

flour to a smooth paste with a little water, stir into the stock and add the pineapple pieces. Simmer for 5–10 minutes, pour over the chicken joints, and serve sprinkled with almonds. (Serves 3)

Chicken Maryland

3 chicken joints	3 bananas
1 egg, lightly beaten	3 tbsps. (*45 ml*) lemon
salt and pepper	juice
1½ oz. (*40 g*) cracker	
crumbs	

Oven temperature: 350°F., 180°C., mark 4
Brush the chicken joints liberally with seasoned egg, then sprinkle with crumbs. Place in a baking dish and bake for 30–45 minutes. Peel the bananas and divide into two lengthwise. Dip into the lemon juice and place in the baking dish, alongside the chicken, 15 minutes before the end of the cooking time. (Serves 3)
Note: For 2 servings, use 2 chicken joints, with 1 oz. (25 g) cracker crumbs, 2 bananas, 2 tbsps. (30 ml) lemon juice, 1 egg and seasoning.

Chicken Louisette

3 chicken joints	½ a cucumber, peeled
salt and pepper	and sliced
1 tbsp. (*15 ml*) oil	2 egg yolks
1 onion, skinned and	1 tbsp. (*15 ml*) milk
sliced	2 oz. (*55 g*) ham,
1 clove of garlic	chopped
¼ pint (*150 ml*) stock	chopped parsley
¼ pint (*150 ml*) dry	
white wine	
bouquet garni	

Season the chicken joints with salt and pepper, and fry in the oil until golden-brown, then pour off all the excess oil. Add onion, crushed garlic, liquids and bouquet garni. Simmer for ½–¾ hour, add the cucumber, season and simmer for a further 4–5 minutes. When the chicken joints are tender, strain off the liquor. Beat the egg yolks with the milk, add the liquor and heat very gently until it thickens. Place the joints on a serving dish, pour the sauce over, and sprinkle with the ham and parsley. (Serves 3)

161

Bordeaux Chicken

4 chicken joints	4 tomatoes, skinned
2 tbsps. (*30 ml*) oil	and sliced
1 onion, skinned and	¼ pint (*150 ml*)
finely chopped	chicken stock or a
1 clove of garlic,	bouillon cube and
skinned and finely	water
chopped	2 tbsps. (*30 ml*) dry
4 oz. (*115 g*) mush-	white wine
rooms, sliced	

Fry the chicken lightly in the oil for 25–30 minutes; remove from the pan and keep hot in the oven. Add the onion, garlic, mushrooms and tomatoes to the pan and cook slowly for about 10–15 minutes. Add the chicken stock and wine, stir and cook until the liquid is reduced to about one-third. Place the mushroom mixture on a serving dish, lay the chicken on top and serve at once. (Serves 4)

Pollo alla Cacciatore

2 tbsps. (*30 ml*) oil	4 oz. (*115 g*) mush-
1 onion, skinned and	rooms, sliced
chopped	1 level tbsp. (*15 ml*)
1 clove of garlic,	tomato paste
skinned and crushed	4 tbsps. (*60 ml*) dry
(optional)	sherry
4 chicken joints	salt and pepper
8 tomatoes, skinned	

Heat the oil and sauté the onions and garlic. Lightly fry the chicken joints until pale golden in colour; pour off any excess oil. Add all the remaining ingredients, cover and cook slowly until the chicken is tender—¾–1 hour. (If it becomes dry add a little stock.) Serve sprinkled with some chopped parsley. (Serves 4)

Chicken and Pepper Pie

12 oz. (*340 g*) cooked	salt and pepper
chicken	¼ pint (*150 ml*)
1 oz. (*25 g*) butter	chicken stock
1 red and 1 green	¼ pint (*150 ml*) milk
pepper, seeded and	7 oz. (*200 g*) short-
chopped	crust pastry
2 level tsps. (*10 ml*)	
flour	

Oven temperature: 400°F., 200°C., mark 6
Dice the chicken and place in a pie plate.

Melt the butter and sauté the peppers for 1–2 minutes. Remove from the butter, draining carefully, and add to the chicken. Add the flour to the remaining butter, mix thoroughly and cook for 1–2 minutes. Gradually add the stock, stirring continuously until smooth. Blend in the milk and adjust the seasoning. Add to the chicken mixture and leave to cool.
Roll out the pastry and use to cover the filling. Bake for 20 minutes, reduce the heat to moderate (350°F., 180°C., mark 4) and continue to cook for a further 20 minutes. (Serves 4)

Minced Chicken Loaf

½ pint (*300 ml*) aspic	6 olives, chopped
jelly	radish lilies
½ lb. (*225 g*) chicken	hard-boiled egg,
pieces	sliced
¼ lb. (*115 g*) ham	lettuce
pieces	

Pour some of the aspic jelly into a dampened loaf tin and leave to set. Mince the chicken and ham very finely and mix with the rest of the aspic and the chopped olives; pour into the loaf tin and leave to set. Turn out and decorate with radish lilies, sliced hard-boiled egg and lettuce. (Serves 3)

Chicken and Tongue Loaf

(*see picture opposite*)

3 level tsps. (*15 ml*)	½ lb. (*225 g*) cooked
gelatine	tongue
4 tbsps. (*60 ml*) water	1 green pepper,
¾ pint (*375 ml*)	seeded
chicken stock	1 red pepper, seeded
salt and pepper	6 olives
½ lb. (*225 g*) cooked	peaches and olives to
chicken	garnish (optional)

Sprinkle the gelatine over the cold water, then dissolve it in the usual way. Add to the stock and season well. Dice the chicken, tongue and peppers, and slice the olives. Place all these in a loaf tin, pour the stock over and leave to set. Serve sliced, garnished with peaches and olives. (Serves 4)

Chicken and Grape Salad

(see colour picture facing page 97)

2 lettuces
3-lb. (*1½-kg*) chicken,
  cooked and cooled
  (or 12 oz. (*340 g*)
  cooked chicken)
1 lemon
chopped parsley

6 salad onions,
  chopped
½ lb. (*225 g*) grapes,
  skinned and pipped
2 hard-boiled eggs,
  sliced

Wash the lettuces and arrange in a dish. Dice the chicken. Peel the lemon, removing the pith and pips, and dice the flesh. Arrange the chicken on the lettuce, and scatter with the lemon, parsley, onions, grapes and egg. (Serves 4)

Chicken and Rice Salad

1 dessert apple
lemon juice
½ lb. (*225 g*) cold
  cooked chicken
4 tbsps. (*60 ml*) dry
  cooked rice
1 celery heart
1–2 oz. (*25–55 g*)
  raisins or dates,
  chopped

1 hard-boiled egg, cut
  up
mayonnaise
salt and pepper
chicory, radishes, etc.

Dice the apple without peeling it, and marinade it in the lemon juice. Cut up the chicken into small pieces and mix with the rice, cut-up celery and apple. Add the raisins or chopped dates and cut-up egg, mix with the mayonnaise and add a little seasoning. Serve in a large bowl or in individual portions on crisp lettuce leaves, with other salad vegetables if desired. (Serves 2)

Chicken and Ham Salad

1 small can of pine-
  apple slices
½ lb. (*225 g*) cooked
  chicken
½ lb. (*225 g*) ham

1 head of chicory
mayonnaise
lettuce
watercress

Drain the pineapple and cut most of it into small pieces. Cut up the chicken, ham and chicory. Mix all these ingredients together with some mayonnaise. Serve with the lettuce and watercress, and the remaining pineapple slices. (Serves 4)

Chicken and Celery Salad

1 chicken, cooked
several sticks of celery
1 green pepper,
  seeded
1 tsp. (*5 ml*) grated
  onion

½ pint (*300 ml*) cheese
  dressing
salt and pepper
lettuce leaves
pineapple chunks and
  asparagus tips

Cut the chicken into pieces, chop the celery and mince the pepper. Mix these ingredients with the onion and dressing, and season well. Pile on to a bed of lettuce leaves, and surround with pineapple and asparagus. (Serves 4)

Chicken and Tongue Loaf

Chicken Mandarin Salad

4 oz. (*115 g*) cooked chicken meat
1 stick of celery, chopped
mandarin segments
2 oz. (*55 g*) grapes
salt and pepper
French dressing
lettuce

Toss all the ingredients together with the dressing. Serve in a lettuce cup. (Serves 1)

Cherry-glazed Duck

(*see colour picture facing page 208*)

1–2 ducks (1 lb., *450 g*, dressed weight per person)
1 lb. (*450 g*) cherries
½ pint (*300 ml*) dry white wine

Oven temperature: 400°F., 200°C., mark 6
Pluck, draw and truss the birds in the usual way. Prick all over with a needle or a very fine skewer, place on a wire rack in a baking dish and cook in the oven, allowing 20 minutes per lb. (45 mins/kg). Simmer all but a dozen of the cherries in the wine until tender, and sieve to remove the stones and skin. Spoon some of this cherry sauce over the ducks 20 minutes before the cooking time is completed; repeat 10 minutes later. Boil the remaining mixture vigorously to reduce the volume by half. Serve the duck on a large dish, with the whole cherries and the remaining cherry sauce. (Serves 8)

Roast Grouse

Oven temperature: 400°F., 200°C., mark 6
After hanging, pluck, draw and truss the bird, season inside and out and lay some fat bacon over the breast. Put a knob of butter inside the bird and place it on a slice of toast. Roast in the centre of the oven for ½ hour, basting frequently. After 20 minutes roasting, remove the bacon, dredge the breast with flour and baste well.
Remove the trussing strings before serving the bird on the toast on which it was roasted. Garnish with watercress and serve with thin gravy, bread sauce and matchstick potatoes.
A lettuce or watercress salad may also be served. (Serves 2)

Roast Partridge

Oven temperature: 450°F., 230°C., mark 8
Select a young bird; pluck, draw and truss it, season the inside with pepper and salt, replace the liver and add a knob of butter. Cover the breast with pieces of fat bacon.
Roast the bird in the centre of the oven for 10 minutes, then reduce the oven to fairly hot (400°F., 200°C., mark 6) and roast for a further 10–20 minutes, according to size; partridge must be well-done.
The usual accompaniments are fried crumbs or game chips and a tossed salad or bread (or orange) sauce. A garnish of lemon quarters and watercress (seasoned and sprinkled with a few drops of vinegar) is often added. (Serves 2)

Casserole of Partridge

2 medium onions, skinned and sliced
2 sticks of celery, scrubbed and sliced
¼ lb. (*115 g*) mushrooms, washed and sliced
4 oz. (*115 g*) bacon, rinded and chopped
1 tbsp. (*15 ml*) oil
1 oz. (*25 g*) butter
2 partridges, plucked, drawn and jointed
3 level tbsps. (*45 ml*) flour
¾ pint (*375 ml*) stock
15-oz. (*425-g*) can of tomatoes
salt and pepper
¼ pint (*150 ml*) red wine

Oven temperature: 350°F., 180°C., mark 4
Fry the onions, celery, mushrooms and bacon in the oil and butter for about 5 minutes, until golden-brown. Remove from the pan with a slotted spoon and line the bottom of a casserole with them. Fry the partridge joints in the oil and butter for about 5 minutes, until golden-brown. Remove from the pan with the slotted spoon and put in the casserole on the bed of vegetables. Stir the flour into the fat remaining in the pan and cook for 2–3 minutes. Gradually stir in the stock, bring to the boil and continue to stir until it thickens. Add the tomatoes, salt, pepper and wine, pour the sauce over the partridge joints, cover and cook in the centre of the oven for 1 hour, until the partridge joints are tender. (Serves 4)

French Rabbit Casserole

1 rabbit	2 tbsps. (*30 ml*) red
lean bacon	wine
salt and pepper	a bay leaf
2 eggs	a little dried thyme

Oven temperature: 350°F., 180°C., mark 4
Cut up the rabbit, reserving the liver, and remove the flesh from the bones. Cut the white parts of the meat into strips, and mince the rest together with the liver; then cut the bacon into strips and line a casserole with some of them. Season the mince with salt and pepper and add the eggs and wine. Place the mince over the layer of bacon, then cover it with strips of white rabbit meat and bacon fat; continue in this way until the casserole is full. Add the bay leaf and thyme; bake for 1½–2 hours. (Serves 4)

Poacher's Pie

6 oz. (*150 g*) short-	salt and pepper
crust pastry	1 tbsp. (*15 ml*)
4 rabbit joints	chopped parsley
2 potatoes	¼ level tsp. (*1.25 ml*)
1 leek	mixed herbs
3–4 rashers of bacon,	stock or water
chopped	beaten egg to glaze

Oven temperature: 425°F., 220°C., mark 7
Make the pastry. Wash the rabbit joints, and prepare and slice the potatoes and leek. Fill a pie dish with alternate layers of rabbit, bacon and vegetables, sprinkling each layer with seasoning and herbs. Half-fill the dish with stock or water, cover with the pastry and make a hole in the centre to let the steam escape. Decorate with leaves made from the pastry trimmings and brush with egg. Bake until the pastry is set, then reduce the temperature to warm (325°F., 170°C.,

mark 3) and cook for about 1¼ hours, until the meat is tender. (Serves 4)

Rabbit and Bacon Blanquette

2 rashers of bacon,	1 stick of celery, sliced
chopped	¼ pint (*150 ml*) stock
2 rabbit joints	salt and pepper
2 carrots, diced	bouquet garni
1 onion, skinned and	¼ pint (*140 g*) fat-free
chopped	natural yoghurt

Fry the bacon until the fat runs; add the rabbit joints and brown them. Add the carrot, onion and celery, pour the stock over, season and add the bouquet garni. Cover and simmer over a low heat until tender—1 hour. Stir the yoghurt into the mixture, adjust the seasoning and cook without boiling for 1–2 minutes longer. (Serves 1)

Rabbit Hot-pot

1 rabbit	1 lb. (*450 g*) potatoes
1 oz. (*25 g*) seasoned	chopped parsley
flour	stock or water
2–3 medium-sized	
onions, skinned and	
sliced	

Oven temperature: 325°F., 170°C., mark 3
Wash and joint the rabbit, dry, then toss the pieces in seasoned flour. Slice the onions and cut the potatoes into quarters or eighths, according to size. Place a layer of onions in a large casserole, put the rabbit on top, sprinkle liberally with chopped parsley, and cover with onion and potato. Add the liquid, nearly covering the rabbit, and bake, covered, for 2–2½ hours. Remove the cover a short time before serving, to brown the potatoes. (Serves 4)

Eggs and cheese

Eggs

Eggs are an excellent source of protein, minerals and vitamins, with no carbohydrates. There are seven weight grades of eggs, though usually they are sold as Large, Standard, Medium and, occasionally, Small.

Large	Grade I	over 70 g
	Grade II	65–70 g
Standard	Grade III	60–65 g
	Grade IV	55–60 g
	Grade V	50–55 g
Medium	Grade VI	45–50 g
Small	Grade VII	below 45 g

Storage

Eggs deteriorate rapidly, particularly in a warm place, due to the evaporation of moisture, and they also absorb odours through the porous shell, so keep them covered and in a cool place. If they are stored in the refrigerator, use the racks or boxes provided, which are designed to protect the eggs, and take them out some time before using, to allow them to return to normal room temperature. Always store pointed end down.

Cheese

Cheese is one of the most versatile foods and may make its appearance in any course of a lunch or dinner. It is a very concentrated food, so a little goes a long way, and is rich in protein, minerals and vitamins, with very little carbohydrate. However, its relatively high fat content means that it should not be eaten in excessive amounts.

Buying and Storage

The drier, harder cheeses will keep well when stored correctly, but the softer cheeses deteriorate more quickly, so should be purchased only as required. To store cheese, wrap it loosely in polythene, aluminium foil or good-quality greaseproof paper, entrapping some air to prevent sweating and mould growth, then place it in a cool larder or refrigerator. If stored in a refrigerator, the cheese should be brought to room temperature before serving. Wrap each variety separately, so that individual characteristics can be retained. Pre-packaged cheese will keep well in a cool place, but once opened it should be removed from its packaging and wrapped and stored as above.

Cottage cheese and cream cheeses are as perishable as milk, and must be kept covered, in the refrigerator.

Cooking

The less cooking cheese receives, the better. Over-heating tends to make it tough and indigestible, so always heat it gently and for a short time.

Boiled Eggs

These should not in fact be boiled but simmered—fast boiling spoils the flavour and toughens the white.
Put the eggs into cold water, covering them completely, and bring to the boil. Reduce the heat immediately to simmering point, and time from the moment of boiling. The exact time depends on the size and on the degree of hardness required.

Eggs	Soft-boiled: mins.	Medium: mins.	Hard-boiled: mins.
Large	3	$4\frac{1}{2}$	8
Standard	$2\frac{3}{4}$	4	7
Medium	$2\frac{1}{2}$	$3\frac{1}{2}$	6

Poached Eggs

Heat the water to boiling point in a heavy, shallow pan. Break each egg into a cup or saucer and slide it into the water, cover the pan and reduce the heat to keep the water simmering. Cook for 4–5 minutes, until a film of white covers the yolk and the white is firm. Remove each egg with a perforated slice, and drain thoroughly.

Scrambled Eggs

4 eggs
$\frac{1}{4}$ pint (150 ml) milk
1 level tsp. (5 ml) salt
a shake of pepper
$\frac{1}{2}$ oz. (15 g) butter

Beat the eggs slightly with the milk and seasonings. Melt the butter in a pan, pour in the egg mixture and cook over a low heat or over hot water. Lift and turn the mixture with a spatula as it sets, keeping it in large, soft masses. Remove the pan from the heat before setting is complete, so as to allow the heat of the pan to finish the cooking. (Serves 2–3)

Scrambled Egg Variations
Add one of the following:

2 oz. (55 g) lightly fried sliced mushrooms
2 skinned tomatoes, chopped and lightly fried with a diced rasher of bacon
2 oz. (55 g) chopped ham, tongue or other cooked meat
2 oz. (55 g) sliced, cooked pork sausages

2 oz. (55 g) Finnan haddock (or other smoked fish), cooked then freed of bones and skin and flaked
2 oz. (55 g) picked shrimps
2–3 oz. grated cheese
$\frac{1}{2}$ level tsp. (2.5 ml) dried herbs or 1 level tsp. (5 ml) finely chopped mixed fresh herbs

Baked Eggs
(see picture below)

Heat the oven to 350°F., 180°C., mark 4. Place the required number of individual ovenproof dishes or cocottes on a baking sheet, with a knob of butter in each. Put them in the oven for 1–2 minutes, until the butter has melted. Break an egg into each dish, sprinkle with a little salt and pepper, place in the centre of the oven and leave until the eggs are just set—about 5–8 minutes. Serve at once.

Baked Eggs

Mexican Scramble

1 tsp. (*5 ml*)
  margarine
1 small green pepper,
  seeded and chopped
1 egg
3 tbsps. (*45 ml*) milk

2 tbsps. (*30 ml*)
  chopped ham
1 oz. (*25 g*) cheese,
  grated
a slice of toast

Melt the fat in a saucepan, sauté the
pepper and scramble the egg in the
normal way. When almost cooked, add
the chopped ham and grated cheese.
Serve on a slice of toast. (Serves 1)

Cheshire Scramble

8 cream crackers
a knob of butter
1 tbsp. (*15 ml*) milk
pepper and salt
4 eggs, beaten

4 oz. (*115 g*) Cheshire
  cheese, grated
parsley, paprika and
  grilled mushrooms

Warm the biscuits in the oven and melt
the butter in a small pan. Beat together
the milk, seasonings and eggs, add to the
butter and heat slowly, stirring with a
fork. When creamy and beginning to set,
add the cheese; stir and continue to cook
till thick but not creamy. Spread the mixture on the crackers, garnish with parsley,
paprika and mushrooms, and serve at
once, with grilled tomatoes and mushrooms (Serves 4)

Scrambled Egg Nests

4 tbsps. (*60 ml*)
  mashed potatoes
flour
bacon fat or dripping
2–3 eggs

salt and pepper
a little milk
a knob of butter
watercress or parsley

Shape the mashed potato into 4 flat
cakes, flouring them lightly. Fry in the
hot bacon fat or dripping until golden-
brown on the underside, then turn them
over, hollow the centre of each cake
slightly with the bowl of a spoon and
leave over a gentle heat to brown underneath. Meanwhile, beat the eggs with
salt and pepper, add the milk and
scramble them in the hot butter. Fill the
'nests' with the scrambled egg and

garnish with sprigs of watercress or
parsley. (Serves 4)
Note: A little chopped cooked bacon may
be added to the potato before it is shaped.

Scrambled Bacon and Corn

1 oz. (*25 g*) butter
1 medium-sized
  onion, skinned and
  finely chopped
3 oz. (*115 g*) bacon,
  chopped

11-oz. (*312-g*) can of
  whole-kernel corn
4 eggs
salt and pepper
Worcestershire sauce
parsley

Melt the butter and fry the onion and
bacon until golden; add the corn. Beat
the eggs, season well and add with a little
Worcestershire sauce to the saucepan.
Stir and heat slowly till the egg is cooked;
garnish with parsley. (Serves 4)

Eggs Fritura

1 green pepper,
  blanched, seeded
  and chopped
½ an onion, chopped
2 oz. (*55 g*) butter
4 tomatoes, skinned
  and chopped
salt

4 eggs
black pepper
4 rounds of toast
butter
2 oz. (*55 g*) Cheddar
  cheese, grated
parsley to garnish

Fry the pepper and onion in the butter.
Add the tomatoes, with plenty of salt and
pepper, and cook for 15 minutes. Meanwhile, poach the eggs. Spoon the vegetable mixture on to the buttered toast and
place a poached egg on top. Sprinkle
with grated cheese and grill quickly.
Garnish with parsley. (Serves 4)

Plain Omelette

2 eggs
1–2 tsps. (*5–10 ml*)
  water per egg

salt and pepper
½ oz. (*15 g*) butter

Season the frying pan by sprinkling salt
into it and warming over a gentle heat;
rub the salt round the base of the pan
with a pad of kitchen paper, tip it out,
then rub the pan with a clean, dry cloth.
Whisk the eggs, water and seasoning
lightly together. Melt the butter in the

168

pan over a medium heat, tilting the pan so that the inside surface is evenly greased. Pour in the egg mixture and gently stir with a fork, the back of the prongs held flat against the base of the pan, so that the uncooked egg can flow to the sides and cook. Once the egg has set, stop stirring and cook the omelette for another minute, until the underside is golden-brown. Using a palette knife, fold the omelette by flicking one-third over to the centre, then folding the opposite third to the centre. Turn the omelette on to a plate, folded side underneath. (Serves 1)

Omelette Fillings and Flavourings
The hot filling is usually placed on the omelette before this is folded.
Bacon and Apple: Lightly fry 1 diced bacon rasher with 1 diced apple until tender; add a dash of lemon juice.
Prawn: Sauté 2 oz. (55 g) thawed frozen prawns (or shrimps) in melted butter, adding a squeeze of lemon; a little chopped green pepper or onion may also be added.
Smoked Haddock: Flake some cooked smoked haddock and heat gently in cheese sauce.
Tuna Fish: Flake a small can of tuna fish and mix with a little condensed mushroom soup.
Cheese: (1) Mix 1 oz. (25 g) grated firm cheese with a little chopped parsley; sprinkle most of this over the omelette before folding, and the remainder on top as it is served.
(2) Melt 1 oz. (25 g) grated cheese, 1 tbsp. (15 ml) milk and butter over a low heat; add ¼ level tsp. (1.25 ml) dry mustard or ¼ tsp. (1.25 ml) vinegar before using.
Mushroom: Dice and lightly fry 1 rasher of bacon and 2 oz. (55 g) sliced mushrooms, cooking until tender.
Spinach: Cook 1 small packet of frozen spinach in butter, and season with salt, pepper and nutmeg. Spread on the omelette and sprinkle with 1 oz. (25 g) chopped ham or grated cheese.
Note: This filling needs to be started well before the omelette is made, to give time for the spinach to thaw.
Tomato: Chop 2–3 tomatoes and fry in butter for 4–5 minutes, until soft and pulped. Add salt, pepper, and a pinch of rosemary, sage or mixed herbs.
Tomato-Cheese: Slice 2 tomatoes and place on the omelette. Sprinkle with finely grated cheese and place under the grill to melt the cheese. (*See colour picture between pages 192, 193.*)

Chinese Omelette

½ lb. (*225 g*) onions	salt
4 bamboo shoots or sticks of celery	2 tbsps. (*30 ml*) dry cider
4 oz. (*115 g*) mushrooms	2 tsps. (*10 ml*) soy sauce
1 clove of garlic	½ pint (*300 ml*) stock or water
1 slice of fresh ginger, if available	4 oz. (*115 g*) shrimps
1 oz. (*25 g*) rice	4 eggs
1 tbsp. (*15 ml*) oil for frying	

Chop the vegetables, garlic and ginger finely and fry them with the rice in the oil for a few minutes; add the salt, cider, soy sauce and stock, and cook for 10–15 minutes until the rice and vegetables are tender, then add all the shrimps. Beat the eggs, add 4 tbsps. (60 ml) water and salt to taste, then cook half the mixture as an omelette; pile half the shrimp and vegetable mixture along the centre, and roll up the omelette. Repeat with the remaining egg and shrimp mixture. Any unused filling may be used for garnishing. (Serves 4)

Spanish Omelette—1

½ oz. (*15 g*) butter	1 cooked potato, diced
½ a small green pepper, seeded and finely chopped	2 eggs
1 small onion, skinned and chopped	salt and pepper

Heat the butter in a frying pan and gently cook the onion and pepper for about 5 minutes. Add the potato and heat through. Whisk together the eggs and seasonings, pour in and cook gently, without stirring, until the egg is set and the underneath golden. Place under the

169

grill to brown the top. Serve without folding. (Serves 1)

Spanish Omelette—2

1 tbsp. (*15 ml*) oil	1 red pepper,
1 onion, skinned and	chopped
chopped	4 eggs
2 tomatoes, skinned	salt and pepper
and chopped	
1 green pepper,	
chopped	

Heat the oil and sauté the onion until clear. Add the tomatoes and peppers and continue cooking for a further 2–3 minutes. Beat the eggs with some salt and pepper and pour over the vegetable mixture. Cook over a low heat until the eggs are beginning to set and the base is golden-brown. Finish cooking under the grill, and serve cut in wedges. (Serves 4)

Mediterranean Omelette

½ oz. (*15 g*) butter	2 tomatoes, skinned
1 small onion,	and sliced
skinned and finely	2 eggs
chopped	8 tbsps. (*120 ml*) milk
1 clove of garlic,	salt and pepper
skinned and crushed	watercress to garnish
or sliced	
4 oz. (*115 g*) mush-	
rooms, sliced	

Melt the butter in the frying pan and sauté the onion until clear but not coloured. Add the garlic and mushrooms and cook for 2–3 minutes; add the tomatoes. Beat the eggs, milk and seasonings together, pour over the vegetable mixture and cook over a low heat until set. Serve cut in wedges, garnished with watercress. (Serves 2)

Cheese Soufflé Omelette

1 tsp. (*5 ml*) butter	pepper
1 large egg, separated	1 oz. (*25 g*) tasty
1 tbsp. (*15 ml*) cold	Cheddar cheese,
water	grated
¼ level tsp. (*1.25 ml*)	
salt	

Melt the butter in a small, heavy frying pan. Beat the egg white until stiff. In a

separate bowl, beat the egg yolk, water and seasonings together until thick. Fold the egg white into the yolk mixture and pour into the pan. Cook over a low heat until the underside is set and lightly browned, then sprinkle with the cheese and melt this under a hot grill. Fold across the centre and invert onto a warmed serving dish. Serve immediately, accompanied by a crisp salad. (Serves 1)

Shirred Eggs with Chicken Livers

Oven temperature: 350°F., 180°C., mark 4
Line some ramekins with partly-fried chicken livers. Pour into each 1 tbsp. (15 ml) tomato juice, then slide in an egg. Sprinkle with salt and pepper and bake for 10 minutes. Sprinkle with chopped parsley and serve.
Alternatively, line the ramekins with cooked sausage cut in ½-inch (1.5-cm) rounds.

Baked Eggs and Mushrooms

½ lb. (*225 g*) mush-	salt and pepper
rooms	2 oz. (*55 g*) Cheshire
2 tbsps. (*30 ml*) oil	or Cheddar cheese,
4–6 eggs	grated

Oven temperature: 350°F., 180°C., mark 4
Wipe and thinly slice the mushrooms, fry in the oil and put into a shallow heat-proof dish. Break the required number of eggs into the dish, season and sprinkle with grated cheese. Bake until the eggs have just set. (Serves 4)

Spaghetti and Egg Casserole

6 oz. (*170 g*)	a little made mustard
spaghetti	salt and pepper
boiling salted water	4 oz. (*115 g*) cheese,
2 oz. (*55 g*) butter or	grated
margarine	1 lb. (*450 g*) runner
1½ oz. (*40 g*) flour	beans, cooked
1 pint (*600 ml*) milk	4 eggs
1 small onion,	a little melted butter
skinned and finely	
chopped	

Cook the spaghetti in the water until just tender, and drain well. Melt the fat and stir in the flour; add the milk gradually and stir until boiling, then add the onion, with mustard, salt, pepper and half the cheese. Put half the spaghetti into a greased casserole, place some of the beans on top, and then half the sauce. Repeat, finishing with a sprinkling of cheese. Bake for about ½ hour. Meanwhile, boil the eggs for 5–8 minutes, until they are hard-boiled; shell, halve and arrange over the spaghetti, with the remaining beans tossed in butter. (Serves 4)

Curried Eggs

2 hard-boiled eggs	½ oz. (*15 g*) flour
1 oz. (*25 g*) butter	¼ pint (*150 ml*) stock
1 small onion, skinned and chopped	salt
	1 tsp. (*5 ml*) lemon juice
a small piece of apple, finely chopped	2 oz. (*55 g*) cooked long-grain rice
½ level tsp. (*2.5 ml*) curry powder	lemon to garnish

While the boiled eggs are still hot, cut one of them into small pieces, and the other into wedges. Melt the butter, fry the onion lightly, add the apple, curry powder and flour and cook for a few minutes. Gradually add the stock, salt and lemon juice. Boil up and skim, then simmer this sauce for about ¼ hour. Add the cut-up egg to the sauce, and when heated place in a hot dish, surrounded by rice. Decorate with the egg wedges, and serve with lemon. (Serves 1)

Egg and Bacon Quiche

4 oz. (*115 g*) ready-made flaky pastry	2 eggs, beaten
3–4 oz. (*85–115 g*) lean bacon, chopped	¼ pint (*150 ml*) milk
4 oz. (*115 g*) Gruyère cheese	salt and pepper

Oven temperature: 400°F., 200°C., mark 6
Roll out the pastry and line 2 4-inch (10-cm) plain flan rings, making a double edge. Cover the bacon with boiling water and leave for 2–3 minutes, then drain well; put it into the pastry cases with the thinly sliced cheese. Mix the eggs and milk, season well and pour into the 2 cases. Bake towards the top of the oven for about 30 minutes, until well risen and golden. (Serves 2)

Poached Egg Mornay

Gently heat 1 tbsp. (15 ml) milk and add 1 oz. (25 g) grated cheese, with some salt and pepper. Stir until smooth. Meanwhile poach an egg, place it on a slice of toast, pour the sauce over, and grill under a moderate heat until browned. (Serves 1)

Egg Mayonnaise Salad
(*see picture below*)

Hard-boil 4 eggs, shell and halve. Wash a lettuce and arrange on a dish. Prepare 10 spring onions; cut a few radishes into 'roses'; slice 3 tomatoes. Arrange all these on the lettuce. Add the halved eggs, coat them with mayonnaise and garnish with strips of tomato. Garnish with cress or parsley. (Serves 4)

Egg Mayonnaise Salad

Egg Flip and Potato Pie

4 eggs
1½ pints (900 ml) milk
salt and pepper
½ lb. (225 g)
  tomatoes, skinned
1 lb. (450 g) cooked
  potatoes

6 oz. (170 g) Cheshire
  or Cheddar cheese
butter
parsley to garnish

Oven temperature: 350°F., 180°C., mark 4
Beat the eggs thoroughly and add the milk, with some salt and pepper. Slice the tomatoes and potatoes and grate the cheese. Butter a pie dish and put in a layer of potatoes and tomatoes and a sprinkling of cheese, salt and pepper. Add 2–3 tbsps. (30–45 ml) of the egg mixture, then another layer of potatoes, tomatoes and cheese. Finish with a layer of grated cheese, and pour in any remaining egg mixture. Bake slowly for about 40 minutes, until the egg 'flip' has set and the cheese topping is golden-brown. Garnish with parsley. (Serves 4)

Scotch Eggs

(see picture right)

4 hard-boiled eggs
1 oz. (25 g) flour
8 oz. (225 g) sausage-
  meat
1 tbsp. (15 ml)
  chopped chives
salt and pepper

1 beaten egg
2 tbsps. (30 ml) milk
breadcrumbs for
  coating
oil or lard for deep
  fat frying

Shell the eggs and roll them lightly in flour. Mix the sausage-meat and chives and season; divide into 4 even-sized portions and mould one evenly and smoothly round each egg. Mix the beaten egg with the milk, coat each Scotch egg, then roll it firmly in breadcrumbs. Heat the oil to 375°F. (190°C.). Fry the eggs until nicely browned—about 7 minutes each. Serve hot or cold. (Serves 4)

Egg Salad

1 hard-boiled egg
1 cooked potato
1 spring onion
1 tbsp. (15 ml) sliced
  celery

2 tbsps. (30 ml) finely
  shredded cabbage
salad dressing
watercress

Cut the egg into slices (reserving 2–3 for garnish), dice the potato and slice the onion. Add the cabbage and celery and blend with the salad dressing to taste. Arrange on a bed of watercress and garnish with the reserved slices of egg. (Serves 1)

Savoury Pancakes

(see picture opposite and colour picture facing page 81)

4 eggs
1 level tbsp. (15 ml)
  flour
¼ level tsp. (1.25 ml)
  salt
¼ level tsp. (1.25 ml)
  dry mustard

4 oz. (115 g) button
  mushrooms, sliced
2 tbsps. (30 ml) stock
parsley sauce
freshly ground pepper
4 oz. (115 g) lean
  ham, chopped

Beat together the eggs, flour and seasonings to make a smooth batter. Gently heat a small, non-stick frying pan (or a lightly-oiled ordinary frying pan). Pour or spoon in just enough batter to cover the base of the pan thinly, and cook quickly until golden-brown underneath. Turn with a palette knife (or toss) and cook the other side until golden-brown. Turn the pancake out on to a warm plate, cover and keep warm. Repeat until all the batter is used (makes 6).

Scotch Eggs

Savoury Pancakes

Slowly heat the ham, mushrooms and stock in a small pan, sprinkle between the pancakes; serve with the sauce. (Serves 4)
Alternative Filling: Chop 2 onions, seed and chop 1 green pepper, mix with 2 tbsps. (30 ml) cooked corn kernels, add 3 tbsps. (45 ml) stock, season to taste, and simmer until the onion and pepper are tender. Drain, fill each pancake with some of the mixture and roll up.

Maryland Soufflé

11-oz. (*312-g*) can of sweet corn	pepper and salt
2 tbsps. (*30 ml*) butter	2 eggs, separated
3 tbsps. (*45 ml*) flour	4 rashers of bacon,
½ pint (*300 ml*) milk	rinded, grilled and crumbled

Oven temperature: 375°F., 190°C., mark 5
Empty the corn into an ovenproof dish. Melt the butter, stir in the flour, add the milk and stir until boiling. Season, and add the egg yolks and bacon. Whisk the egg whites to a stiff froth, fold lightly into the mixture and pour over the sweet corn, leaving sufficient room for it to rise when baking. Bake for 45–50 minutes, until golden-brown and firm. Serve at once. (Serves 3–4)

Cheese and Corn Soufflé

1 oz. (*30 g*) butter	3 oz. (*85 g*) Cheddar
1 oz. (*30 g*) plain flour	or Cheshire cheese, grated
½ pint (*300 ml*) hot milk	3 large eggs, separated
salt and pepper	
4 tbsps. (*60 ml*) sweet corn purée	

Oven temperature: 375°F., 190°C., mark 5
Melt the butter in a thick saucepan, stir in the flour and cook for 3 minutes. Remove from the heat and add the milk gradually, then return the pan to the heat, bring to the boil and cook for a further 3 minutes. Add salt, pepper, the sweet corn and cheese. Beat the egg yolks thoroughly and blend well with the corn mixture. Beat the whites until very stiff, fold into the mixture, pour into a prepared 2-pint (1.2-litre) soufflé dish and bake for 40–45 minutes. Serve immediately. (Serves 4)

Cheese and Mushroom Soufflé

2 rashers of bacon	3 oz. (*85 g*) cheese, grated
11-oz. (*312-g*) can of ready-to-serve mushroom soup	paprika and salt
	2 eggs, separated

Oven temperature: 350°F., 180°C., mark 4
Rind and chop the bacon and fry lightly. Put the soup into a saucepan, add the cheese and heat, stirring until smooth. Season with paprika (and salt if required), then stir in the egg yolks and the bacon pieces. Whisk the egg whites and fold them into the mixture, pour into a greased dish and bake until well risen and golden-brown—about 40 minutes. (Serves 3–4)

Tomato and Cheese Fondue

½ pint (*300 ml*) cooked and sieved tomatoes	4 oz. (*115 g*) Cheddar cheese, grated
2 oz. (*55 g*) soft white breadcrumbs (starch-reduced)	3 eggs, separated
	salt and pepper

Oven temperature: 350°F., 180°C., mark 4
Gently heat the tomatoes and add the breadcrumbs and cheese. Blend with the lightly beaten egg yolks. Beat the egg whites until stiff, fold into the tomato mixture and season to taste. Turn the mixture into 4 individual dishes and place in a pan of hot water. Bake for ¾–1 hour, until firm when tested with a knife. (Serves 4)

Macaroni Cheese

4 oz. (*115 g*)
  macaroni
4 eggs
1½ pints (*900 ml*) milk
salt and pepper
6 oz. (*170 g*) cheese,
  grated

Oven temperature : 350°F., 180°C., mark 4
Cook the macaroni in boiling salted water until tender (about 20 minutes), stirring occasionally to prevent it sticking to the pan. Drain, and run water through it to separate the tubes. Beat the eggs lightly, then add the milk, seasonings and three-quarters of the cheese. Place the macaroni in an ovenproof dish, pour the egg mixture over and sprinkle with the remaining cheese. Bake for 45 minutes. (Serves 4)

Welsh Rarebit de Luxe

½ oz. (*15 g*) butter
8 oz. (*225 g*) cheese,
  grated
½ level tsp. (*2.5 ml*)
  dry mustard
salt and cayenne
  pepper
¼ pint (*150 ml*) milk
1 egg, beaten
4 rounds of buttered
  toast
grilled tomatoes to
  garnish

Melt the butter in the top of a double saucepan and add the cheese, mustard, seasonings and milk. When smooth and creamy, add the beaten egg and stir for 2–3 minutes, until it is cooked. Pour over the buttered toast and garnish with the grilled tomatoes. (Serves 4)

Cheese and Egg Pie

4 oz. (*100 g*) short-
  crust pastry
¾ oz. (*20 g*) butter
¾ oz. (*20 g*) flour
½ pint (*300 ml*) milk
5 oz. (*140 g*) Cheddar
  cheese, grated
2 large tomatoes
3 eggs, hard-boiled

Oven temperature : 350°F., 180°C., mark 4
Line a 7-inch (18-cm) flan case with the pastry and bake blind for 20 minutes. Melt the butter, add the flour and gradually stir in the milk, bring to the boil and add 3 oz. (85 g) of the grated cheese. Chop the tomatoes roughly into fairly small pieces and add to the sauce. Slice the hard-

boiled eggs and place a layer over the bottom of the flan case. Pour a layer of sauce over, then add more egg and sauce. Sprinkle the top with the remaining cheese, and brown in a very hot oven (450°F., 230°C., mark 8) or under the grill. (Serves 4)

Quiche Anglaise
(*see picture below right*)

4 oz. (*100 g*) short-
  crust pastry
½ lb. (*225 g*) pork
  sausages, grilled and
  sliced
1 onion, skinned and
  finely chopped
2 eggs
4 tbsps. (*60 ml*) milk
2 oz. (*55 g*) cheese,
  grated
1 tbsp. (*15 ml*)
  chopped parsley
salt and pepper

Oven temperature : 400°F., 200°C., mark 6
Line a 7-inch (18-cm) flan ring with the pastry, crimping the edges; fill with the sausages and onion. Beat the eggs and milk together and add the cheese, parsley, salt and pepper. Pour into the flan case and bake for about 30–40 minutes. (Serves 3–4)

Cheese and Asparagus Flan

11-oz. (*312-g*) can of
  asparagus pieces,
  drained
8-inch (*20-cm*) cooked
  shortcrust flan case
2 oz. (*55 g*) Cheddar
  cheese, grated
4 eggs
salt and pepper

Oven temperature : 350°F., 180°C., mark 4
Place the asparagus in the cooked flan case and sprinkle with the grated cheese. Lightly beat the eggs, season with salt and pepper and pour over the asparagus. Bake for 30–40 minutes, until the filling is set. (Serves 4)

Spicy Rarebit

1 tsp. (*5 ml*) butter
2 oz. (*55 g*) Cheddar
  cheese, grated
1 tbsp. (*15 ml*) milk
1 tsp. (*5 ml*) chopped
  parsley
a pinch of cayenne
  pepper
a pinch of mixed
  spice
salt
1 egg, lightly whisked
toast or cooked
  asparagus or other
  vegetables

Melt the butter over a very low heat, then stir in the cheese and heat until smooth and creamy. Stir in the milk gradually, add the parsley, pepper, spice and a little salt, and continue stirring for 2–3 minutes. Take the pan off the heat, beat in the egg yolk, then put the pan back over a very low heat. Stir until the mixture thickens, but do not let it boil. Pour over the toast or cooked vegetables. (Serves 1)

Mock Pizza

4 oz. (*115 g*) self-raising flour	½ level tsp. (*2.5 ml*) dried sage, mixed herbs or oregano
pinch of salt	
cooking oil	3 oz. (*85 g*) cheese, diced
3–4 tbsps. (*45–60 ml*) water	a few anchovy fillets
a small can of tomatoes	a few stuffed olives

Mix the flour and salt to a soft dough with 1 tbsp. (15 ml) of oil and the water. Roll out into a 6-inch (15-cm) round and fry gently in a little oil in a shallow pan, for about 5 minutes, or until browned on the underside. Turn it over and cover with the well drained tomatoes, herbs and cheese; garnish with the anchovy fillets and sliced olives. Fry on the second side for a further 5 minutes, then place under a hot grill until the topping is golden-brown. Serve with a simple green salad. (Serves 2)

Pizza Napoletana
(*see picture over*)

For the Dough:	oil
½ lb. (*225 g*) plain bread flour	2 15-oz. (*425-g*) cans of Italian tomatoes, drained
1 level tsp. (*5 ml*) salt	
1 tsp. (*5 ml*) lard	2 level tsps. (*10 ml*) dried marjoram
¼ pint (*150 ml*) water	salt and pepper
¼ oz. (*7 g*) fresh bakers' yeast	4 oz. (*115 g*) Bel Paese cheese, grated
oil	2 2-oz. (*55-g*) cans of anchovy fillets, drained
For the Topping:	black olives
1 lb. (*450 g*) onions, chopped	

Oven temperature: 450°F., 230°C., mark 8
Mix together the flour and salt and rub in the lard. Blend the yeast and water and then pour them into the flour. Hand-mix until the dough leaves the bowl clean, then knead on a floured board until smooth and elastic. Put the dough in an oiled plastic bag, and leave in a warm place to double in size. Turn the dough out on to a floured surface, and roll it out to a long strip. Brush with oil and roll up like a Swiss roll. Repeat all this 3 times. Grease a 12-inch (30-cm) plain flan ring, placed on a baking sheet, roll out the dough to fit the base and brush with oil.

Sauté the onions in a little oil until soft but not coloured, and spread to within ½ inch (1 cm) of the edge of the dough. Arrange the tomatoes on top, and sprinkle with marjoram and seasoning. Bake in the centre of the oven for 20 minutes.

Quiche Anglaise

Pizza Napoletana

Sprinkle the cheese over, lattice the anchovies across the top and arrange olives between. Cover loosely with foil and cook for a further 20 minutes. Serve hot, cut in wedges. (Serves 4)

Cheese and Ham Rolls

Allow 1 slice of ham and 2 oz. (55 g) cottage cheese per person. Spread the ham with the cheese, and season with mustard and freshly ground pepper and 1 or 2 chopped stalks of chives. Roll up tightly and chill before serving.

Cheese Picnic Baskets

Cut a slice off the top of some crusty rolls and scoop out a little of the middle. Spread the hollow with butter, and fill with a savoury mixture such as one of the following: diced cheese and celery or scrambled egg and cress. Butter the slice cut off the top of each roll and replace it to make the 'lid'. Other good fillings are shrimps or prawns and shredded lettuce; chopped cooked liver and watercress; chopped ham and tomato.

Tomato Consommé (see page 108), Sweet and Sour Pork (see page 142), Ginger Fruit Salad (see page 196)

176

Vegetables

Vegetables play a very important rôle in both maintenance and slimming diets, for they provide bulk without contributing many calories.

Their carbohydrate content varies, depending on the part of the plant used. Thus stem and leaf vegetables (cabbage, celery, etc.) have a high percentage of carbohydrate in the form of cellulose—but since this substance is not utilised by the human body, it can be eaten liberally. 'Underground' vegetables—potatoes, carrots, etc.—have a high proportion of starch and must therefore be eaten cautiously. Succulent vegetables —for example, new peas, onions and beetroot—are rich in plant sap and consequently contain a comparatively high percentage of sugar, which limits their extensive use.

All vegetables contribute minerals and vitamins to the diet, and for this reason they are particularly valuable. However, this virtue can be easily cancelled out by incorrect cooking methods. Vegetables should be placed in a minimal amount of boiling salted water, covered tightly and cooked at a moderate rate until tender yet firm, then drained and served immediately. Never soak vegetables prior to cooking, as this causes loss of the water-soluble vitamins. Prolonged heating will also destroy the vitamins, so avoid keeping cooked vegetables hot for any length of time.

Vegetables should be carefully selected: the fresher they are, the better the flavour, texture and colour. Older vegetables have tough fibres, starchy texture and marked deterioration of colour. Once vegetables are picked, store them in a cool, airy place and use as soon as possible.

Vegetable Seasons

Aubergines, Beetroot, Cabbage, Carrots, Leeks, Onions, Potatoes, Turnips, Mushrooms } all the year

Artichokes (Globe)—July–Oct.; (Jerusalem)—Nov.–June
Asparagus—Sept.–June
Beans (String)—Feb.–June; (Broad)—April–July; (Runner)—June–Sept.
Broccoli—Oct.–April
Brussels Sprouts—Sept.–March
Cauliflower—June–March
Celery—Aug.–Feb.; April–May
Celeriac—Sept.–March

Courgettes—Nov.–June
Parsnips—Sept.–April
Peas—May–Oct.
New Potatoes—May–Sept.
Chicory—Sept.–June
Spinach—April–Nov.

Salad Vegetables

Lettuce (Cos), Endive, Cucumber, Watercress, Capsicums (peppers), Tomatoes, Radish } all the year

Webb's lettuce—available in the summer months.

Chicken Liver Pâté (see page 98), Grilled Salmon (see page 117),
Strawberry Cream (see page 198)

Aubergines à la Provençale

2 aubergines	1 onion, skinned and
salt and pepper	chopped
1 oz. (*25 g*)	2 oz. (*55 g*) bread-
margarine	crumbs
4 small tomatoes	2 oz. (*55 g*) cheese,
skinned and	grated
chopped	parsley sprigs and
1 shallot, skinned and	baked tomatoes to
chopped	garnish

Don't peel the aubergines, but wipe them and steam or boil for about ½ hour; when they are tender, cut them in half lengthways, scoop out the flesh, chop and season. Heat the fat in a pan and sauté the chopped tomatoes, shallot and onion. Lastly, add the aubergine flesh and a few breadcrumbs. Stuff the aubergine cases with this mixture, sprinkle with breadcrumbs and then with the grated cheese. Grill until golden brown on top, and serve garnished with the parsley and tomatoes. (Serves 4)

Baked Stuffed Aubergines

2 aubergines	1 egg, beaten
2 oz. (*55 g*) starch-	2 oz. (*55 g*) cheese,
reduced bread-	grated
crumbs	1 tbsp. (*15 ml*)
1 onion	chopped parsley
2 oz. (*55 g*) mush-	salt and pepper
rooms	a little milk
1 oz. (*25 g*) butter	

Oven temperature: 350°F., 180°C., mark 4
Cut each aubergine in half lengthways, scoop out some of the inside flesh and put the cases into a greased ovenproof dish. Chop the aubergine flesh and mix with most of the breadcrumbs. Chop the onion and mushrooms and cook in the hot fat, turning them occasionally and not allowing them to colour. Add to the aubergine and breadcrumbs, together with the beaten egg, half of the cheese, the parsley, seasonings, and if required a little milk to moisten. Put the mixture into the aubergine cases, sprinkle the surface with the rest of the cheese and crumbs, and bake for 35–45 minutes. Serve with tomato sauce. (Serves 4)

Green Beans Sorrento

1 oz. (*25 g*) bacon,	1 medium-sized
rinded and chopped	tomato, chopped
2 oz. (*55 g*) onion,	2 8-oz. (*225-g*) pkts.
skinned and finely	frozen haricot verts,
chopped	half-thawed
1 clove of garlic,	½ level tsp. (*2.5 ml*)
skinned and	oregano
chopped	1 level tsp. (*5 ml*) salt
2 oz. (*55 g*) green	black pepper
pepper, seeded and	4 tbsps. (*60 ml*) water
finely chopped	

Sauté the bacon in a pan until lightly browned. Add the onion, garlic and green pepper and sauté until golden-brown. Stir in the tomato, beans, oregano, salt, pepper and water, bring to the boil, cover and simmer until the beans are tender—about 10 minutes. Serve immediately. (Serves 4)

Harvard Beets

1 tbsp. (*15 ml*) butter	1 lb. (*450 g*) cooked
2 level tsps. (*10 ml*)	beetroot
cornflour	salt and pepper
¼ pint (*150 ml*) mild	artificial sweetener
vinegar	

Melt the butter and add the cornflour. Stir in the vinegar gradually, and continue stirring until the sauce boils. Add the diced beets and simmer gently till the sauce is a rich red, then add salt, pepper and sweetener to taste. (Serves 4)

Pickled Beets

½ lb. (*225 g*) beetroot,	¾ pint (*375 ml*) water
cooked and sliced	¼ pint (*150 ml*)
4 level tsps. (*20 ml*)	vinegar
powdered gelatine	artificial sweetener

Dissolve the gelatine in the water in the normal way. Add the vinegar and sweetener to taste, pour over the beetroot and leave in a cool place to set. (Serves 4)

Cauliflower au Gratin

Put a large cauliflower, stem end downwards, in sufficient salted water to half-cover it and cook until tender. Break it into small pieces and put into a heatproof dish, then cover with $\frac{1}{2}$–$\frac{3}{4}$ pint (300–375 ml) Mornay sauce and sprinkle with grated cheese and browned crumbs. Brown under a grill or in a hot oven, garnish with parsley sprigs and serve very hot. (Serves 4)

Baked Celery Cheese

1 head of celery, scrubbed and chopped	1 oz. (25 g) flour
	$\frac{1}{4}$ pint (150 ml) milk
	3 oz. (85 g) Cheddar
salt and pepper	cheese, grated
1 oz. (25 g) butter	

Oven temperature: 375°F., 190°C., mark 5
Cook the celery in a little boiling salted water for 10–15 minutes. Drain well, retaining $\frac{1}{4}$ pint (150 ml) of the liquor. Melt the butter, blend in the flour and cook for 2–3 minutes. Gradually add the celery liquor and milk, stirring continuously until smooth. Add 2 oz. (55 g) cheese, and stir to blend. Fill an ovenproof dish with alternate layers of celery and sauce, and sprinkle with cheese. Bake until lightly browned. (Serves 4)

Courgettes Créole

2 lb. (900 g) courgettes	salt and pepper
1 tbsp. (15 ml) oil	15-oz. (425-g) can of tomatoes
2–3 spring onions, chopped	

Wash the courgettes and slice diagonally, $\frac{1}{2}$ inch (1 cm) thick. Heat the oil and sauté the spring onions. Add the courgettes, salt and pepper and simmer over a low heat for 10 minutes. Add the tomatoes and simmer for 5 minutes longer. (Serves 4–5)

Baked Courgettes and Aubergines

2 aubergines	salt and pepper
6–7 courgettes	3 level tbsps. (45 ml) tomato paste
6–8 shallots	
1 clove of garlic	$\frac{1}{4}$ pint (150 ml) stock
olive oil	olives to garnish

Slice the aubergines, courgettes and shallots and chop the garlic very finely. Rub an ovenproof dish with oil, put a layer of aubergine in the bottom, and sprinkle with salt and pepper; now put in a layer of shallot and a little garlic, then a layer of the courgettes. Continue in this way until the dish has been filled. Mix together the tomato paste and stock, pour this over the vegetables and bake for 1 hour. Serve hot or cold, garnished with a few olives. (Serves 4)

Courgettes in Cheese Sauce

1 lb. (450 g) courgettes	$\frac{1}{2}$ level tsp. (2.5 ml) dry mustard
salt and pepper	sliced tomatoes and watercress
$\frac{1}{2}$ pint (300 ml) milk	
4 oz. (115 g) cheese, grated	

Wash the courgettes and remove the stalks; slice diagonally and cook in boiling salted water for 2–3 minutes. Drain and place in a shallow ovenproof dish. Heat the milk and add the cheese, salt, pepper and mustard; stir until the cheese has melted. Pour over the courgettes and place under a moderate grill until lightly browned. Serve garnished with the tomatoes and watercress. (Serves 3–4)

Belgian Cucumber

4 small cucumbers	$\frac{1}{4}$ pint (150 ml) mayonnaise
salt	
2 egg yolks	chopped dill
$\frac{1}{2}$ pint (300 ml) yoghurt	

Peel the cucumbers, cut into 2-inch (5-cm) lengths and cook in fast-boiling salted water until tender (about 20 minutes); drain. Arrange the cucumbers in a hot dish. Beat the egg yolks, mix with the yoghurt and the mayonnaise and warm gently, without boiling. Pour over the cucumber and sprinkle with chopped dill. (Serves 4)

Leek and Bacon Savoury

4 leeks (about 1 lb. (450 g))	1 oz. (25 g) flour
	2 oz. (55 g) cheese
4 rashers of bacon	salt and pepper
1 oz. (25 g) margarine	$\frac{1}{4}$ pint (150 ml) milk
	parsley

Oven temperature: 350°F., 180°C., mark 4
Wash the leeks, cutting off the roots and green leaves, and cook them for 10 minutes in salted water. Rind the rashers and cook them for 5 minutes in the oven. Strain the leeks, saving a little of the stock. Wrap a rasher of bacon around each leek and place in an ovenproof dish. Make a sauce with the fat, flour, cheese, seasoning and milk, including the leek stock; pour this over the leeks and cook for 20 minutes. Sprinkle a little chopped parsley on top before serving. (Serves 4)

Marrow and Tomato Bake

½ a vegetable marrow, cubed	toast triangles (use starch-reduced bread)
salt and pepper	
½ lb. (*225 g*) tomatoes	parsley to garnish
½ pint (*300 ml*) cheese sauce	

Grease a casserole and put in the cubed marrow, with salt and pepper. Cover and cook gently until the marrow is almost tender. Add the skinned and quartered tomatoes and the cheese sauce. Leave the lid off to brown the top, and serve with the toast triangles and parsley garnish. (Serves 3–4)

Stuffed Marrow

a 3-lb. (*1.5-kg*) marrow	1 tsp. (*5 ml*) chopped parsley
2 onions, skinned and sliced	salt and pepper
2 oz. (*55 g*) butter	a pinch of dried thyme
1 red pepper, sliced and seeded	4 hard-boiled eggs, chopped
½ lb. (*225 g*) mushrooms, sliced	baked tomatoes
6 oz. (*170 g*) cooked rice	

Oven temperature: 325°F., 170°C., mark 3
Wash the marrow, then place it in a greased baking tin with a little water. Cover with greased paper and bake until tender (about ¾ hour). Fry the onions in the butter until they are golden brown, then add the red pepper and mushrooms and cook for several minutes; add this mixture to the rice, together with the

parsley, seasoning and thyme, and mix lightly together. Lastly, add the hard-boiled eggs. When the marrow is tender, remove a portion of the top for a lid, scoop out the seeds and fill up the centre with the rice mixture. Replace the top, and serve with baked tomatoes. (Serves 4)

Mushroom Casserole

1 lb. (*450 g*) mushrooms, sliced	salt and pepper
4 tomatoes, skinned and sliced	1 tbsp. (*15 ml*) chopped parsley
2 onions, cut in rings	6 tbsp. (*90 ml*) stock or water
4 sticks of celery, chopped	

Oven temperature: 350°F., 180°C., mark 4
Thoroughly grease a casserole. Fill the dish with alternate layers of mushrooms, tomatoes, onions and celery, seasoning each layer well and finishing with a layer of mushrooms on top. Sprinkle with a little parsley, add the liquid and bake until tender (about 30 minutes). Pack the vegetables closely, to allow for considerable shrinkage during the cooking. (Serves 4)

Spanish Stuffed Onions

6 large onions, skinned	1 level tsp. (*5 ml*) dried thyme
salt and pepper	grated rind of ½ a lemon
½ lb. (*225 g*) pork, minced	1 egg, beaten
¾ lb. (*340 g*) pie veal, minced	oil
12 stuffed olives, halved	

Oven temperature: 375°F., 190°C., mark 5
Cook the onions in boiling salted water for ½–¾ hour, according to size; drain them and carefully ease out the centres. Mix together the pork, veal, olives, thyme, lemon rind, egg and seasoning. Place the onions in a greased ovenproof casserole, then stuff each with meat mixture. Brush the onions with oil, cover and bake for 40–50 minutes. Serve immediately. (Serves 4–6)

Stuffed Onions

4 large onions	2 oz. (*55 g*) walnuts,
salt and pepper	chopped
4 oz. (*115 g*) carrot,	4 tbsps. (*60 ml*) fat-
grated	free yoghurt
3 oz. (*85 g*) cheese,	
grated	

Oven temperature: 350°F., 180°C., mark 4
Cook the onions in salted water for $\frac{1}{2}$–$\frac{3}{4}$ hour; scoop out the centres and chop them. Mix the carrot, 2 oz. (55 g) of the cheese and the walnuts with the onion and the yoghurt; season to taste. Fill the onion shells with this mixture, sprinkle the remaining grated cheese on top and bake for about 30 minutes. (Serves 4)

Scalloped Potatoes

1 lb. (*450 g*) potatoes,	1 pint (*600 ml*) cheese
cooked and sliced	sauce
4 rashers of lean	grated cheese
bacon, roughly	chopped parsley
chopped	
4 hard-boiled eggs,	
sliced	

Oven temperature: 375°F., 190°C., mark 5
Layer the potatoes, bacon, eggs and sauce in 4 individual dishes. Top with grated cheese and bake for 20–30 minutes, until golden-brown and bubbling. Serve sprinkled with parsley. (Serves 4)

Spinach with Poached Eggs

2 lb. (*1 kg*) spinach	2 tbsps. (*30 ml*) stock
salt	1 tbsp. (*15 ml*) cream
1 oz. (*25 g*) butter	or top of the milk
1$\frac{1}{2}$ tbsps. (*22.5 ml*)	4 eggs
flour	

Wash the spinach thoroughly, cook with a little salt until tender, then drain well by pressing in a colander and finally sieve it. Melt the fat in a pan and stir in the flour, add the spinach and a little stock and cook for a few minutes. Remove from the heat, stir in the cream and put into a hot dish. Poach the eggs and place on top. (Serves 4)

Spinach with Cheese

1$\frac{1}{2}$ lb. (*700 g*) spinach	1 egg yolk
salt	1–2 oz. (*30–55 g*)
$\frac{1}{2}$ oz. (*15 g*) butter	cheese, finely grated

Wash the spinach thoroughly and cook in a pan with a little salt but no additional water. When it is tender, drain it thoroughly in a colander and chop with a sharp knife. Put the butter into the pan and add the spinach; toss in the butter, then add the egg yolk and grated cheese. Mix well and serve at once, without further heating. (Serves 3)

Tomato and Onion Bake

3–4 onions, skinned	salt and pepper
and sliced	1 oz. (*25 g*) butter
3–4 tomatoes, sliced	

Oven temperature: 350°F., 180°C., mark 4
Put in an ovenproof dish alternate layers of onion and tomato; sprinkle with salt and pepper, add a knob of butter and cover. Bake for $\frac{1}{2}$–$\frac{3}{4}$ hour, until the onion is tender. (Serves 3–4)

Ham-topped Tomatoes

Oven temperature: 350°F., 180°C., mark 4
Cut 4 large tomatoes in halves, and mix 2 oz. (55 g) minced ham with a little pepper. Pile some of the mixture on to the cut side of each tomato half, and bake for about 20–30 minutes. Serve the tomatoes garnished with parsley. (Serves 4)

Stuffed Baked Tomatoes—1
(*see picture over*)

2 tomatoes	chopped parsley
2 oz. (*55 g*) mush-	salt and pepper
rooms, chopped	

Oven temperature: 350°F., 180°C., mark 4
Remove the centres from the tomatoes, and mix the pulp with the mushrooms, parsley and seasoning. Refill the tomatoes and bake 20–30 minutes. (Serves 2) For a special occasion, serve with asparagus and garnish with egg.

Stuffed Baked Tomatoes—2

4 large tomatoes	7-oz. (*198-g*) can of
2 oz. (*55 g*) butter	tuna fish, drained
1 onion, skinned and	2 tbsps. (*30 ml*)
chopped	chopped parsley
4 oz. (*115 g*) button	
mushrooms, sliced	

Oven temperature: 350°F., 180°C., mark 4
Remove the top from each tomato, cutting in a zig-zag fashion. Using a tea-spoon, carefully scoop out the soft core and pips and discard these. Place the tomato shells on a baking sheet. Heat the butter in a frying pan, add the onion and cook until soft, without colouring. Add the mushrooms and continue cooking for a few minutes; flake the tuna fish and add to the pan, together with the parsley. Mix well together. Divide the mixture between the tomatoes, cover with foil and bake in the centre of the oven for about 20–30 minutes. (Serves 4)

Cold-weather Vegetable Casserole

1 rasher of lean bacon, rinded and diced	½ pint (*300 ml*) milk and stock mixed
1 oz. (*25 g*) butter	salt and pepper
1 large onion, skinned and sliced	parsley and grated cheese
1 lb. (*450 g*) potatoes, peeled and sliced	

Oven temperature: 375°F., 190°C., mark 5
Put the diced bacon into a pan with the butter and onion and fry lightly without browning; add the potatoes, and sauté for a further few minutes. Add the liquid and seasoning and bring to the boil, then turn the mixture into a casserole and cook in the oven until tender—about ½ hour. Just before serving, sprinkle with chopped parsley and grated cheese. (Serves 3)

Alternatively, this dish may be cooked in a saucepan; cover and simmer gently until tender—about 20 minutes—and then turn it into a hot dish and sprinkle with the parsley and cheese.

Ratatouille Niçoise
(see colour picture facing page 96)

2 onions, cut into rings	½ a marrow, peeled and diced (or 5 courgettes, sliced)
2 red peppers, seeded and sliced	3 tomatoes, skinned and chopped
2 green peppers, seeded and sliced	salt and pepper
1 tbsp. (*15 ml*) oil	chopped parsley
2 aubergines, diced	

Oven temperature: 350°F., 180°C., mark 4
Fry the onions and peppers in the oil. Add the aubergines and marrow, mix well, then add the tomatoes and season-ing. Put into a casserole, cover and bake for 20–30 minutes. Garnish with parsley before serving. (Serves 4)

Vegetable Salad

1 lettuce, torn into pieces	3 carrots, shredded
1 small cauliflower, divided into florets	a few radishes
3 tomatoes, sliced	a few spring onions
	French dressing
	chopped mint

Toss all the vegetables together in the dressing and sprinkle with the mint.

Stuffed Baked Tomatoes—1

Salads and salad dressings

Virtually all vegetables can be used in a salad (see colour picture between pages 96, 97). Salads bring great variety to the meals, contributing something crisp to counteract the softer accompaniments. They help to achieve a well-balanced diet by supplying vitamins and minerals which have no chance of being destroyed by incorrect cooking methods.

Salads can be divided into two groups: those that accompany a main dish—simple salads tossed in a French dressing; and those heartier salads containing meat, fish or poultry with a richer dressing, that form the main dish.

Salads should be freshly prepared as near to the time of serving as possible. The various salad plants can be washed and stored in a plastic bag in the bottom of the refrigerator.

Dressing the Salad

The dressing can make or mar a salad. The most usual mistake is to use too much dressing, swamping the salad instead of making it appetising. No surplus dressing should be seen at the bottom of the bowl—there should be just sufficient clinging to the salad ingredients to flavour them. There are now a number of low-calorie dressings available for extra variety.

Herbs in Salads

Parsley is an addition to any salad. Do not chop it very finely but snip it with scissors straight on to the salad, just before serving. A few leaves of fresh mint, sage, thyme, dill or tarragon (one at a time, not all together) can be chopped and sprinkled over a salad. Some people like verbena or rosemary, but don't be too liberal with these slightly scented flavours unless you know the tastes of the people you are serving.

Garlic

Many of those who say they dislike garlic don't really know how to use it. True, it is pungent and needs using with discretion—you will find one 'clove' ample for the average bowl of salad.

First remove the papery outside skin of the garlic clove, then crush the clove with a broad-bladed knife (do this on a plate, unless you have a board that you keep specially for onion-chopping). Scrape the crushed garlic into the salad bowl or add it to the dressing. Alternatively, use a garlic press, if you have one.

To make Salad Garnishes

Celery Curls: Cut a celery stick into strips about $\frac{1}{2}$ inch (1 cm) wide and 2 inches (2.5 cm) long. Make cuts along the length of each, close together and to within $\frac{1}{2}$ inch (1 cm) of one end. Leave the pieces in cold or iced water for 1–2 hours, until the fringed strips curl. Drain well before using.

Cucumber Cones: Use thin slices of cucumber. Make a cut in each slice from the centre to the outer edge, then wrap one cut edge over the other to form a cone.

Crimped Cucumber: Run a fork down the sides of the cucumber to remove strips of peel and slice the cucumber thinly in the usual way—this gives the slices an attractive deckled edge.

Gherkin Fans: Use whole gerkins, choosing long, thin ones. Cut each lengthwise into thin slices, but leave these joined at one end. Fan out the strips of gherkins so that they overlap each other.

Radish Roses: Trim the radishes. Make 4 or 8 small, deep cuts, crossing in the centre at the root end. Leave the radishes in cold or iced water for 1–2 hours, till the cuts open to form 'petals'.

Tomato Lilies: Choose firm, even-sized tomatoes. Using a small sharp-pointed knife, make a series of V-shaped cuts round the middle of each, cutting right through to the centre. Carefully pull the halves apart.

Quick Garnish: Sprinkle finely chopped parsley on potato salad; finely chopped onion on beetroot; chopped spring onion on tomato; chopped mint, chives, tarragon or parsley on green salad.

Note: In this chapter we do not give numbers of servings at the end of the recipes, because these depend so much on whether the salad is being served as an accompaniment or as a main dish.

Green Salad

1 lettuce	a piece of cucumber
1 small bunch of	1 tomato (optional)
watercress	French dressing
1 chicory	

Wash the lettuce, watercress and chicory. Tear the lettuce, trim the watercress, slice the cucumber and tomato, remove the outer leaves of the chicory and slice finely. Toss all in the dressing.

Hot-weather Green Salad

Wash a lettuce or endive and tear the leaves into small pieces. Clean a bunch of watercress, retaining only the top part and the small leaves. Peel half a cucumber, cut it in very thin slices, and cut up a dozen spring onions finely. Mix all the ingredients and toss them in a French dressing to which a little white wine has been added.

Algerian Salad

Mix together some shredded lettuce, chopped celery and chives. Scatter with quartered tomatoes and top with a little French dressing.

Apple and Cabbage Salad

Dice some red apples without peeling them. Sprinkle with lemon juice and mix with some finely chopped cabbage.

Apple and Celery Salad

Dice some red apples without peeling them; mix with some diced celery and moisten with French dressing. Heap into a lettuce 'cup' and scatter with seedless grapes.

Apple, Celery and Egg Salad

Slice 1 cooking apple, finely slice a little celery and add 1 small chopped onion (or spring onion) and 1 hard-boiled egg. Season, add a little lemon juice and garnish with parsley, or serve on a bed of lettuce.

Apple and Tomato Salad

Peel, core and dice 2 dessert apples, and peel and slice ½ lb. (225 g) tomatoes. Put into a bowl with sufficient salad dressing to bind. Place on lettuce leaves, or serve garnished with mustard and cress or watercress.

Apple-Tuna Salad

(see colour picture between pages 96, 97)

6-oz. (*170-g*) can of tuna fish	4 medium red-skinned apples
1 small green pepper, seeded and chopped	cheese dressing lettuce

Drain and flake the tuna and mix with the pepper. Wash the apples and scoop out the inside of each, leaving a ¼-inch (0.5-cm) wall. Chop the scooped-out apple and add to the tuna mixture, then add 1–2 tbsps. cheese dressing and toss. Pile into the apple shells and chill. Serve on a lettuce base.

Glorified Apple Salad

3 oz. (*85 g*) carrot, grated	6 oz. (*170 g*) cottage cheese
3 oz. (*85 g*) celery, chopped	2 tbsps. (*30 ml*) mayonnaise
1 red apple, cored and sliced	lettuce

Toss the carrot, celery, apple, cottage cheese and mayonnaise together in a bowl. Chill until just before serving, then arrange the lettuce leaves on a platter and place the apple mixture in the centre.

Atlantic Salad

Mix together some finely shredded lettuce, cut-up, cooked beans, cooked peas, diced celery and carrot curls. Pour a little French dressing over and toss lightly. Sprinkle with mustard and cress.

Beef Cabbage Salad

1 white cabbage, finely shredded	4 oz. (*115 g*) peanuts
2 red apples, cored and diced	4 oz. (*115 g*) cooked beef, diced
1 onion, skinned and finely chopped	French dressing diced cooked beetroot tomato wedges

Put the cabbage, apples, onion, nuts and beef in a bowl. Toss the salad in the dressing, and serve garnished with beetroot and tomato.

Belmont Salad

Mix together some finely shredded lettuce, seeded and chopped red and green peppers and diced apples. Add lemon juice and toss lightly.

Brazilian Salad

½ lb. (*225 g*) tomatoes, skinned and sliced	1 good lettuce heart juice of 1 lemon
1 celery heart, cut up	1 tbsp. (*15 ml*) fat-free yoghurt
4 oz. (*115 g*) pine-apple pieces	cayenne pepper

Mix the tomatoes and celery with the pineapple pieces. (Although fresh pine-apples should be used if possible, well-drained canned pineapple can be substituted.) Shred the lettuce heart and mix this with the other ingredients. Put the mixture into a dish and pour over it the lemon juice, yoghurt and some cayenne pepper, blended well together.

California Salad

Dice some cucumber and celery, and thinly slice 2 apples, 1 banana and 4 tomatoes. Sprinkle the tomato and cucumber with salt and pepper, and squeeze the juice of ½ a lemon over the apples and banana. Mix together all the ingredients, mask lightly with salad dressing and arrange on a bed of lettuce.

Cauliflower Salad

Divide a raw cauliflower into florets. Finely chop a small onion, neatly dice a small beetroot and finely shred the heart of a cabbage. Add all these ingredients to the cauliflower florets, and pour over them a French dressing to which a few capers have been added. Serve chilled.

Cheddar Cheese Salad

4 oz. (*115 g*) Cheddar cheese	mayonnaise
	a little made mustard
½ lb. (*225 g*) tomatoes, skinned and thinly sliced	a lettuce
	watercress
	chopped chives

Cut the cheese into very small cubes and mix with the tomatoes, mayonnaise and mustard. Make a bed of torn lettuce leaves and watercress sprigs, put the cheese and tomato on top and sprinkle with the chopped chives.

Cheese and Carrot Salad

1 lettuce	2–3 carrots, grated
French dressing	4 tomatoes, skinned and sliced
2 oz. (*55 g*) cheese, grated	½ a cucumber, sliced

Wash the lettuce and toss it in the dressing. Arrange the other ingredients on the bed of lettuce leaves.

Cheese and Pineapple Salad

8 oz. (*225 g*) pine-apple, finely chopped	8 oz. (*225 g*) cottage cheese
	salt and pepper
1 red pepper and 1 green pepper, seeded and chopped	small lettuce leaves, or large ones, torn or shredded

Fold the pineapple and peppers into the cottage cheese; salt and pepper to taste. Pile into lettuce 'cups', or serve on a base of shredded lettuce.

Cheese and Chopped Ham Salad

Mix 2 oz. (55 g) chopped ham with 8 oz.

(225 g) cottage cheese. Pile on a platter and surround with a sweet-sour salad of chopped apple tossed in lemon juice, grated young carrot, sliced orange and chopped green peppers (or sweet pickle), and serve with a dressing of plain yoghurt.

Cheese Nest Salad

Add a little finely chopped parsley and spring onion to some grated cheese or cream cheese, with just enough thick mayonnaise to bind, then form into balls the size of small bird's eggs. Make 'nests' of salad vegetables on crisp lettuce leaves, and put 4–5 cheese 'eggs' in each one. Serve in individual dishes, with mayonnaise.

Cole Slaw Bowl

1 large round cabbage	1 tbsp. (*15 ml*) chopped chives
4 raw carrots, grated	salt and pepper
1 spring onion, chopped	mayonnaise
2 oz. (*55 g*) Cheddar cheese, grated	1 tomato, skinned, seeded and sliced

Remove any tough outside leaves from the cabbage, then hollow it out with a sharp knife to make a 'bowl'. Slice the inside part of the cabbage (removing the coarse ribs), mix with the carrot, onion, cheese and chives, and season well. Add a little mayonnaise to bind together and pile the mixture back into the cabbage. Garnish with the tomato.

Crab Salad Mornay

Mix together equal quantities of cottage cheese and flaked crab. Season with Worcestershire sauce, lemon juice, salt and freshly ground pepper. Pile into lettuce 'cups'. Decorate with chopped gherkins and serve with sliced tomatoes and cucumber.

Crunchy Salad

2 sticks of celery, chopped	1 eating apple, chopped
1 small cooked beetroot, chopped	2–3 tbsps. (*30–45 ml*) mayonnaise

Mix all the ingredients well to combine with the mayonnaise

Cucumber Salad

2 cucumbers	¼ pint (*150 ml*) water
1 level tbsp. (*15 ml*) salt	juice of ½ a lemon pepper
¼ pint (*150 ml*) vinegar	liquid artificial sweetener

Wash the cucumbers and slice finely. (Remove the skin only if tough.) Sprinkle with salt and leave to stand; discard the juice and rinse off the salt. Make a dressing of vinegar, water, lemon juice, pepper and sweetener to taste. Pour over the cucumber and leave to stand for ½ hour in a cool place before serving.

Dressed French Beans

1 lb. (*450 g*) French beans, cooked	2 tbsps. (*30 ml*) salad oil
salt and pepper	1 tbsp. (*15 ml*) tarragon or white vinegar
¼ level tsp. (*1.25 ml*) dry mustard	

Drain the beans well, season and allow to cool. Blend the remaining ingredients, including ¼ level tsp. (1.25 ml) salt, and use as a dressing, mixing well with the cooled French beans.

Frankfurter Salad

Endive and Tomato Salad

1 endive	3 tomatoes
1 clove of garlic, skinned	French dressing

Wash, drain and dry the endive. Crush the garlic and rub the side of the bowl with it to give a slight flavour to the salad, then discard the garlic pieces. Place the endive in the bowl. Slice the tomatoes and add them to the salad, pour the prepared dressing over and toss with two spoons so that the leaves are coated with the dressing. Serve at once.

Ensalada Isabella

2 celery hearts	*For the mayonnaise:*
1 lb. (*450 g*) potatoes, cooked	1 clove of garlic, skinned
4 apples, peeled and cored	1 egg yolk salt and pepper oil lemon juice

Remove the outer stalks of the celery, leaving the crisp hearts; wash, and leave in cold water until required. Slice the potatoes and apples. Crush the garlic; add the egg yolk and seasoning and stir in the oil, a few drops at a time, until the mixture is thick; stir in a little lemon juice to taste. Cut up the drained celery and toss this with the apples and potatoes in the mayonnaise.

Frankfurter Salad

(*see picture left*)

2 frankfurters, sliced	chopped mint
2 sticks of celery, sliced	2 tbsps. (*30 ml*) French dressing
1 cooked potato, diced	a large lettuce leaf

Mix the salad ingredients together with the dressing. Pile into a lettuce 'cup'.

Fruit, Nut and Cheese Salad

8 oz. (*225 g*) curd cheese	6 canned peaches, well drained
1 tbsp. (*15 ml*) raisins	4 walnut halves cucumber and water-
lettuce	cress to garnish

Beat the cheese until smooth. Put the raisins into boiling water for 1–2 minutes to soften them, drain well and cool, then mix with the cheese. Place the lettuce on a dish in about 4 individual portions, and put a roughly heaped tbsp. of the mixture on each. Arrange on top a couple of slices of peach and half a walnut, and garnish with cucumber slices and water-cress sprigs.

Grapefruit Slaw

Peel, segment and chop 1 grapefruit. Toss it with 1 cup of finely shredded white cabbage. Add 1 skinned and sliced tomato and 1 tbsp. (15 ml) French dressing, and season with freshly ground pepper.

Grapefruit and Banana Salad

Prepare some small cress, draining it well and reserving a little for garnish. Cut 2 grapefruits in half, scoop out the flesh and cut it into neat pieces. Add 2 sliced bananas and some chopped cress to the fruit, blend with a little salad dressing and fill the grapefruit cups with this mixture. Garnish with remaining cress.

Grapefruit and Shrimp Salad

(see picture below)

lettuce	¼ pint (150 ml) picked
1 grapefruit	shrimps
cucumber	French dressing

Grapefruit and Shrimp Salad

Prepare the lettuce and arrange a neat bed of the heart leaves in a shallow salad bowl. Peel the grapefruit, remove the pith and divide it into sections; cut each section into three, and put the juice and grapefruit into a basin. Wash the cucumber, cut it into thin strips and add it with the shrimps to the grapefruit. Pour on some French dressing and mix lightly. Pile the mixture on the lettuce leaves and garnish with a few of the shrimp heads.

Ham and Cheese Salad

1 stick of celery, diced	1 hard-boiled egg,
1 spring onion, finely	sliced
chopped	1 slice of boiled ham,
4 oz. (115 g) cottage	cut 1 in. (2.5 cm)
cheese	thick and diced
2 tomatoes, sliced	

Mix the celery, onion and cottage cheese together and pile in the centre of a dish. Arrange the tomatoes, hard-boiled egg and diced ham around the edges.

Health Salad

2 lb. (1 kg) white	4 carrots, peeled and
cabbage	finely diced
1 green pepper,	cheese dressing
seeded and diced	

Shred the cabbage very finely. Add the diced pepper and carrot and toss with a little cheese dressing.

Hot Slaw Salad

2 lb. (1 kg) cabbage,	3 eggs
cooked	½ pint (300 ml) milk
2 tbsps. (30 ml)	2 rashers of back
vinegar	bacon, grilled and
salt	crumbled
mustard	chopped parsley
liquid sweetener	

Slice the cabbage finely. Mix the vinegar with salt, mustard and sweetener to taste; sprinkle over the cabbage. Beat the eggs and milk together and heat, stirring, until thickened; pour over the cabbage. Toss lightly, and serve sprinkled with the bacon and parsley.

Main-dish Salad Bowl

1 clove of garlic	4 oz. (*115 g*) cooked
1 lettuce	chicken
some curly endive	4 oz. (*115 g*) Gruyère
1 head of celery	cheese
French dressing	1 egg, hard-boiled
4 oz. (*115 g*) ham	watercress

Rub the cut garlic round a salad bowl. Prepare and shred the lettuce, endive and celery and toss them in some of the dressing. Cut the ham, chicken and cheese into small slivers and toss in dressing. Put all these ingredients into the bowl, sprinkle with sieved egg and garnish with watercress.

Kentucky Salad

1 lettuce	2 sweet peppers,
2 tomatoes, skinned	seeded and sliced
and sliced	finely
4 oz. (*115 g*) tongue,	2 sticks of celery,
cut in strips	sliced finely
2 slices of ham, cut in	cress
strips	French dressing

On a bed of lettuce place the sliced tomato. Sprinkle with the strips of tongue, ham, pepper and celery. Garnish with cress and serve with dressing.

Leek and Lemon Salad

Wash and slice some raw leeks finely and separate into rings. Add 1 tbsp. (15 ml) chopped mint and toss in lemon juice.

Melba Salad

Core and slice 2 apples, without peeling. Remove the stones from 2 peaches and slice. Toss the fruit together in lemon chive dressing and pile on some endive.

Mushroom Salad

6 oz. (*170 g*) button	salt to taste
mushrooms	1 tsp. (*5 ml*) finely
juice of 1 large lemon	chopped chives
4 tbsps. (*60 ml*) olive	1 tbsp. (*15 ml*) finely
oil	chopped parsley
freshly ground pepper	

Wash the mushrooms and remove the stems; slice thinly and arrange in an hors d'oeuvre dish or salad bowl. Mix the lemon juice and olive oil, add pepper and salt and pour over the mushrooms. Chill in the refrigerator for 2 hours. Just before serving, sprinkle with chopped chives and parsley.

Orange Salad

Combine some sliced oranges and onions with small black olives; add a dressing of oil, salt and paprika pepper.

Orange and Celery Salad

Peel 2 oranges and separate into segments. Finely chop 2–3 sticks of celery, mix with the orange segments and toss in a light French dressing.

Pasta Salad

4 oz. (*115 g*)	chopped chives
macaroni	French dressing
salt	

Cook the macaroni in boiling salted water until tender. Drain thoroughly, allow to cool, then cut into 1-inch (2.5-cm) lengths. Add the chopped chives and toss in French dressing.

Pear and Grape Salad

Prepare 2 eating pears by peeling them and cutting into halves. Spread cottage cheese over the 4 cut surfaces. Prepare $\frac{1}{4}$ lb. (115 g) grapes by halving them and removing the pips, then arrange them on top of the cream cheese. Place the pears in a dish and decorate with halved walnuts, sprigs of parsley and slices of another eating pear.

Plum Salad

12 ripe red dessert	3 tbsps. (*45 ml*)
plums	tarragon dressing
1 tbsp. (*15 ml*) cock-	
tail onions	

Stone and slice the plums; chop the onions. Mix them together, make the dressing (see end of chapter), spoon it over and serve very cold.

Peach Cheese Salad

Peach Cheese Salad

(see picture above)

¼ lb. (*115 g*) sliced cold meat
8 oz. (*225 g*) cottage cheese
6 peach halves
watercress
4 walnut halves

Overlap the slices of meat (brawn, luncheon meat, ham, etc.) round the edge of an oval dish. Pile the cottage cheese in the centre and circle with the peach halves and sprigs of watercress. Arrange the walnut halves over the cheese.

Poinsettia Salad

Cut some tomatoes in quarters, leaving them joined at the base so that the sections can spread apart while remaining attached. Place the tomatoes on lettuce leaves, and fill the centres with diced cucumber and celery; sprinkle with salt and pepper and add a little French dressing.

Potato Salad

Take 3 large potatoes, cooked but very firm, and cut them into neat dice or slices. Finely chop 2 spring onions and add them to the potatoes. Blend the vegetables with a salad dressing, pile lightly on a dish, sprinkle with chopped parsley and garnish with watercress.

Red Cabbage Salad

1 lb. (*450 g*) red cabbage
salt
1–2 apples, grated
2–3 tbsps. (*30–45 ml*) salad oil
2–3 tbsps. (*30–45 ml*) water
2–3 tbsps. (*30–45 ml*) lemon juice or vinegar
½ tsp. (*2.5 ml*) ground caraway seeds

Wash the cabbage and shred it finely; salt lightly, then add the apple. Prepare a marinade with the salad oil, water, lemon juice and caraway seeds, and let the cabbage steep in it for about 1 hour. Drain well before serving.

Rice, Celery and Apple Salad

2 oz. (*55 g*) long-grain rice
salt
4 sticks of celery, chopped
2 pimientos, chopped
2 apples, cored and chopped
2 tbsps. (*30 ml*) French dressing
mustard and cress

Cook the rice in boiling salted water; drain and rinse several times in cold water, to remove as much starch as possible. When cold, add the chopped vegetables and fruit, pour the dressing over and toss lightly with a fork. Scatter with mustard and cress.

Rice and Meat Salad

1 oz. (*25 g*) long-grain rice
salt
1 tbsp. (*15 ml*) French dressing
2 sticks of celery, chopped
1 small can of chopped ham and pork, diced
1 small green pepper, finely chopped
lettuce

Cook the rice in boiling salted water until tender; drain and rinse thoroughly. When cool, add all the ingredients and toss lightly in the dressing. Serve on lettuce.

Rice, Pimiento and Tomato Salad

2 oz. (*55 g*) long-grain rice
salt
2 pimientos (red peppers)
2 tomatoes
½ an onion, skinned and chopped
French dressing
1 tbsp. (*15 ml*) chopped parsley

Wash the rice and cook in boiling salted water until the grains are tender. Meanwhile, cut up the pimientos and tomatoes and add them to the cooled rice, together with the onion. Add the dressing and parsley and mix very thoroughly, to combine all the ingredients. Chill.

Salade Anna

Peel and segment 2 oranges and 2 grapefruit and place on a lettuce base. Add 4 oz. (115 g) seeded grapes. Top with some cheese dressing, and sprinkle with chopped walnuts.

Salade Niçoise

½ lb. (225 g) ripe tomatoes	lemon rind
½ small cucumber, thinly sliced	3 black olives, halved and shredded
salt and black pepper	garlic flavoured French dressing
1 tbsp. (15 ml) chopped parsley	4 anchovy fillets (optional)

Scald and skin the tomatoes and cut into slices. Lay tomato and cucumber slices in alternate rows on a dish, season well and sprinkle with chopped parsley. Grate lemon rind over, scatter the olives over the top and season again. Spoon the dressing over. Split each anchovy fillet in half and arrange lattice fashion on top of the salad.

Salade Royale

Place some diced apples and sliced chicory on a lettuce base. Garnish with sliced red peppers; add French dressing.

Shrimp Mint Salad

½ a cucumber	7-oz. (198-g) can of shrimps, drained
chopped mint	lemon dressing
7-oz. (198-g) can of chopped ham and pork, diced	lettuce

Divide the cucumber in half and cut into Julienne strips. Mix with the mint, ham and shrimps, add the lemon dressing and toss. Chill, then serve on lettuce.

Sunshine Salad

Toss together some finely shredded white cabbage, finely shredded carrots and finely chopped pineapple, with a little oil, lemon juice and seasoning.

Spring Salad

On a bed of lettuce place equal quantities of watercress and diced pickled beetroot. Add chopped olives, and serve with French dressing.

Sweet and Sour Cucumber Salad

¼ pint (150 ml) white vinegar	½ a cucumber, thinly sliced
¼ pint (150 ml) water	1 stick of celery, thinly sliced
2–3 sprigs of dill	1 carrot, thinly sliced
4–5 saccharin tablets	
1 onion, skinned and sliced	

Mix together the vinegar, water and dill, bring to the boil for 5 minutes and strain; add the sweetener to taste. Layer the vegetables on a dish and pour the boiling mixture over. Cover and refrigerate. Serve cold in individual dishes.

Sweet Pepper Salad

Take an equal quantity of red and green peppers and wash them thoroughly. Cut them in halves and remove all the seeds, then cut the flesh into very fine strips and toss these in French dressing combined with 1 tbsp. (15 ml) chopped parsley.

Sweet Slaw Salad

8 oz. (225 g) white cabbage, finely chopped	1 orange, peeled and segmented
2 red-skinned apples, cored and diced	French dressing
	mustard and cress to garnish
4 oz. (115 g) grapes, halved	

Toss all the ingredients together with the dressing, and top with mustard and cress.

Salad Tomatoes

4 large tomatoes (or 8 medium-sized)	1 medium-sized carrot, shredded
4 oz. (115 g) cottage cheese	1 tbsp. (15 ml) diced cucumber
chopped fresh chives	salt and pepper

Halve the tomatoes and scoop out the pulp, reserving it. Mix together the cheese, chives, carrot and cucumber. Season to taste and blend together with a little of the tomato pulp. Pile into the tomato halves and chill thoroughly.

Tomato Baskets

Halve some firm tomatoes and scoop out the pulp. Fill each half with a few green peas, 1 or 2 small spring onions, a young carrot, shredded, a leaf of lettuce heart, shredded, and sprigs of cress, etc. Put some crisp lettuce leaves on individual dishes, sprinkle with French dressing, and place one of the Tomato Baskets on each.

Tossed Winter Slaw

1 close cabbage heart	1 tbsp. (*15 ml*)
1 dessert apple	chopped chives
2–3 carrots	2 tbsps. (*30 ml*)
1 oz. (*25 g*) chopped nuts	French dressing

Shred the cabbage heart very finely, chopping it crossways if necessary. Add the rest of the ingredients, finely chopped or grated as convenient, blend with the French dressing and mix well.

Waldorf Salad

Mix some diced apple and cut-up celery with mayonnaise or French dressing. Arrange on lettuce leaves, garnish with grapefruit segments and stoned grapes and sprinkle the whole with some roughly chopped walnuts.

Whirligig Salad

2 large ripe apples	8 oz. (*225 g*) cottage
2 tsps. (*10 ml*) lemon juice	cheese
2 grapefruit, seeded and segmented	1 tbsp. (*15 ml*) raisins parsley to decorate

Slice the cored but unpeeled apples and sprinkle with lemon juice to keep them white. Arrange the apple and the grapefruit segments in a circle on a plate. Pile the cottage cheese in the centre, sprinkle with raisins and decorate with parsley.

White Salad Platter

Break some raw cauliflower into small florets, slice peeled cucumber very finely and cut onions and celery finely. Arrange in a dish, sprinkle with French dressing.

Cheese Dressing

4 oz. (*115 g*) cottage cheese	juice of ½ a lemon salt and pepper

Combine the ingredients and sieve or blend until smooth and creamy. Adjust the seasoning. If the lemon is very acid, add 1 or 2 drops of liquid sweetener.

Garlic Dressing

2 pimientos (a 3¼-oz., *92-g*, can)	2 tbsps. (*30 ml*) white vinegar
2 tbsps. (*30 ml*) salad oil	1 clove of garlic, skinned and crushed

Sieve or blend the pimientos. Beat in the oil, vinegar and garlic.

Lemon Dressing

Mix together 1 tsp. (5 ml) soy sauce and the juice of 1 lemon, with liquid sweetener to taste.

Lemon Chive Dressing

8 oz. (*225 g*) cottage cheese	salt and pepper
1 tbsp. (*15 ml*) PLJ	1 tbsp. (*15 ml*) chopped chives
1 tbsp. (*15 ml*) salad oil	

Sieve or blend the cheese, then add the remaining ingredients. Chill before using.

Tarragon Dressing

1 egg yolk	sweetening tablets,
1 tbsp. (*15 ml*) tarragon vinegar	crushed freshly ground pepper
2 tbsps. (*30 ml*) fat-free yoghurt	and salt

Mix together the egg, vinegar and yoghurt, cook over hot water until thick and add sweetening tablets to taste; cool. Adjust the seasoning, blending in a little extra yoghurt if the flavour is too strong.

Mexicalli Soup (see page 107), Open Sandwich (see page 154)

Fruit desserts and drinks

Fruits are valuable as a food because they not only contain essential vitamins and minerals, but also furnish bulk. Except for bananas and avocados, most fruits have a high water content and are low in fat. They are not a good source of protein, and carbohydrates are present in the the form of sugars and cellulose.

A basket of some attractive fresh fruit is welcome at any meal.

Buying and Storing

Highly perishable fruits, such as berries, should be bought and used on the same day and should not be washed until about to be used. Bananas, melons and pears can be bought before they are fully ripe and allowed to ripen at room temperature. Apples, oranges and grapefruit can be bought in reasonable quantity and stored in a cool, dry place.

Apple Crumble

1 lb. (*450 g*) apples, thinly sliced	4 oz. (*115 g*) plain flour
4 saccharin tablets, crushed	a pinch of salt
	2 oz. (*55 g*) butter

Oven temperature: 400°F., 200°C., mark 6
Place the apples in a baking dish and sprinkle them with the crushed tablets. Mix together the remaining dry ingredients and rub in the butter until the mixture resembles fine breadcrumbs, then sprinkle over the fruit. Bake for about 45 minutes. (Serves 3–4)
Note: 1 oz. (25 g) of the flour may be replaced by 1 oz. (25 g) dried milk powder.

Apple Soufflé
(*see picture right*)

2 lb. (*900 g*) cooking apples	5 oz. (*140 g*) natural fat-free yoghurt
2 eggs, separated	2 level tbsps. (*30 ml*) gelatine
juice of 1 lemon	
6 saccharin tablets	2 tbsps. (*30 ml*) water

Slice the apples and cook in a very little water, then strain off the juice and sieve; add the beaten egg yolks and cook for 1–2 minutes. Add the lemon juice and sweeten to taste. Cool, then blend in the yoghurt. Dissolve the gelatine in the water and add to the apple. Beat the egg whites until stiff and fold into the mixture, pour into a prepared 6-inch (15-cm) soufflé dish and leave to set. (Serves 4–6)

Apple Soufflé

Chilled Meat Loaf (see page 146), Roast Chicken Drumsticks, Open Sandwiches (see page 154)

Apple Whip

large can of
  evaporated milk
1 pint (*600 ml*) apple
  purée
pinch ground cloves

pinch ground
  coriander
finely grated rind of 1
  lemon

Beat the milk until thick and doubled in volume. Blend in the purée, spices and lemon rind. Pour into a serving dish or individual glasses. (Serves 4–6)

Baked Apples

4 large, even-sized
  cooking apples

1 oz. (*25 g*) butter
a little water

Oven temperature: 400°F., 200°C., mark 6
Wash the apples, remove the cores and with a sharp knife-point cut round the middle of each apple, piercing the skin only. Place in an ovenproof dish, put a piece of butter on top and pour round enough water to cover the bottom of the dish. Cover and bake for about 40 minutes, until the apples are soft but not collapsed. (Serves 4)

Apricot Creams

(see colour picture facing page 112)

1½ lb. (*700 g*) fresh
  apricots
¼ pint (*150 ml*) water
4–5 saccharin tablets
1 egg

½ pint (*300 ml*) milk
4 level tsps. (*20 ml*)
  gelatine
¼ pint (*140 g*) natural
  fat-free yoghurt

Stew the apricots in the water until tender and add sweetener to taste. Strain off the juice and sieve the fruit. Make a custard with the egg and milk, mix with the puréed fruit and allow to cool. Dissolve the gelatine in the fruit juice in the usual way. Fold the yoghurt into the purée, stir in the gelatine, pour the mixture into individual sundae glasses and chill. (Serves 4)

Apricot and Pineapple Whip

(see colour picture facing page 208)

2 lb. (*900 g*) fresh
  apricots
1½ pints (*900 ml*)
  unsweetened pine-

apple juice
3 level tbsps. (*45 ml*)
  powdered gelatine
4 tbsps. (*60 ml*) water

Simmer the apricots in the pineapple juice until tender, then chill well. Sieve or blend to combine thoroughly. Dissolve the gelatine in the water in the usual way and stir into the fruit mixture. Pour into glasses and leave to set. (Serves 8)

Baked Apple Surprise

2 medium-sized
  bananas, peeled
1 tbsp. (*15 ml*) lemon
  juice
¼ level tsp. (*1.25 ml*)
  grated nutmeg

artificial sweetener
a dash of salt
6 medium-sized
  cooking apples
¼ pint (*150 ml*)
  orange juice

Oven temperature: 375°F., 190°C., mark 5
Put the bananas into a medium-sized bowl, mash them with a fork and mix with the lemon juice, nutmeg and salt. Add sweetener to taste. Wash and core the apples and place in a large baking dish. Fill the centres with the banana mixture and pour the orange juice over them. Bake for 1 hour, or until tender, basting occasionally with the orange juice. Cool slightly and serve warm, or chill and serve cold, topped with the orange sauce. (Serves 6)

Apricot Sponge

(see colour picture facing page 145)

2 large eggs,
  separated
1 level tbsp. (*15 ml*)
  caster sugar
1 tbsp. (*15 ml*) cold
  water
3 saccharin tablets,
  crushed

2 level tbsps. (*30 ml*)
  plain flour
2 level tsps. (*10 ml*)
  cornflour
½ lb. (*225 g*) apricots,
  stewed and hot

Oven temperature: 375°F., 190°C., mark 5
Beat the egg whites until foamy, add the sugar and beat until stiff. Beat the egg yolks and water together until stiff and add the saccharin. Fold the yolks into the whites, then gently fold in the dry ingredients. Turn the mixture into a lightly greased 2-pint (1.2-litre) ring tin and bake for 18–20 minutes. Turn out, and fill the centre with the hot apricots. (Serves 4) If serving the sweet cold, allow the cake to cool before piling the cooled fruit into the centre.

Banana Sherbet

3 bananas, peeled
¼ pint (*150 ml*) lemon
  juice
½ pint (*300 ml*) low-
  fat milk
1 pint (*600 ml*)
  unsweetened orange
  juice
artificial sweetener

Mash or blend the bananas with the lemon juice. Add the milk and orange juice, with sweetener to taste. Freeze for 1 hour, then turn the mixture into a bowl and beat until smooth. Pour back into the tray and freeze until firm—overnight if necessary. Spoon into glasses and decorate with a twist of orange or lemon peel. (Serves 4)

Banana Nut Creams

(see picture right)

4 bananas
juice of ½ a lemon
½ pint (*300 ml*)
  evaporated milk
liquid sweetener
2 oz. (*55 g*) almonds,
  chopped and
  browned

Peel the bananas, slice off about 2 inches (5 cm) and brush the slices with lemon juice; mash the rest of the bananas with the remaining lemon juice. Whisk the evaporated milk until thick. Fold in the banana pulp, add sweetener to taste, put into sundae glasses and top with the chopped almonds and the lemon-brushed banana slices. (Serves 4)

Blackberry Whip

1 lb. (*450 g*) black-
  berries
½ lb. (*225 g*) cooking
  apples, peeled and
  sliced
¼ pint (*150 ml*) water
4 level tsps. (*20 ml*)
  gelatine
artificial sweetener
3 tbsps. (*45 ml*) hot
  water
2 egg whites
desiccated coconut

Cook the blackberries and apples with the water until tender, then sieve. Add the gelatine and sweetener to taste and dissolve. Set aside to get cold and thick, but not become set. Whisk until thick and creamy, then fold in the stiffly beaten egg whites. Pour into individual glasses and sprinkle with coconut. (Serves 4)

Crispy Top

1½ lb. (*700 g*) apples,
  peeled, cored and
  sliced
2 oz. (*55 g*) butter
2 oz. (*55 g*)
  Demerara sugar
2 tbsps. (*30 ml*) corn-
  flakes

Oven temperature: 350°F., 180°C., mark 4
Cook the apples to a pulp with the minimum of water, adding a little more as required, then put them in an oven-proof dish. Melt the butter, stir in the sugar and cereal and cover the apples with this mixture. Bake for 20–30 minutes, till the top is brown. (Serves 4)

Baked Custard

2 eggs
¾ pint (*375 ml*) milk,
  scalded
artificial sweetener
vanilla essence
¼ level tsp. (*1.25 ml*)
  ground nutmeg

Oven temperature: 350°F., 180°C., mark 4
Beat the eggs lightly, add the milk, sweetener and ¼ tsp. (1.25 ml) essence and stir to combine thoroughly. Pour the mixture into 4 cups and sprinkle with nutmeg. Place in a pan of hot water and bake for ½–¾ hour, until firm when tested. Turn out, and serve hot or cold. (Serves 4)

Banana Nut Creams

Ginger Fruit Salad

(see colour picture facing page 176)

2 apples, cored but
  not peeled
2 apricots, peeled
1 orange, peeled and
  segmented
1 bottle of low-calorie
  ginger ale
2 bananas
2 tbsps. (*30 ml*) lemon
  juice
2 oz. (*55 g*) green
  grapes

Dice the apples and apricots, add the orange segments and ginger ale and leave to stand. Slice the bananas and mix with the lemon juice and grapes. Mix all the fruits and juices together and serve in individual glasses. (Serves 4)

Grape Jelly

(see colour picture facing page 112)

4 level tsps. (*20 ml*)
  powdered gelatine
¼ pint (*150 ml*)
  boiling water
¾ pint (*375 ml*)
  unsweetened grape
  juice
green colouring
½ lb. (*225 g*) white
  grapes, peeled
8 oz. (*225 g*) cottage
  cheese
½ pint (*300 ml*) fat-
  free yoghurt

Dissolve the gelatine in the water and add the grape juice, with a few drops of the colouring. Pour into 6 glasses. Divide the grapes between the glasses and leave tilted in a cool place to set. Blend or sieve the cheese until smooth. Fold in the yoghurt and top up the glasses. Chill. (Serves 6)

Orange Mousse

2 oranges
3 eggs, separated
artificial sweetener to
  taste
1 level tsp. (*5 ml*)
  powdered gelatine
tangerine to garnish

Grate the rind of the oranges and squeeze out the juice. Add the egg yolks and sweetener to the juice and whisk over boiling water until thick and fluffy (15–20 minutes), then leave to cool. Meanwhile dissolve the gelatine in 1 tbsp. boiling water, and keep in a warm place while whisking the egg whites very stiffly. When the yolk mixture is nearly cold, stir in the grated orange rind and dissolved gelatine and

196

lastly fold in the whisked egg whites. Turn the mixture into a bowl and serve cold, decorated with tangerine pieces. (Serves 4)

Honeycomb Castles

1 pint (*600 ml*) milk
2 eggs, separated
4 level tsps. (*20 ml*)
  gelatine
2 tbsps. (*30 ml*) hot
  water
vanilla essence
artificial sweetener

Heat the milk without boiling. Beat the egg yolks and pour on the hot milk, stirring. Strain into a double saucepan and heat until the custard thickens. Add the gelatine, dissolved in the hot water, and a few drops of essence, with sweetener to taste. Carefully fold in the stiffly beaten egg whites, and pour into wetted castle pudding tins; turn out when set. (Serves 4)

Peach and Orange Flan

6-inch (*15-cm*) short
  crust flan case
  (allow 4 oz., *100 g*,
  shortcrust pastry)
1 level tsp. (*5 ml*)
  powdered gelatine
1 tbsp. (*15 ml*) water
¼ pint (*150 ml*)
  orange juice
2 oranges
4 peaches

Make the flan case in the usual way. Dissolve the gelatine in the water. Add the orange juice and leave to set to the consistency of egg white. Peel and segment the oranges, removing all pith and membrane. Peel and slice the peaches. Arrange the fruit in the flan case and glaze with the thickened fruit juice. (Serves 4)

Porcupine Pudding

1 oz. (*25 g*) butter
2 level tbsps. (*30 ml*)
  sugar
1 pint (*600 ml*) milk
1½ level tbsps. (*22.5
  ml*) cornflour
1 tsp. (*5 ml*) coffee
  essence
browned shredded
  almonds to decorate
  the pudding

Melt the butter and sugar in a saucepan and heat, stirring gently, until a rich golden-brown in colour. Remove at once from the heat, allow to cool slightly, then add ½ pint (*300 ml*) of the milk and stir over a gentle heat until smooth. Stir in the cornflour, blended with the remainder of the milk, bring to the boil, stirring, and cook for 2 minutes, still stirring. Now add the coffee essence, mix well and pour into a wetted jelly mould. Leave to set. To serve, turn out, and stick all over with shredded almonds. (Serves 4)

Plum and Orange Salad

1 lb. (*450 g*) red
  plums
2 oranges
liquid sweetener

Stone and slice the plums. Add the juice of the oranges and the finely grated rind of half an orange. Add a few drops of sweetener and leave the salad in a cool place for at least 2–3 hours before serving. (Serves 4)

Queen of Puddings

2 eggs, separated
1 pint (*600 ml*) milk,
  scalded
saccharin tablets
vanilla essence
2 oz. (*55 g*) soft white
  breadcrumbs
½ lb. (*225 g*) apricots,
  cooked

Oven temperature: 350°F., 180°C., mark 4
Lightly beat the egg yolks and stir in the milk; add crushed saccharin to taste, ½ tsp. (2.5 ml) vanilla essence and the breadcrumbs. Turn the mixture into a baking dish, place in a pan of water and bake for ¾–1 hour. Place the apricots in a layer on top of the custard. Beat the egg whites with 4 crushed saccharin tablets until stiff, and pile on to the apricots. Return the dish to the oven immediately and cook for 10 minutes, until the meringue is lightly browned. (Serves 4)

Raspberry Crème

Blend together 1 pint (600 ml) fat-free yoghurt and 1 lb. (450 g) raspberries. Adjust the sweetness by adding crushed saccharin tablets, or liquid sweetener. Serve in individual glasses, topped with a few raspberries. (Serves 4)

Raspberry Delight

(see colour picture facing page 112)

Divide ¾ lb. (340 g) of raspberries between 4 glasses. Pour 1 tbsp. (15 ml) of orange juice into each glass, and chill. Serve decorated with mint leaves. (Serves 4)

Raspberry Whip

4 level tsps. (*20 ml*)
  gelatine
½ pint (*300 ml*) low-
  fat milk
4 eggs, separated
vanilla essence
artificial sweetener
1 lb. (*450 g*) frozen or
  fresh raspberries

Mix the gelatine with the milk and heat, then blend in the lightly beaten egg yolks; return the mixture to the heat and stir until beginning to thicken. Add ½ tsp. vanilla essence and sweetener to taste, then cool. Sieve the raspberries and blend into the custard. Beat the egg whites until stiff and fold into the fruit mixture. Pour into individual glasses and leave to set. (Serves 4–6)

Rhubarb Almond Crème

1 lb. (*450 g*) rhubarb
¼ pint (*150 ml*) water
artificial sweetener
1 pint (*600 ml*) fat-
  free yoghurt
toasted almonds to
  decorate

Cut the rhubarb into ½-inch (1.25-cm) lengths and simmer gently in the water for 1–2 minutes, until tender but not mushy. Add the sweetener to taste and cool. Blend with the yoghurt and serve in individual glasses, topped with toasted almonds. (Serves 4)

Spanish Cream

(see colour picture facing page 112)

1 pint (*600 ml*) milk
1 level tbsp. (*15 ml*)
  gelatine
3 eggs, separated
6 saccharin tablets
½ tsp. (*2.5 ml*) vanilla
  essence

Blend 2 tbsps. milk with the gelatine and dissolve over hot water. Lightly beat the egg yolks with the remaining milk and heat gently, stirring continuously (do not boil). Remove from the heat and add the gelatine mixture, saccharin tablets and vanilla. Mix thoroughly, then cool. Beat the egg whites until stiff, fold into the custard, pour the mixture into 4 glasses and leave to set. (Serves 4)

197

Variation

Replace the vanilla essence by coffee essence.

Snow Peaks

(see colour picture facing page 209)

3 egg whites	¼ pint (*140 g*) fat-
6 saccharin tablets,	free yoghurt
crushed	1 lb. (*450 g*) straw-
3 level tsps. (*15 ml*)	berries, sliced
granulated sugar	
1 pint (*600 ml*) apple	
purée	

Oven temperature: 325°F., 170°C., mark 3

Beat the egg whites until stiff and beat in the sweeteners. Pipe onto an oiled baking sheet to form 8 meringues and bake for about ½ hour until crisp. Cool. Blend together the apple purée and yoghurt and lightly fold in the strawberries. Pour into individual dishes and top with the meringue. (Serves 8)

Spiced Pear Grill

1 lb. (*450 g*) dessert	a small piece of
pears, peeled and	cinnamon
sliced	artificial sweetener
¼ pint (*150 ml*) water	2 oz. (*55 g*) cornflakes
finely grated rind of ½	1 oz. (*25 g*) butter
a lemon	

Cook the pears in the water with the lemon rind and the cinnamon. Add sweetener to taste. Place in a shallow flameproof dish, sprinkle with cornflakes and dot with butter. Place under a moderate grill for 5 minutes. (Serves 4)

Strawberry Cream

(see colour picture facing page 177)

1½ lb. (*700 g*) fresh	¼ pint (*140 g*) fat-
ripe strawberries	free yoghurt
¼ lb. (*115 g*) cottage	liquid sweetener
cheese	

Divide the strawberries between 6 glasses. Beat together the cottage cheese and yoghurt, adding sweetener to taste. Pour over the strawberries and chill. (Serves 6)

Strawberries in Burgundy

Divide ¾ lb. (340 g) strawberries between 4 individual glasses and sprinkle 1 tbsp. (15 ml) Burgundy or claret in each glass. Cool in the refrigerator for 1 hour, and serve decorated with a sprig of mint leaves. (Serves 4)

Strawberry Sponge

4 level tsps. (*20 ml*)	1 egg white
gelatine	3 tbsps. (*45 ml*)
¼ pint (*150 ml*) water	evaporated milk
½ pint (*300 ml*) straw-	
berry purée	

Dissolve the gelatine in the water in the usual way. Add to the puréed fruit. When cold and of the consistency of egg white, add the egg white and evaporated milk and beat until foamy. Divide between 4 glasses. When set, decorate with small whole strawberries. (Serves 4)

Summer Fruit Sundae

(see picture below)

1 tbsp. (*15 ml*)	2 eggs, separated
powdered gelatine	½ pint (*300 ml*)
3 tbsps. (*45 ml*) cold	cultured buttermilk
water	artificial sweetener
1 pint (*600 ml*) fruit	
pulp	

Sprinkle the gelatine over the water, leave to swell, then dissolve over hot

Summer Fruit Sundae

water. Add to the fruit pulp, with the beaten egg yolks and buttermilk. Add artificial sweetener to taste. Pour into freezing trays and freeze for ½ hour, until partially set. Beat vigorously and add the beaten egg whites; return the mixture to the freezer trays and freeze. Serve it in individual glasses. (Serves 6–8)

Egg Custard Sauce

1 egg	artificial sweetener
½ pint (*300 ml*) milk, scalded	vanilla essence

Beat the egg lightly and stir in the milk. Return the mixture to the heat and—stirring continuously—bring almost to boiling point. Remove from the heat, add sweetener to taste and a few drops of essence; cool before serving. Serve with stewed fruit, etc.

Sweet Orange Sauce

½ pint (*300 ml*) orange juice	2 level tsps. (*10 ml*) cornflour
½ oz. (*15 g*) butter	artificial sweetener

Heat the orange juice and butter together. Mix the cornflour to a smooth paste with a little water, add the orange juice and stir continuously until the mixture thickens. Allow to continue cooking for 1–2 minutes and then add sweetener to taste. Serve hot or cold, with such things as baked bananas.

Summer Party Punch
(*see colour picture facing page 113*)

2 pints (*1 litre*) cold tea, strained	liquid saccharin
1 pint (*600 ml*) unsweetened pineapple juice	4 pints (*2 litres*) soda water, chilled
1 lb. (*450 g*) strawberries, sieved	fruit kabobs (see below)

Mix together the tea, pineapple juice and strawberries, then chill. Add the chilled soda water and saccharin to taste just before serving the punch in tall glasses, each topped with a fruit kabob. (Makes about 20 ¼-pint, 150-ml, servings.)
Fruit Kabobs: On cocktail sticks impale cubes of green-skinned eating apple, alternating with pineapple cubes; top each off with a strawberry.

Hot Egg Nog

Place 1 egg in a tall heat-resisting glass and beat it lightly with a fork. Heat ½ pint (300 ml) milk and when almost boiling, pour on to the egg, stirring all the time. Flavour if desired with vanilla, rum or brandy. Adjust the sweetening with saccharin. (Serves 1)

PART FIVE

Slimming with the freezer

Freezers are gradually becoming very much more widely used. They are a boon to the frantic mother, busy housewife and working wife, to those who entertain frequently and to those who need to budget carefully. What more useful piece of equipment could there be for the potential slimmer? An entire slimming campaign can be planned, prepared and frozen down eliminating all necessity for delays and excuses in weak moments. Simply take the food from the freezer, cook and eat it!

Our recipes cater for family situations but if planning a solitary campaign just pack and freeze in single serving portions.

Packaging: wrapping methods

Successful freezing depends on careful packaging. The best prepared food if incorrectly packaged will quickly become a disaster. Freezing converts water to ice within the cell structure of the food and this is the state that must be maintained. Careless packaging allows the moisture to be drawn from the cells causing dehydration and freezer burn, with subsequent loss of nutrients.

Solids must be packaged tightly to expel as much air as possible—aluminium foil fits where it touches and is therefore ideal for many foods. If filling a rigid container with insufficient food then the vacant space must be filled with crumpled waxed, non-stick or freezer paper before sealing. When filling a polythene bag, remove excess air by using a straw to suck out the surplus.

Liquids are the reverse. A headspace of at least $\frac{1}{2}$ in. (1 cm) is essential to allow for the natural expansion during freezing. A combination of liquid and solids as with stews and casseroles needs care. The solids should be completely submerged in the liquid and a small headspace of $\frac{1}{2}$ in. (1 cm) allowed.

Sealing and labelling methods

PACKAGING	SEALING	LABELLING
Polythene bags	Plastic covered wire, twist ties, or heat sealing	Write clearly the contents, date of freezing, number of portions, and perhaps re-heating time. Tie clearly marked labels to the bags
Self-cling film (double)	Self sealing	Waterproof labels
Foil, non-stick or waxed paper	Seal with freezer tape	Waterproof labels
Waxed containers	Freezer tape	Waterproof felt pen
Tupperware-type plastic containers	No additional seal required	As above

Golden rules for freezing

Whatever kind of food you're dealing with, these general notes apply.

1. Always start with good-quality foods and freeze them at peak freshness. Food can only come out of the freezer as good as you put it in.
2. Keep handling to a minimum and make sure everything is scrupulously clean. Freezing doesn't kill bacteria and germs.
3. Pay special attention to packaging and sealing. Exposure to air and moisture damage frozen foods.
4. Cool food rapidly if it's been cooked or blanched; never put anything hot—or even warm—into your freezer.
5. Freeze as quickly as possible, and in small quantities.
6. Freeze in the coldest part of the freezer, and don't pack the food to be frozen too closely together—spread it out until it is frozen.
7. Transfer newly added items to the main part of the cabinet once they've been frozen.
8. Remember to return the switch from 'fast freeze' to 'normal' once newly added foods have been frozen, i.e., after about 24 hours.
9. Maintain a steady storage temperature of $-18°C.$ ($0°F.$), and don't do anything that will cause temperatures within the freezer to keep fluctuating.
10. Label and date food so that you can ensure a good rotation of stock. Ideally, keep a record and tick off items as you eat them, then you can tell at a glance which supplies are getting low.

11. Defrost the freezer at a time when stocks are low, and if possible on a cold day.

12. Be prepared for emergencies. Make sure you know what steps to take in case of a breakdown or power cut.

WHEN YOU'RE FREEZING COOKED FOODS

1. When preparing a dish for the freezer, keep a light hand with the seasoning.

2. Use shallow rather than deep dishes.

3. As already directed above, cool everything as rapidly as possible, and freeze at once.

4. To ensure best results, don't keep cooked dishes in the freezer for more than two months, unless otherwise stated.

SPECIAL WARNING: Remember, polythene bags or film must always be removed before food is re-heated.

Plate meals

A little extra food can be prepared as part of the family meal and put to one side to be plated up, frozen and stored until required. Any ovenproof plates can be used or 8-in. (20-cm) foil plates. Seal by double wrapping in foil—it is important to keep an even density of wrapping over the entire plate—then label giving entire menu and date. Meals will keep satisfactorily for up to 3 months. To use start from a cold oven set at 400°F., 200°C., mark 6 and heat for 40 minutes. If the oven has been previously heated then reduce the cooking time by 10 minutes.

Suitable foods for plate meals:

ROAST MEAT: Freeze in slices of even thickness. Any cut of meat or poultry, with its trimming, in gravy or suitable sauce, freezes well—lamb with mint sauce; pork with apple sauce etc.

BRAISING STEAK: Prepare in the usual way but undercook slightly to allow for re-heating time.

SAUSAGES: Grill these first or dry bake; plate up with a tomato or barbecue sauce.

MIXED GRILL: Chops, sausages, lambs' liver, or lambs' kidneys can all be used. Grill to brown before plating up.

POTATOES: Most potatoes, except chips or other fried variations freeze well but must be fully cooked before plating up.

PEAS: Plate up while still frozen.

FRESH GREEN VEGETABLES: Unfortunately these are not suitable as they tend to dry out and burn on the plate.

ROOT VEGETABLES: Good, especially if not diced too small.

ONIONS: Button onions are good.

Mixed Grill for One

1 lamb chump chop	3 oz. (*85 g*) creamed
1 chipolata sausage	potato
1 bacon, rasher,	2 mushrooms
rolled	2 oz. (*50 g*) frozen
1 large firm tomato	peas
salt and pepper	

To make: Place the chop, sausage and bacon roll on the grill rack and cook until the sausage is swollen and the chop well browned. Place the meats on a suitable plate. Cut the tomato in half and season with salt and pepper; add to the plate. Place the potato in an even thickness on the plate. Sauté the mushrooms in a little oil—$\frac{1}{2}$ tsp. (2.5 ml)—drain well and add to the plate. Add the peas still frozen.

To pack and freeze: Cover the complete meal with a double layer of foil. Freeze rapidly until firm.

To use: Loosen the foil, but leave it lightly covering the meal. Bake from frozen at 400°F., 200°C. (mark 6) for about 40 minutes.

Slimmers' menus—with the help of your freezer

Lunch/Supper

Tomato Soup*
Apple-Tuna Salad
Crispbread

Liver Terrine*
2 thin slices Toast
Green Salad; Tomatoes

Cheese and Ham Cocottes*
Toast Fingers
Apple

Spicy Aubergine*
Slice of Cold Meat
Fresh Fruit

Cheese and Bacon Quiche*
Cole Slaw Bowl

Oeufs à la Maison*
Celery Sticks
Fresh Fruit

Cheese and Leek Soup
Ratatouille Salad*

Stuffed Tomatoes*
Haricot Verts
Fresh Fruit

Ham and Celery au Gratin*
Endive and Tomato Salad
Fresh Fruit

Cabbage Parcels*
Gravy
Bread Roll; Cheese
Fresh Fruit

Tuna Flan*
Tossed Green Salad

Kedgeree*
Apple and Celery Salad

Vegetable Soup
Farmhouse Pâté*
Toast Fingers

Thatched Haddock*
Leek and Lemon Salad
Fresh Fruit

Dinner

Barbecued Spare Ribs
Small Jacket Potato
Leeks

Californian Trout*
Green Beans
Fresh Fruit

Beef Roll Casserole*
Winter Fruit Salad*

Chicken Goulash*
Noodles
Courgettes

Hamburgers with Spicy
    Tomato Sauce*
Broccoli
Creamed Potatoes

Curry Fish Fry*
Brussels Sprouts
Apple Whip

Moussaka*
Tossed Green Salad
Baked Apple

Cinnamon Pork Parcels*
Baked Potato
Broccoli

Cod with Mushrooms
Carrots
Green Beans

Noisettes of Lamb*
Baked Tomato
Creamed Potato
Baked Apple

Casseroled Liver Balls*
Small Jacket Potato
Green Beans
Plum and Orange Salad

Pork Chops with Orange and
Ginger Stuffing*

Asparagus Spears
Fresh Fruit

Chicken Tettrazini*
Dressed Green Salad
Fresh Fruit

Braised Lamb Hearts*
Creamed Potato
Cabbage

Recipes marked * are in the
following pages.

Tomato Soup

½ oz. (25 g) butter	2 tbsps. (30 ml) water
1 small onion, skinned and chopped	salt
	freshly ground pepper
	¼ pint (150 ml) milk
8-oz. (226-g) can tomatoes	

To make: Melt the butter and sauté the onion until clear. Add the tomatoes and water and cook for 2 minutes. Season well with salt and pepper. Blend or sieve.
To pack: Allow to cool. Pour into a rigid container, label and seal.
To freeze: Freeze rapidly until solid.
To use: Release the soup from the container by running cold water over the surface, then turn it into a saucepan. Heat gently stirring occasionally. Add the milk and heat to boiling point, but do not boil. (Serves 3)

Liver Terrine

1 lb. (450 g) pigs' liver	¼ pint (150 ml) thick white sauce
¼ lb. (115 g) fat bacon	salt and pepper
4 eggs, beaten	12 rashers streaky bacon, rinded
1 small clove garlic, skinned and crushed	

To make: Mince the liver and fat bacon finely, then put the mixture through the mincer again. Mix with the beaten eggs, garlic, sauce and seasoning to taste. Line a 2-pint (1.2-litre) terrine or loaf tin with the rashers, fill with the liver mixture and place in a dish containing some cold water. Bake at 325°F., 170°C., mark 3, for 2 hours. Cover the top of the liver mixture with greaseproof paper and place a weight on top. Leave for 24 hours in a cold place.
To pack and freeze: Cut into ½-inch (1.25-cm) slices, and separate them with pieces of non-stick paper. Wrap in foil then overwrap in polythene. Seal and label. Freeze rapidly until solid.
To use: Thaw in the refrigerator for approx. 3 hours. (Serves 6–8)

Cheese and Ham Cocottes

½ oz. (15 g) butter, melted	2 eggs
1 small onion, skinned and chopped	2 oz. (55 g) cooked ham, chopped
	salt and pepper
8 oz. (225 g) cottage cheese	1 tbsp. (15 ml) chopped tarragon or parsley

To make: Melt the butter and sauté the onion until clear. Beat the cottage cheese and eggs together, add the onion, ham and seasonings. Mix well. Spoon into 4 lightly greased individual ovenproof dishes.
To pack and freeze: Freeze uncovered until firm. Cover each with a disc of freezer paper and place the dishes one on top of the other. Wrap in foil then place in a polythene bag. Seal and label. Replace in the freezer.
To use: Unwrap and place in a single layer in a pan with a little cold water. Bake at 375°F., 190°C., mark 5 for 40 minutes. Serve sprinkled with a little chopped tarragon or parsley. (Serves 4)

Spicy Aubergine

2 tsps. (*10 ml*) oil
1 small onion,
  skinned and
  chopped
1 small clove garlic,
  skinned and
  crushed

1 aubergine, peeled
  and diced
8 tbsps. (*120 ml*)
  tomato juice
1 level tsp. (*5 ml*)
  tomato paste
salt and pepper

To make: Heat the oil and sauté the onion until clear. Add the garlic and diced aubergine. Fry for 4 minutes. Mix together the tomato juice, tomato paste and seasonings. Add to the vegetables and cook for a further 2 minutes.

To pack and freeze: Turn the mixture into a rigid foil container and allow to cool. Seal and label. Freeze rapidly until solid.

To use: Cook at 350°F., 180°C., mark 4 for 30 minutes, or turn into a small saucepan and heat gently until piping hot. Serve sprinkled with a little grated cheese. (Serves 2)

Cheese and Bacon Quiche

6 oz. (*150 g*) short-
  crust pastry
6 lean bacon rashers,
  rinded and chopped
2 large eggs
¼ pint (*150 ml*) milk

salt
freshly ground black
  pepper
4 oz. (*115 g*) Cheddar
  cheese, grated
chopped parsley

To make: Set an 8-inch (20-cm) flan ring on a baking sheet and line with the prepared pastry. Leave in the refrigerator while preparing the filling.

Fry the bacon until the fat runs, then allow to cool. Beat together the eggs, milk and seasonings. Stir in the bacon, cheese and chopped parsley. Spoon into the pastry case.

To pack and freeze: Put in the freezer until firm. When frozen cover the top with a round of non-stick paper. Place on a large sheet of foil and remove the flan ring. Parcel up, overwrap in polythene. Seal and label.

To use: Unwrap and place on a baking sheet. Replace the flan ring, cover loosely with foil and bake from frozen at 375°F., 190°C. (mark 5) for 45 minutes. Remove foil and cook for a further 15 minutes until golden. (Serves 4)

206

Oeufs à la Maison

4-oz. (*113-g*) pkt.
  frozen peas
1 onion
4 tomatoes
pinch garlic salt

freshly ground black
  pepper
3 large eggs
½ pint (*300 ml*) milk

To make: Cook the peas according to the directions on the packet. Skin and finely chop the onion. Peel and chop the tomatoes. Add the onion to the peas 2 minutes before the end of cooking time, drain and divide the vegetables between four individual ovenproof dishes. Season with garlic salt and pepper. Whisk the eggs and milk in a bowl and pour over the vegetables.

To pack and freeze: Place the containers on a baking tray and freeze rapidly until firm. Overwrap in polythene bags, seal and label.

To use: Remove from the polythene bags and place the dishes in a shallow dish containing ½ inch (1.25 cm) water. Cook at 350°F., 180°C., mark 4 for about 50 minutes or until set. Serve garnished with chopped parsley. (Serves 4)

Ratatouille Salad

2 aubergines
salt
3 tbsps. (*45 ml*) oil
2 onions, skinned and
  sliced finely
2 green peppers,
  sliced
1 lb. (*450 g*)
  courgettes, sliced
freshly ground black
  pepper
4 tomatoes, peeled
  and quartered
chopped parsley

For dressing:
3 tbsps. (*45 ml*) oil
1 tbsp. (*15 ml*) wine
  vinegar
1 tsp. (*5 ml*) French
  mustard
½ tsp. (*2.5 ml*)
  Worcestershire sauce
1 level tbsp. (*15 ml*)
  tomato paste
6 tbsps. (*90 ml*)
  tomato juice

To make: Slice the aubergines and sprinkle with salt. Leave to stand for 30 minutes. Drain and dry. Heat the oil and fry the aubergines, onions, peppers and courgettes, tossing them gently. Season well with salt and pepper. Cover and simmer for 30 minutes, shaking occasionally to prevent sticking. Allow to cool.

To pack and freeze: Turn the mixture

into 1 large or 4 small foil dishes. Seal, label and freeze.

To use: Allow to thaw at room temperature for 4–5 hours. Turn the salad into a serving dish and add the tomatoes. Place all the ingredients for the dressing in a screw-top jar and shake vigorously to mix. Pour over the salad vegetables, toss and allow to stand for a further ½ hour. Serve sprinkled with chopped parsley. (Serves 4)

Stuffed Tomatoes

4 large firm tomatoes	1 oz. (*25 g*) cheese,
3½-oz. (*100-g*) can	grated
tuna fish	1 tsp. (*5 ml*) chopped
1½ oz. (*40 g*) bread-	parsley
crumbs	salt and freshly
	ground black pepper

To make: Cut the tops from the tomatoes, scoop out the core and seeds and stand the cups upside down to drain. Drain and flake the tuna. Mix it with the breadcrumbs, cheese and parsley and season well with salt and pepper. Add 1–2 tsp. (5–10 ml) of the tomato juices, sufficient just to bind the mixture. Fill the tomato shells with stuffing.

To pack and freeze: Place in a shallow rigid foil container. Seal and label. Freeze in the usual way.

To use: Remove the lid and bake at 350°F., 180°C., mark 4 for 35 minutes. (Serves 4)

Ham and Celery au Gratin

6 sticks celery (each	⅓ pint (*200 ml*) milk
4 in., *10 cm*)	2 oz. (*55 g*) Cheddar
2 slices cooked ham	cheese, grated
½ oz. (*15 g*) butter	salt and freshly
2 level tbsps. (*30 ml*)	ground black pepper
flour	

To make: Place the celery in boiling water and cook for 5 minutes, then drain. Place two bundles of 3 sticks celery together and wrap in a slice of ham. Place these side by side in a foil dish. Melt the butter, stir in the flour and cook for 2 minutes. Gradually add the milk, stirring until thick and smooth. Stir in the cheese, season with salt and pepper and pour over the ham rolls. Allow to cool.

To pack and freeze: Seal the foil container, label and freeze.

To use: Place the covered foil container on a baking sheet and bake at 350°F., 180°C., mark 4 for 30 minutes. Remove the lid, raise the temperature to 400°F., 200°C., mark 6 and cook for a further 10 minutes until lightly browned. (Serves 2)

Cabbage Parcels

1 tbsp. (*15 ml*) oil	1 oz. (*25 g*) long-
1 onion, skinned and	grain rice, cooked
chopped	3 oz. (*85 g*) cheese,
1 lb. (*450 g*) minced	grated
beef	salt and pepper
1 level tbsp. (*15 ml*)	5 or 6 large Savoy
tomato paste	cabbage leaves

To make: Heat the oil and cook the onion until soft. Add the beef and cook, stirring frequently until lightly browned. Stir in the tomato paste and rice. Allow to cool before mixing in the cheese and seasoning well with salt and pepper.
Blanch the cabbage leaves for 5 minutes, refresh in cold water and drain well. If necessary, cut away the coarse stems with scissors. Divide the meat mixture between the leaves and fold the top, sides and bottom to form a square parcel.

To pack and freeze: Pack close together in a shallow rigid container. Cover, overwrap, seal and label. Freeze.

To use: Remove the overwrap and thaw overnight in the refrigerator. Place in an ovenproof dish, brush with a little oil, cover and cook at 350°F., 180°C., mark 4 for about 45 minutes. Uncover for the last 10 minutes. Serve with a savoury tomato sauce. (Serves 4)

Tuna Flan

6 oz. (*150 g*) short-	3 eggs
crust pastry	¼ pint (*150 ml*) milk
7-oz. (*198-g*) can tuna	chopped parsley
fish	

To make: Set an 8-inch (20-cm) flan ring on a baking sheet and line with the prepared pastry. Flake the tuna and spread over the pastry. Beat together the eggs and milk and season well with salt and pepper. Mix in the parsley and pour over the fish.

To pack and freeze: Put in the freezer until firm. When frozen, cover the top with a round of non-stick paper. Place on a large sheet of foil and remove the flan ring. Parcel up, overwrap in polythene, seal and label.

To use: Unwrap and place the ring on a baking sheet. Replace the flan ring, cover loosely with foil and bake from frozen at 375°F., 190°C., mark 5 for 45 minutes. Remove foil and cook for a further 15 minutes until golden.

This recipe can be used to make 4 4-inch (10-cm) individual flans—reduce cooking time by 10 minutes. (Serves 4)

Kedgeree

½ lb. (*225 g*) smoked haddock fillet	2 hard-boiled eggs, shelled and chopped
3 oz. (*85 g*) long-grain rice, freshly cooked	1 tbsp. (*15 ml*) chopped parsley
½ oz. (*15 g*) butter	pinch cayenne pepper salt oil

To make: Gently poach the fish in boiling water for 7–10 minutes until the flesh is tender. Drain, skin and flake the fish. Combine with the rice, butter, egg, parsley and seasonings. Allow to cool.

To pack and freeze: Place the kedgeree in a well oiled 1¼-pint (725-ml) foil dish or two ½-pint (300-ml) foil dishes. Seal and label. Freeze rapidly.

To use: Loosen the coverings but leave in position. Heat through in the oven at 400°F., 200°C., mark 6 for about 45 minutes, forking through occasionally. Pile into a hot serving dish and garnish with parsley sprigs and lemon wedges. (Serves 2)

Farmhouse Pâté

½ lb. (*225 g*) belly pork	freshly ground black pepper
½ lb. (*225 g*) lean veal	1 level tsp. (*5 ml*) salt pinch powdered mace
¼ lb. (*115 g*) pigs' liver	3 tbsps. (*45 ml*) dry white wine
¼ lb. (*115 g*) fat bacon	small clove garlic, skinned and crushed

To make: Finely mince the pork, veal and liver 2 or 3 times. Cut 2 oz. (55 g) of the fat bacon into small dice. Add to the minced meats. Season with the pepper, salt, mace, wine and garlic. Blend thoroughly and leave to stand for 2 hours in a cool place. Stir thoroughly then turn into a 1-pint (600-ml) ovenproof dish. Cover with thin strips cut from the remaining fat bacon. Stand in a dish containing ½ inch (1.25 cm) water and cook at 325°F., 170°C., mark 3 for 1¼–1½ hours. When nearly cold, cover with greaseproof paper, press with a weight and leave in a cool place until really cold.

To pack and freeze: Turn the pâté out, cut into portions, interleave with freezer paper and wrap in foil. Freeze rapidly until solid. Store for up to 1 month.

To use: Thaw in the refrigerator. (Serves 4)

Chicken Goulash

small knob butter	8-oz. (*226-g*) can tomatoes
1 tbsp. (*15 ml*) oil	¼ pint (*150 ml*) chicken stock
salt and pepper	
4 6-oz. (*170-g*) chicken joints	1 level tbsp. (*15 ml*) cornflour
1 large onion, skinned and chopped	¼ pint (*140 g*) natural yoghurt
1 level tsp. (*5 ml*) paprika	chopped parsley
1 level tbsp. (*15 ml*) tomato paste	

To make: Heat the butter and oil together and rub the seasonings into the joints. Brown the chicken in hot fat, drain well and transfer to a shallow casserole. Sauté the onion until clear, stir in the paprika and tomato paste and cook for 2 minutes. Add the tomatoes and stock. Stir to mix. Pour the sauce over the chicken and cover. Cook at 350°F., 180°C., mark 4 for 30 minutes. Allow to cool.

To pack and freeze: Place the joints and juices in family-pack foil container or 4 individual containers. Cover, label and freeze rapidly until solid.

To use: Reheat from frozen, lightly covered, in the oven at 375°F., 190°C., mark 5 for 1½ hours. Remove from the oven. Thicken the juices with cornflour mixed to a smooth paste with a little water. Stir in the yoghurt and adjust

Moulded Prawn Salad (see page 118), Cherry-glazed Duck (see page 164), Apricot and Pineapple Whip (see page 194)

seasonings. Re-heat, uncovered for a further 10 minutes. Serve sprinkled with a little chopped parsley. (Serves 4)

Barbecued Spareribs

3 lb. (*1.3 kg*) spare ribs, American cut
2 tbsps. (*30 ml*) oil
2 large onions, skinned and chopped
1 clove garlic, skinned and crushed
2 level tbsps. (*30 ml*) tomato paste
3 tbsps. (*45 ml*) vinegar
2 tbsps. (*30 ml*) golden syrup
½ level tsp. (*2.5 ml*) ginger
1 beef stock cube
½ pint (*300 ml*) water

To make: Cut the rib sections into single ribs and place in a shallow roasting pan, in a single layer. Heat the oil in a saucepan, add the onion and sauté until tender. Add the garlic, tomato paste, vinegar, golden syrup, ginger and beef cube dissolved in hot water. Simmer gently for 10 minutes. Brush the ribs with a little of the sauce then roast at 375°F., 190°C., mark 5 for 30 minutes. Pour off the fat and coat with the remaining sauce. Allow to cool.
To pack and freeze: Pack in a 9½ × 6½-inch (23 × 16-cm) rectangular foil container. Cover with lid and overwrap with polythene. Seal, label and freeze.
To use: Remove the wrappings and cook from frozen at 375°F., 190°C., mark 5 for about 1½ hours. (Serves 4)

Hamburgers

2 oz. (*55 g*) soft breadcrumbs
6 tbsps. (*90 ml*) milk
1 lb. (*450 g*) minced beef
1 level tsp. (*5 ml*) salt
freshly ground black pepper
½ level tsp. (*2.5 ml*) mustard
1 small onion, skinned and grated
1 egg, beaten

To make: Soak the breadcrumbs in milk for 10 minutes. Mix with a fork before adding the beef, seasonings, onion and egg. Shape into 4 patties.
To pack and freeze: Separate each patty with a piece of freezer paper, double wrap

in foil then overwrap in a polythene bag. Freeze rapidly until solid.
To use: Pre-heat the grill and unwrap the patties and cook from frozen for about 30 minutes, turning occasionally to ensure even browning. Serve with Tomato Sauce (below). (Serves 4)

Tomato Sauce

8 oz. (*225 g*) streaky bacon, rinded and chopped
1 small onion, skinned and chopped
1 clove garlic, skinned and crushed
2 oz. (*55 g*) plain flour
2¼-oz. (*64-g*) can tomato paste
3 lb. (*1.3 kg*) fresh tomatoes, peeled and seeded
3 pints (*1.75 litre*) chicken stock
bouquet garni
2 level tsp. (*10 ml*) salt
freshly ground black pepper

To make: Fry the bacon in a large saucepan until the fat runs. Add the onion, garlic and flour. Cook for 5 minutes. Blend in the tomato paste, tomatoes and stock and add the bouquet garni and seasonings. Stir well, bring to the boil and simmer for 15 minutes. Allow to cool.
To pack and freeze: Pack in ½-pint (300-ml) portions in polythene bags placed inside rigid preformers. Seal, label and freeze. Remove the preformers for storage.
To use: Turn out and thaw the sauce in a saucepan over a gentle heat. Adjust seasonings.

Moussaka

2 aubergines, thickly sliced
2 tbsps. (*30 ml*) oil
3 onions, skinned and sliced
1 lb. (*450 g*) minced lamb
15-oz. (*425-g*) can tomatoes
2 level tbsps. (*30 ml*) tomato paste
salt and pepper
1 egg
1 oz. (*25 g*) flour
¼ level tsp. (*1.25 ml*) dry mustard
¼ pint (*140 g*) natural yoghurt
salt and pepper
paprika pepper

To make: Spread the sliced aubergines out on a tray and sprinkle with salt. Leave to stand for 30 minutes. Pour off the liquid and dry. Cut into dice. Heat the oil and fry the aubergines and onions together.

Shrimp Courgettes (see page 118), Swiss Veal (see page 139), Salads, Snow Peaks (see page 198)

Place the minced lamb in a bowl with the tomatoes and tomato paste. Season well with salt and pepper. Place the vegetables and meat in layers in a casserole, cover and cook at 350°F., 180°C., mark 4 for 1 hour. Cool.

To pack and freeze: Freeze rapidly in its casserole. Secure lid with freezer tape and overwrap in polythene. Seal and label.

To use: Allow to thaw then cook covered at 375°F., 190°C., mark 5 for 30 minutes. Blend the egg, flour and mustard. Stir in the yoghurt and seasonings. Spoon on to the moussaka and cook for a further 20 minutes. Serve sprinkled with a little paprika pepper. (Serves 4)

Cinnamon Pork Parcels

4 pork chops	½ level tsp. (*2.5 ml*)
1 lb. (*450 g*) dessert	cinnamon
apples	
1 tbsp. (*15 ml*) lemon	
juice	

To make: Trim the rind from the chops and remove the excess fat. Snip round the outer edge at ½-inch (1.25-cm) intervals. Place the chops under a moderate grill and brown them, 5 minutes on each side. Grate the apples and mix with the lemon juice and cinnamon. Lightly oil 4 large pieces of foil and spread a little apple mixture on each, top with a chop and then with the remaining apple. Parcel up the foil.

To freeze: Freeze rapidly until solid. Overwrap in polythene, seal and label.

To use: Remove from the polythene, place the foil parcels on a baking sheet, loosen the foil slightly and bake at 375°F., 190°C., mark 5 for 1 hour. (Serves 4)

Noisettes of Lamb

2 best ends of neck (6 noisettes each)

To make: Ask the butcher to bone and roll the best ends. Wipe the meat with a clean damp cloth, then cut each best end into 6 noisettes, cutting between the strings.

To pack and freeze: Place pieces of freezer paper between the noisettes so that they will separate easily before cooking. Cover with a double layer of foil. Overwrap in polythene, seal and label and freeze rapidly.

To use: Place on a large plate and allow to thaw for 12 hours in the refrigerator or 5 hours at room temperature—or cook from frozen. Unwrap, then season to taste and brush with a little oil. Whether frozen or ready thawed, brown them quickly under a hot grill, then reduce the heat and cook for a further 10–15 minutes if thawed or 30 minutes if frozen. Baste frequently. (Serves 4–6)

Chicken Tettrazini

12 oz. (*340 g*) cooked	1½ oz. (*40 g*) flour
chicken meat	½ pint (*300 ml*)
6 oz. (*170 g*)	chicken stock
spaghetti	½ pint (*300 ml*) milk
1 oz. (*25 g*) butter	salt and pepper
8 oz. (*225 g*) button	4 tbsps. (*60 ml*) dry
mushrooms	white wine
8-oz. (*225-g*) can	2 oz. (*55 g*) cheese,
tomatoes	grated

For sauce:
1½ oz. (*40 g*) butter

To make: Cut the chicken meat in pieces. Cook the spaghetti in boiling salted water until tender. Drain and rinse thoroughly in cold water several times. Melt the butter and sauté the mushrooms. To prepare the sauce, melt the butter and stir in the flour. Cook for 1 minute then gradually stir in the stock and milk, bring to the boil, stirring continuously and cook for 2 minutes. Add seasonings and wine, then cool slightly before stirring in the cheese. Add half the sauce to the chicken and the other half to the spaghetti with the mushrooms. Allow to cool.

To pack and freeze: Line a shallow ovenproof dish with foil. Spoon in the spaghetti mixture, top with tomatoes then cover with chicken in sauce. Freeze until solid. Remove from the dish and wrap the foil over. Place in a polythene bag, seal and label. Return to the freezer.

To use: Unwrap then re-heat in the serving dish with a light foil covering, at 350°F., 180°C., mark 4 for 1 hour. Fork through once or twice during heating. Serve garnished with chopped parsley. (Serves 4)

Pork Chops with Orange and Ginger Stuffing

4 pork chops	1 oz. (25 g) preserved
2 large oranges	ginger
4 oz. (115 g) soft	salt and pepper
breadcrumbs	
1½ oz. (40 g) melted	
butter	

To make: Select thickly cut pork chops. Trim away any rind and excess fat and carefully cut through the chop from the skin side to the bone to form a pocket. Finely grate the rind of the oranges and mix with the breadcrumbs. Add the melted butter and chopped ginger. Mix thoroughly and season well with salt and pepper. Press the mixture into the pockets. Place in a shallow ovenproof dish and bake at 400°F., 200°C., mark 6 for 15–20 minutes or until lightly browned. Allow to cool and place in a shallow rigid foil container. Squeeze the juice from 1 orange; remove the pith from the other and cut into slices. Arrange the slices on top of the chops. Add the juice.

To pack and freeze: Cover with a lid, seal and label. Freeze rapidly.

To use: Release seal but do not remove the lid. Cook from frozen at 375°F., 190°C., mark 5 for 1½ hours. (Serves 4)

Casseroled Liver Balls

1 lb. (450 g) lambs'	freshly ground black
liver	pepper
6 oz. (170 g) lean	1½ oz. (40 g) flour
bacon, rinded	1½ oz. (40 g) butter
8 oz. (225 g) onions,	15-oz. (425-g) can
skinned	tomatoes
4 oz. (115 g) fresh	¼ pint (150 ml) stock
breadcrumbs	rosemary
1 egg, beaten	
¼ level tsp. (1.25 ml)	
salt	

To make: Mince the liver with the bacon; mince the onion. Combine the meats, onion, breadcrumbs, egg and seasonings. Shape into 12 balls, pressing the mixture lightly together, and coat with flour. Melt the butter in a pan and fry the balls until evenly browned. Remove from pan, drain well and cool. Sprinkle any flour remaining into the pan and stir to loosen any residue. Add the tomatoes with their juice, the stock, and a sprig of fresh rosemary. Stir to blend. Pour into a rigid foil container, add the liver balls and cool rapidly.

To pack and freeze: Freeze rapidly, uncovered, until firm. Cover with a lid or foil, seal and label.

To use: Re-heat from frozen. Cook at 400°F., 200°C., mark 6 for 1¼ hours, turning the liver balls half way through cooking. Adjust seasonings before serving. (Serves 4)

Braised Lambs' Hearts

4 lambs' hearts	2 oz. (55 g) chopped
1 oz. (25 g) butter	mushrooms
2 onions, skinned and	1 rasher bacon,
chopped	rinded and chopped
salt and pepper	1 level tsp. (5 ml)
¾ pint (375 ml) stock	dried mixed herbs
	salt and pepper
For stuffing:	1 egg, beaten
1 oz. (25 g) bread-	
crumbs	

To make: Prepare the hearts by trimming away the tubes etc.; rinse and dry them. Mix the ingredients for the stuffing and use to stuff the hearts. Sew up the openings with thread or fine string. Grill to seal, then place in a casserole with the chopped onions, seasonings and stock. Cover and cook at 350°F., 180°C., mark 4 for 1 hour. Cool.

To pack and freeze: Place hearts and juices in a rigid foil container. Cover, seal and label. Freeze rapidly.

To use: Place frozen in the oven at 350°F., 180°C., mark 4 and cook for 1¼ hours. Strain off the juices and thicken lightly with a little cornflour mixed to a smooth paste with water. Adjust seasonings and sprinkle with chopped parsley. (Serves 4)

Beef Roll Casserole

1½ lb. (700 g) skirt steak	¾ pint (375 ml) beef stock
4 oz. (115 g) lean bacon, rinded and chopped	4 carrots, peeled and diced
1 onion, skinned and chopped	½ lb. (225 g) shallots, skinned
1 level tsp. (5 ml) mustard	2 level tbsps. (30 ml) tomato paste
2 level tbsps. (30 ml) flour	1 lb. (450 g) courgettes, sliced
2 tbsps. (30 ml) oil or dripping	salt and pepper

Roll up tightly and secure with cotton or string. Roll in the flour, heat the oil and brown the rolls. Drain them well and transfer to a casserole. Stir in any remaining flour and cook for 2 minutes. Stir in ½ pint (125 ml) stock and bring to boiling point, stirring. Pour over the meat, cover and cook at 350°F., 180°C., mark 4 for 1 hour. Add the carrots, shallots and remaining stock mixed with the tomato paste. Cook for 15 minutes. Allow to cool.

To pack and freeze: Turn into a foil container. Label and seal. Freeze rapidly until firm.

To use: Open the seal but do not remove the cover. Heat through at 375°F., 190°C., mark 5 for 1½ hours. Add the courgettes 15 minutes before cooking is complete. Adjust the seasonings and thickening before serving. If using frozen courgettes add ¼ hour earlier. (Serves 4)

Cod with Mushrooms

4 frozen cod steaks	¼ pint (140 g) low-fat yoghurt
8 oz. (225 g) mushrooms, sliced	few drops Worcestershire sauce
4 tsps. (20 ml) lemon juice	chopped parsley
salt and pepper	lemon wedges

Lightly oil 4 pieces of foil and place a frozen steak on each. Top with mushrooms and season lightly with salt and pepper. Mix the yoghurt and Worcestershire sauce together and divide between the 4 steaks. Parcel up lightly and place on a baking sheet. Bake at 350°F., 180°C., mark 4 for 40 minutes. Serve sprinkled with a little chopped parsley and accompanied by wedges of lemon. (Serves 4)

Curry Fish Fry

6 frozen cod steaks	freshly ground black pepper
1½ oz. (40 g) flour	3 tbsps. (45 ml) oil
2 level tbsps. (30 ml) curry powder	lemon wedges
½ level tsp. (2.5 ml) salt	parsley

Using a freezer knife, cut the fish into bite-size portions. Mix together the flour, curry powder, salt and pepper and use to coat the fish. Heat the oil and fry the fish until lightly browned and the fish flakes easily when tested with a knife. Serve with lemon wedges and parsley garnish. (Serves 6)

Californian Trout

1½ pints (900 ml) water	2 oranges
1 tsp. (5 g) salt	1 lemon
2 bay leaves	½ oz. (15 g) butter
1 onion, skinned and chopped	2 level tbsps. (30 ml) cornflour
4 frozen, smoked trout	chopped parsley

Put the water, salt, bay leaves and onion into a large shallow pan, bring to the boil and simmer for 5 minutes. Add the frozen fish and simmer for 15 minutes. Transfer the fish to a serving dish and strain the liquor.

Extract the juices from the oranges and lemon and make up to ½ pint (300 ml) with fish stock. Add the butter and bring to the boil. Mix the cornflour to a smooth paste with a little of the stock and stir into the boiling juices. Stir until smooth, thick and clear. Simmer for 3 minutes. Pour over the fish and serve sprinkled with a little chopped parsley. (Serves 4)

Thatched Haddock

oil	2 oz. (55 g) fresh breadcrumbs
2 large frozen haddock fillets	2 oz. (55 g) cheese, grated
salt	1 oz. (25 g) butter, grated
freshly ground black pepper	chopped chives
juice of 1 lemon	
1 lb. (450 g) tomatoes	

Lightly oil 2 sheets of foil large enough to wrap each frozen fillet. Place a fillet on each and brush with a little oil. Season with salt and pepper and sprinkle with lemon juice. Blanch, peel and seed the tomatoes then dice the flesh. Add to the fish. Package with foil and place on a baking sheet. Cook at 325°F., 170°C., mark 3 for 30 minutes. Mix together the breadcrumbs, cheese, butter and chives. Season lightly and spread over the cooked fish. Flash under a hot grill until golden. Serve in the package or transfer to a warm serving dish, garnished with a slice of lemon. (Serves 2)

PART SIX

What else will help?

Everybody who has ever grimly soldiered on through a slimming diet must have stopped at times to ask why on earth science hasn't come up with an easier and better answer. Admittedly you do lose weight by dieting, there is no question that simple obesity can be cured that way, but it is a slow, hard business.

One can visualise three obvious ways of approaching the problem. You could give people pills to make them feel less hungry. This would enable them to eat less—in effect to diet—without feeling miserable and deprived. Or you could invent a new sort of food which would be just as nourishing as ordinary food, but much less fattening. Or, best of all, you could invent a pill or an injection which would melt away people's fat deposits while they continued to eat normally.

This last suggestion is naturally the most appealing, as it would take away all need for struggle or calculation. Unfortunately, this is the one field where scientists have so far had no success. Despite the claims that are made periodically for some wonder drug or series of injections, no one has yet found a method of using up, or mobilising, the body's store of fat, except by dieting. This is the area where most research is being concentrated at the moment, as it is potentially the most useful. But so far no fat-mobilising substance has been discovered which could be used to treat human beings. Some people have claimed to have unearthed such a substance, and periodically new clinics spring up offering a series of injections which will melt away fat without effort. But on investigation the injections always prove to be linked to a strict diet and it is of course the diet, and not the injections, which brings the weight down.

Slimming aids

In the meantime, while we wait for scientists to produce the final answer, we can make use of some of the aids they offer.

Substitute foods
The most important of these, and the most noticeable feature of the diet scene in the last 15 years, has been the introduction and widespread acceptance of substitute foods.

The search was for a substance that would contain all the nutriments necessary to a healthy life, but with a much diminished calorie content. Then people could give up all the tedious business of counting calories, and simply use the food substitute instead.

Perhaps the most successful of all the substitute foods was Metercal, an American invention which swept through the States when it was first invented, until the newspapers seemed full of accounts of Metercal parties, Metercal jokes and cartoons and ecstatic endorsements from people who had finally managed to lose weight after years of struggle. The cause of all the excitement was a slightly vanilla-flavoured powder consisting of soy flour, powdered milk, coconut oil, yeast, vitamins, minerals and a few other ingredients. Its protein content was 30 per cent, and the proper amount, mixed with water, added up to four sensibly balanced, tolerably palatable liquid meals of 900 calories (3766 joules) a day.

For a time it was so successful it seemed as if no other answer would ever be needed. Then sales began to decline. This was not due to any fault in the product—Metercal was and is all it has claimed to be. But, as everyone in the diet field realises sooner or later, food is an immensely tricky and unpredictable topic. It is impossible to forecast how the market will turn next. There was no doubt that Metercal worked. But once the novelty wears off, drinking four cups of liquid a day is extremely boring. People missed the social side of eating. Sitting around a table over a leisurely meal is an opportunity for sharing business problems, for chatting to old friends, for keeping in touch with busy acquaintances, for enjoying oneself. Sitting alone at home or in the office with a beaker of substitute food is in no way an adequate alternative.

There are a number of liquid meal replacements on the market now. Complan, a British product, has been available since about 1955. It was developed as a food for invalids too sick to cope with eating proper meals, yet needing adequate nourishment to aid their recovery. The company was caught rather off-balance when it discovered that what it had on its hands was a potentially very profitable meal-replacement diet drink; it began to market Complan more widely and extended the range to include chocolate, butterscotch and strawberry flavours. Carnation produce 'Slender', a liquid meal replacement aimed directly at slimmers which comes in four flavours. Limmits make a similar one in two flavours. Nutriplan instant soups are intended to replace one normal meal each day and are very useful for office lunches. They come in six flavours and are quickly made by just adding boiling water to the contents of the sachet and stirring briskly with a fork. Heinz also produce a range of slimmers' soups in cans, in eight different flavours. The variety of flavours now available goes a long way to overcome the monotony of a liquid type of diet.

Although the liquid diet proved too boring to be totally successful, it can still play a useful rôle as part of an ordinary slimming diet. The chief advantage is that the meal-in-a-cup is quick, easy and nourishing. In the winter, especially, a hot drink will probably seem more appealing than the other replacement foods, biscuits and chocolate.

Lots of people who want to lose weight or to avoid putting it on find it helps to take a liquid meal for breakfast. This is usually the time of day when they have least time to spare for cooking, anyway, and they might otherwise be tempted to make do with the easiest thing—bread or toast and coffee. The liquid meals are also very convenient for anyone who for the time being is working too hard to stop for a proper meal. A housewife in the middle of spring-cleaning will find a meal in a cup keeps her going every bit as long as a plate of sandwiches, and with far better effects on her figure. The same is true also for someone working at a rush period.

Latest versions

The failure of the liquid foods to maintain their early success led to a search for more satisfactory food replacements. One lesson had been learnt—the food replacement would have to offer variety, or people would become bored with it. And so there was a growing trend towards biscuits, with a cream filling which could be given different flavours. Most of the firms making these biscuits recommend that their products should be taken with a glass of milk, and this snack meal of milk and biscuits is a little closer to a normal diet than the meal-in-a-cup ever got.

Most diet biscuits, when taken with milk, give a daily 1,050–1,250 calorie (4393–5230 joules) diet, which is low enough to make one lose weight. There are two types—heavy biscuits, of which you eat two per meal, and crackers, of which you eat four. Most firms offer sweet and savoury flavours, though the savoury ones seem to be increasing in popularity.

All these biscuits, remember, are intended to replace a meal, not to be added to one. They would not help you to lose weight if you took them in addition to an ordinary meal. On the contrary, since they are intended to provide enough nourishment to replace a normal diet, they are naturally quite filling. If added to an ordinary diet, they could be disastrous. The Food Standards Committee points out that the phrase 'slimming foods' is a contradiction in terms, since such foods do give energy and, if eaten in over-large quantities, would be fattening. The most they can aspire to is to be a slimming 'aid'.

The main criticism (apart from their cost) of these meal-replacement biscuits is that they are no substitute for proper eating habits. The person who diets solely by taking a meal-replacement product is learning nothing

216

about how to control his ordinary eating habits. In fact, these products may even encourage bad eating patterns by making people accustomed to eating large numbers of biscuits every day. A woman who has used chocolate biscuits as a substitute for food for any length of time when on a diet will almost certainly still want to eat chocolate biscuits when her diet is over. And if she does so, she runs of course a serious risk of putting back all the weight she has so painfully lost.

Most of the products come with an accompanying leaflet of practical advice about diet, which usually points out that many people find it helpful to use these meal-replacements occasionally rather than full-time. And this would seem to be their most useful function. It is obviously better to eat normal food as much as possible. Not only is that the only way of ever learning permanently to cope with your appetite, it also offers the widest possible selection of flavours and tastes. Real food is, after all, very nice. But while you are learning to cope with ordinary food and adjusting your intake to the amount you need, you may find it helpful occasionally to eat a substitute food to speed things up. More recently manufacturers have broadened the substitute food market by introducing a greater variety of products such as omelette mixes and mixed cereals with fruit and nuts.

Substitute foods are also useful if you are trying to maintain a weight loss. If you find yourself putting on weight again immediately, it often helps to take a meal-replacement, say, once a day, and to cut down on the rest of your intake. Having one of the meal-replacement foods regularly will help to sustain you while you eat less, until your stomach has got used to the reduced quantity and stops complaining. These foods may also be a blessing if you are faced with a social function which includes a meal; it's quite a good idea to eat one of the meal-replacements on the day itself and perhaps the day after, so that your one big dinner does no harm.

The range of diet biscuits as meal replacements has increased to include a greater variety of both sweet and savoury flavours. A diet consisting solely of meal replacements of this nature is not a good long-term plan, because it encourages people to maintain their liking for foods which are normally fattening. But not all fat people are sensible, or strong-minded, and there is no point in insisting on impossible standards for those people who will never reach them.

There are also bars of diet chocolate—milk or plain with nuts or fruit. It is better to try to lose the craving for chocolate than to pander to it—but some people do find this particularly difficult. They will probably be happier cutting out an occasional evening meal and eating a bar of diet chocolate while they watch television, rather than trying to resist the temptation of sweets altogether.

Diet extras

As well as the products which are intended to replace a complete meal, manufacturers have also turned their attention to individual items of diet. There are now a wide variety of low-calorie fruit squashes and low-calorie canned or bottled drinks available as well as unsweetened fruit juices, all of which are very useful for slimmers.

These would also be useful for an overweight child, since all children seem to demand huge quantities of fruit drinks. It goes against all the mother's natural instincts to deprive a child of food, so these diet drinks, even though they only solve one problem, will be a great help. There are also diet versions on the market now of the drinks to partner gin, vodka and white rum. These do little to affect the calorie-content of the spirit itself (see chart on page 232), but they do help to limit the damage for anyone who can't give them up.

Among the other minor aids to slimming is a starch-reduced wheatflake breakfast cereal made by Energen, which contains only half the carbohydrate of ordinary cornflakes. Kellogg's make a high protein breakfast cereal, Special K, which is lighter than ordinary breakfast cereals and so provides fewer calories per serving. Also for breakfast is Limmits muesli in their 250 range, Nutriplan mixed cereals with fruit and nuts, and Kousa Naturally Light which can be taken as a substitute for any meal. Energen also make six varieties of jam, including orange marmalade, which contains only 11.4 grams of sugar per ounce against 19.3 grams in ordinary jam.

Bread replacements

All these products, however, add up to only a fraction of the slimming food market. Total sales are going up, and will certainly continue to do so. But there is one food that people find particularly hard to give up, and for which substitutes are most eagerly sought—bread. The slimming biscuits market was reported to have brought in £2½ million in 1968. But the turnover for starch-reduced breads and rolls was £25 million.

It is easy to see why. Of all foods, bread is the most basic in our civilisation, and provokes the most basic responses. It was the discovery of cereal cultivation that turned mankind from being nomadic hunters to settled farmers who could provide their own food, plan ahead, stay in one place and build, grow and develop. Seeing the corn grow, mature, die and grow again gave man his vision of birth, death and resurrection. And the smell of good, fresh bread, crusty and hot from the oven, still provokes a feeling of pleasure, of security, of satisfaction, that no other food provides. It is probably because bread has all these emotional overtones and associations that people cling to it with near-fanatical persistence.

There is no easy solution to this problem. If you really want to lose a good deal of weight you *must* cut out ordinary bread, as well as drastically reducing *all* other carbohydrates. You just cannot make exceptions. But if you are only trying to lose a small amount, or want to keep your weight steady, you might find starch-reduced bread the answer. Energen, founded as long ago as 1914, were first in the field, and indeed pioneered the starch-reduced roll as an aid to slimming. Six of these rolls contain less starch than 1 oz (25 g) of ordinary bread and will keep indefinitely. Energen starch-reduced crispbreads contain 49 per cent starch against 78 per cent in ordinary crispbreads. Their range includes cheese and chicken flavoured ones as well as wheat, bran and rye, which all add interest and variety to your diet. Ryvita now make a Swedish rye crispbread in addition to the original rye flavour. The range of crispbreads on the market at the moment is quite extensive with products such as Ry-King, Primula, Peek Freans, plus all the supermarket own brands, readily available.

Outline, a low-calorie alternative to butter or margarine, has been a welcome addition to the range of slimmers' foods on the market. This spread provides about half the number of calories per ounce and so represents quite a substantial saving. It cannot, however, be used in cooking.

Crispbreads themselves were for a long time thought to be less fattening than ordinary bread, probably because they are lighter and drier. People made the same mistake about toast, thinking that it too was less fattening than ordinary bread. Both, in fact, are very high in carbohydrates. With all bread, unless a loaf is clearly marked 'starch-reduced' (the term is Government-controlled), there is little hope of its helping in a diet.

There are a number of proprietary brands of bread on the market which are intended for slimmers. Among these are Procea which has 40 calories per slice, and Nimble and Slimcea which have 35 calories per slice. These breads have the same calories per ounce as ordinary bread but are much lighter and so each slice provides about half the calories. These light breads are made by aerating the dough by adding air, carbon dioxide or other gas, which increases the volume of the loaf without increasing its weight. The manufacturers sometimes argue that this leads to a smaller intake, as the bread looks the same but is actually less. The implication is that many people eat a set amount of food as a matter of habit, and that if they always eat the same number of slices of bread at breakfast, four slices of light bread will give them fewer calories than four slices of normal bread.

The Food Standards Committee, however, warns that 'Such claims have not been backed by reputable scientific trials.' There is no proof that the amount of food to be eaten is determined by the eye, irrespective of weight and irrespective of any feeling of insufficiency. If, on the contrary, people simply eat sufficient bread to satisfy their appetite, they will eat five or six slices of the light bread to four slices of normal bread, and will be no better off.

The diet food companies have not been content with simply meeting their clients' nutritional needs. They know that to lose weight you must eat less, and that to some extent this depends on adopting a new pattern of eating, but they also know how hard it is for the person who has got used to having little snacks and nibbles all day long to give them up. Where the nutritionist can only plead with or bully patients into breaking this habit, the food manufacturers have developed products to satisfy the need.

Thus, Bisks produce water biscuits at 35 calories a biscuit and cream crackers at 40 calories each which, they suggest, can be nibbled between meals without ruining your diet. They also do a digestive sweetmeal biscuit at 50 calories which can also be eaten as a snack, but not so often. Boots also sell their own brand of water biscuits at 35 calories per biscuit. The main thing to remember about snacks like these is to keep track of the total number of calories eaten in the day.

There is no reason to suppose that the manufacturers' imaginations are in any way exhausted yet. As long as there is a need, they will struggle to meet it. Just as the breathalyser provoked the invention of new drinks which manage to look like beer though without having any of its joyful but sometimes dangerous effects, so the need for foodless foods will doubtless bring new goodies to our tables. Until the day when a researcher finally isolates the longed-for fat mobilising agent, or until a new breed of man arises with massive self-control, the demand for an easy diet will persist. These formulas are all successful for a time. As Dr Fernstein of the Rockefeller Institute put it: 'The novelty of some of these approaches may sometimes evoke from the patient and physician an enthusiasm which helps the patient maintain the diet.' Any product that postpones for a time the moment when you have to admit that the only way to lose weight is to eat less, appears to have a future.

Sweeteners

Until recently, artificial sweeteners were the most widespread and most widely-accepted aid to slimming. The first branded sugar-substitute, Saxin, came on to the market in Britain in 1897. Artificial sweeteners have recently been withdrawn from the market in America and their use is currently under review in Britain but no decision has yet been reached.

Saccharin is still the main widely accepted substitute for sugar (apart from honey and glucose, which to the slimmer are as harmful as sugar). It is a white, odourless powder which is immensely sweet. It dissolves easily in hot water, not so well in cold, and would still taste sweet if diluted 100,000 times. It is sometimes said to have a slightly bitter taste, which is probably the result of being used in too high a concentration. Saccharin has been on the market in one form or another for over 80 years.

There are various different saccharin products on the market, all fairly similar. The liquid products are very useful in cooking, as the tablets would sometimes be inconvenient. They do not, of course, replace the bulk of sugar, so they cannot be used in baking, nor do they have the preserving quality of sugar which makes it essential in jam-making. But they can be used successfully to make desserts and light puddings. Sugar substitutes intended for use by diabetics are not ideal for slimmers as they usually have virtually the same calorific value as sugar. There are also a number of sugar plus saccharin preparations on the market now. The effect of such a combination is to increase the sweetness of the sugar two, three or even four times. Ideally the slimmer reduces the amount of sugar consumed to adjust to this 'super sweetness' thus reducing the number of calories actually consumed. Like any other saccharin preparation it must be added after cooking is completed.

If you hope to diet successfully it is almost essential to find some substitute for sugar. In the last hundred years we have got so used to eating large quantities that most people find it extremely difficult to give it up. Yet the very fact that it tastes so particularly pleasurable means that we are likely to eat too much of it. Many people have tried to give up sugar in their tea either by cutting it out completely in one sudden burst, or by taking one spoonful less each week, and have failed on both counts. It is better, in such cases, to use a sugar substitute. Experience has shown that people on a sugar-free or low-sugar diet, whether because of illness or obesity, will only keep strictly to the diet if their food and drink are sweetened, and this is best done by saccharin.

It also helps in the difficult business of slimming overweight children. If you make their jellies and desserts with a saccharin solution instead of sugar, children will enjoy them just as much. (The manufacturers of liquid saccharins have produced useful recipe leaflets for dishes using their products, which are readily available.) Most of the manufacturers of saccharin wisely stress, however, that the use of sweeteners as a sugar substitute will not bring about the desired decrease in weight unless the slimmer adheres strictly to a diet at the same time. A sugar substitute can help a diet, but it cannot do the whole job by itself.

Non-starters

There are other substances used as alternatives to sugar, chiefly honey, glucose and Sorbitol (an alcohol made from glucose). These may be useful in the kitchen as an alternative to sugar, but they have no value at all in a true reducing diet. They contain almost as many calories per gram as sugar, but they are not as sweet. Thus you would have to use larger amounts to reach the required level of sweetness—adding calories all the time. If you are buying jam, canned fruit or cakes and any of these three sugar substitutes is included in the list of ingredients, then the food will be just as fattening as if it contained sugar. But then, no serious slimmer would be thinking of buying such things, anyway.

No longer available

The other well-known substitute, sodium cyclamate, has been banned in the U.K. pending further research into possible side-effects when it is taken in any quantity. Sodium cyclamate, like saccharin, is a white, odourless powder, but it is only one-tenth as sweet. It has no noticeable flavour, unless it is used in extremely concentrated doses, and is less likely than saccharin to add a taste to tea or coffee—hence the growing popularity it was enjoying.

Pills

An increasing number of people who go to their doctors for advice about losing weight are prescribed tablets or pills. There is no pill that can actually make anyone lose weight—all they can do is either to affect the food intake by curbing the appetite, or to impede the body's absorption of the food eaten by acting as a laxative. In rare cases a third approach is tried, by using hormones, but these are extremely tricky to calculate and are usually avoided. Some hormones will induce wasting of the body, but the hormone balance is so delicately poised, and so essential to health, that interfering with it just for the purpose of slimming is thought to be too great a risk.

To be avoided

Aperients, purgatives and laxatives can be obtained without a doctor's prescription, and many of the old-fashioned slimming cures, and a few of the new ones, contain some purging agent. It is undoubtedly the most ridiculous means of tackling the problem of slimming. The very idea of going to all the trouble of buying, preparing, cooking, serving and eating food only to try and take it out again immediately at the other end is farcical. Yet laxatives have had a long innings as slimming agents, and have done much harm. The chief objection to them is that they are indiscriminate. They eliminate not only useless bulk, but vital nutriments as well. A prolonged course of purging could lead to a loss of essential salts and minerals and do genuine harm. It is far better to choose which foods to do without while they are still on the table.

Drugs to promote diarrhoea are equally dangerous. It is tempting to think that since the body is largely water, getting rid of some of the water will also reduce the weight. But the balance of water in the body is very delicately and perfectly maintained. The body takes exactly as much as it needs and releases the rest. You can increase the water loss by taking a drug, but unless you continue with the drug the body will simply take up an extra quantity of water at the next opportunity, to bring itself back into balance. In any case, it isn't water you want to lose, it's fat—that solid material lying all over your body and in great rolls around your middle. Getting rid of your water won't take that away.

Cheating the stomach

Among the pills taken to reduce the appetite are some that contain a cellulose filler which swells up in the stomach to make it feel full and satisfied. Cellulose, which is not absorbed by the body to any great degree, is used as a filling agent in most diet foods. Methyl cellulose is used in Britain in Harley Discs, Limmits Pastilles, Kirby 10 Day, Pastille 808, Slendettes, Slim-maid, Slimway, Slim Discs and Trihextin. These pills do work in so far as you tend to eat smaller amounts of food than before. But because they fill the stomach, they play no part in getting it accustomed to having smaller quantities of food. They may help in the first few difficult days, but if they are used over a long period, the dieter will never retrain his appetite. As the *Journal of American Medicine* put it: 'complete dependance on formulas does not constitute a rational approach to weight reduction and weight control over the long term.'

For anyone reluctant to use such things, but feeling a need to boost the will power, some of the slimming companies have introduced sweets to be eaten before meals. Ayds, for example, sell caramel-flavoured candies. These help to take the edge off the appetite if eaten immediately before a meal. They contain no drugs, and the effect could be duplicated by eating almost any other sweet or chocolate. The American Federal Trade Commission in an enquiry into Ayds pointed out that 'this candy or any other sweet' might curb the appetite, but that it could not reduce weight unless the reducer would also diet. And in such a case the success would be due to the diet, not the candy.

223

Anybody tempted to buy over the counter pills for slimming would be well-advised to read carefully the text on the sides of the box. If they say they are merely 'to assist' you with your slimming, you might stop and wonder whether you need their help that badly and expensively. The American Food and Drug Administration points out that 'Most reducing products which can be purchased without a prescription are food supplements (i.e. they contain calories), which have no effect on food intake. What you pay for, if you expect any results, is the little circular containing the diet plan which tells you to eat less.'

On prescription only

The medicine most widely prescribed by doctors to deal with obesity is amphetamine. This is used to curb the appetite and to increase energy and a feeling of well-being. In 1967 it was estimated that 2.3 million prescriptions were issued for amphetamine preparations. The amphetamine group includes Benzedrine, Dexedrine and other pep pills which work on the nervous system and do indeed depress the appetite. It is of course the resulting reduced food intake, and not the pill itself, which actually leads to a loss of weight. Most responsible doctors only use amphetamines for a short period, often as a crutch to help patients starting on a diet. They would advise against using them for longer stretches, because in such cases the patient would never learn to curb his appetite, and when he came off the diet would probably return to a pattern of over-eating.

There is a further disadvantage in the use of amphetamines. It is possible for them to give rise to unpleasant side-effects, such as heart palpitations, irritability and insomnia. This last effect can lead in a vicious spiral to patients taking more drugs to get to sleep. Amphetamines have also been known to raise blood pressure, induce nausea and vomiting and cause constipation. But the worst danger is that of addiction. The body easily builds up a tolerance to these preparations, and even after a short time, small doses become ineffective. The dose is therefore increased and addiction may result.

It has been increasingly suggested recently that amphetamines should be added to the list of addictive drugs, along with heroin, LSD and cocaine. Certainly the situation in Britain gives cause for concern. In 1967 a conference of the Pharmaceutical Society was told that the largest single category of prescription forgery was that done by women aged between 30 and 50, forging prescriptions for amphetamines. In most cases these had been given initially as part of a slimming programme; the patients had experienced a lowered sense of fatigue and a feeling of euphoria, and become addicted. In these unfortunate cases the effects of taking slimming pills have proved more harmful than the dangers of being overweight.

A working party set up by the British Medical Association recommended in 1968 that 'amphetamines and amphetamine-like compounds should only be prescribed for those conditions for which no reasonable alternative exists . . . they should be avoided so far as possible in the treatment of obesity'. Perhaps their most important use lies in helping a patient to continue with his diet once the initial enthusiasm has worn off, and for people who are sub-normal, who need to diet for health reasons, but who are unable fully to understand the principles of a reducing diet.

A newer alternative is fenfluramine; this compound is being increasingly used (under medical supervision), and recently published evidence shows it to be free of serious or troublesome side effects.

Exercise

No society in history has ever been quite as immobile as our own is today. The business of living demands less and less of our physical resources, and we have become almost static. It is a recent phenomenon, mushrooming especially in the last two decades. We assume more and more that we should not be expected to exert ourselves. We use lifts and escalators at work and in large stores. We use trolleys to carry our shopping and luggage. We go from front door to front door in our cars, and spend our evenings watching television, or watching other people play games, or sitting in a pub.

It is probably because we are so inactive that exercise has lost its appeal and is usually relegated to a very subordinate rôle in any slimming programme.

Now there can be no doubt that the only sure way to lose weight is to diet. Exercise will never be a substitute for that. But exercise can play an important rôle in helping a diet and, even more so, in seeing that weight once lost is never put back on. Admittedly, exercise is a slow way of losing weight. It has been estimated that it takes 20 hours of fast walking, 14 hours of cycling or 7 hours of swimming to burn up one pound of fat. To get rid of a single excess cheese sandwich, you would have to play squash for an hour. But you must remember that you also put on weight slowly, and there is no reason why it should all come off overnight. A certain amount of exercise, added to a diet, will speed up the effect a little, and will also restore a feeling of fitness that most people have not experienced for years.

Did lack of exercise make you plump ?

The amount of exercise people take varies with their jobs and their habits. But there is an increasing body of evidence to show that obese people take considerably less exercise than average people, which of course aggravates their problem. A survey of housewives in 1967 found that overweight housewives on average spend an hour longer in bed than lean housewives, and spend 15 per cent less time on their feet each day. And a report in *The Lancet* put forward the suggestion that, 'In obesity, sloth may be more important than gluttony.'

Recent American research seems to bear this out. A study showed that 'the great majority of obese adolescents eat *less* than average non-obese adolescents', a fact they have probably been protesting for years, without being believed. But although they eat fewer calories, they nevertheless have more calories left over to turn into fat, because they use up so few in activity. The intake is not exorbitant, but the output is meagre. The American study concludes: 'We have shown that in such individuals, stepping up exercise, even without paying much attention to diet, invariably results in weight loss. Thus, if there is any basic rule in managing obese adolescents, the chances are it would be *to increase their physical activity.*'

New views on the value of exercise

For a long time one of the most telling arguments against exercise has been the suggestion that it simply helps you to work up an appetite, so that you eat more at the next meal and put back all the weight you have so laboriously lost. There is just a little truth in it: a sudden burst of strenuous exercise might well make you feel hungry. But exercise is not concerned solely with thrashing about in a swimming pool or playing games to exhaustion. Exercise for slimming is more a matter of everyday affairs like walking to the station or the bus stop in the morning, climbing a flight of stairs instead of waiting for the lift, or just getting up to find your own letters in the file instead of calling to your secretary to do it. Dr Jean Mayer, a Harvard physiologist, writes: 'If you don't walk at all, you may well become a little *less* hungry if you start walking for an hour every day. If you're already active and increase your activity, your appetite will go up, but not so much that you won't profit from the activity.' It is also thought that a sensible amount of exercise may perhaps help in avoiding a coronary.

This message has got through to the men whose health and well-being are a matter of widespread public concern. Harry Truman was famous for his early morning marches; General Eisenhower was at times thought to spend more hours on the golf course than in his office, and Lyndon Johnson used to stride around the White House lawns, trailing reporters and beagles. These men had the best possible medical advice, and this advice included taking exercise.

Which exercise ?

Walking is the most obvious form of exercise to adopt for general fitness, because it is the easiest. Walking at a normal pace uses up about 300 calories (1255 joules) an hour (or more for a heavy person); walking at a brisk four miles an hour will burn up about another 100 calories (418 joules) an hour. If this doesn't seem very much, remember that an hour's walk a day would take off 20 pounds (10 kg) of fat in a year, other things being equal. And an hour's walk, which represents three miles, also represents the difference between the average number of miles walked daily by fat women and by thin. So it should not be difficult for the overweight woman to walk this additional distance and take the same amount of exercise as her thinner contemporaries. Men tend to find golf as pleasant a way as any of keeping up with their walking.

Everything you do uses up some calories. You use more calories standing still, for instance, than sitting still, and using an ordinary typewriter instead of an electric typewriter will burn off an additional 16 calories an hour. But if you want to be more active, you should suit the activity to your age and health. For middle-aged people who want to take more exercise but who are afraid to start suddenly with something too strenuous, the best thing would probably be swimming. This allows the body to be supported while the actual work is being done, so it exercises the muscles without throwing too great a strain on the heart. Younger people, less worried about their hearts, may prefer to take up tennis or squash and turn their slimming into a pleasurable social occasion.

Exercise and the adolescent

Exercise, as already indicated, is especially important as part of the slimming programme of overweight teenagers. But they frequently find the usual forms of exercise embarrassing or distressing, since their friends tease them about their slowness and poor performance. This poor ability at games has been shown to be of greater significance as a cause of unpopularity among schoolchildren than the fatness itself. There may also be a tendency for teachers to exclude overweight children from physical activities at school, especially if these leave the children breathless, whereas in fact they should be having extra physical training in this respect.

If the child is shy about joining in his friends' games, swimming might offer a satisfactory alternative. Once in the water, he will be less conspicuous and his extra fat should give him additional buoyancy and help to make him a good swimmer. This would encourage him to go on, and give him some necessary pride in himself. Again, this exercise should be taken daily, if possible.

Fat children can be strikingly immobile. They show none of the frequent fidgety movements that thin children make while they are awake, and to some extent in their sleep, too, which make a considerable contribution to the total energy expenditure. Because they are fat they find walking difficult, and for this reason the mother is often tempted to put the child in a pram when she takes him shopping, so that she can get about more easily, even when the child is quite old. It would be better if she could try to persevere with making him walk these journeys, as the plump toddler needs all the exercise he can get to break the pattern of inactivity.

Beauty bonus

Besides burning off extra calories, there is another useful aspect to exercise. While you are fat, your muscles grow flabby and useless, because they lack employment, and this in turn contributes to a sagging, drooping appearance. A few specific exercises taken as the weight begins to come off can help to tone the muscles and lead to a better posture. Many women find, for example, that they still have a rather protruding stomach even when they have started to lose weight. This is partly due to the fact that they have worn corsets for years, because their stomach muscles could not be expected to cope with so much weight, and so the muscles have become weak. The result is that when the stomach diminishes, and the muscles could be expected to play their proper part again, they are no longer in a condition to do so. This should be tackled with a few physical jerks each morning.

Similar exercises will trim the waist muscles so that you can stretch and twist easily. Most fat people have long ago given up any vanity in their bodies—in fact some hate the sight of themselves and go out of their way to avoid looking in a mirror. A few exercises each morning will help to tone up your body, and as your diet makes the fat melt away, you will see a new, firmer and fitter body emerging. You can't reshape yourself completely by exercise, of course. If wide hips run in your family, then you too will have wide hips. But standing well and carrying yourself well can make a great difference. While you are making yourself slim, you might as well make yourself more beautiful.

228

That fit feeling

The feeling of well-being that comes from being fit will also help to sustain you through the gloomy days of your dieting. The man who eats a few calories more than he needs, but exercises these away every day is probably healthier than the man who eats only exactly what is necessary and takes no exercise at all. This man will always feel slightly under the weather, because he has no energy to spare to cope with any sudden demands. If you keep yourself feeling well, you will feel more able to cope with the rigours of your diet. It is when you feel slightly run down and sad that food presents its maximum temptation.

Carbohydrate counting

Overweight is due not to the number but the kind of calories taken in. In terms of fuel, 1 gram of protein supplies four calories (17 joules), but because the protein is utilised in many ways, the fuel value is not so quickly available.

Fats, supplying vitamins and essential fatty acids, are digested slowly and thereby contribute to more prolonged satisfaction. One gram of fat supplies nine calories (38 joules).

One gram of carbohydrate supplies four calories (17 joules)—but these offer energy only.

One gram of alcohol contributes seven calories (29 joules), but the number of grams of carbohydrate per drink is comparatively low, with the exception of beer, ale, sweet wines and liqueurs.

Because you may not be eating too many calories, but more calories in carbohydrate form than the body can burn up, we would suggest that you avoid counting calories, and concentrate on controlling the carbohydrates. The chart below gives figures for the number of grams of carbohydrate per ounce of various foods, and alongside are the calorific values. In many instances the calorific values are high, although the carbohydrate value is low, and vice versa. Try to limit the daily intake of carbohydrate to 60 grams.

Note: The energy values of·foods in the following tables are given in Kilocalories (kcal) and kilojoules (kJ). Throughout the text of the book the colloquial terms 'calorie' and 'joule' are used for the same units.

Fruit	Grams of carbohydrate per oz.	kcal	kJ
Apples	3.5	13	54
Apricots, raw	1.9	8	34
dried	12.3	52	218
Bananas	5.5	22	90
Blackberries	1.8	8	34
Blackcurrants	1.9	8	34
Cherries	3.4	13	54
Damsons	2.7	11	46
Dates	15.0	62	260
Gooseberries,	1.0	5	21
ripe	2.6	10	42
Grapes, black	4.4	17	71
white	4.6	18	75
Grapefruit	1.5	6	25
Lemons	0.9	4	17
Melons	1.5	7	29
Olives in brine	trace only	30	126
Oranges	2.4	10	42
Peaches	2.6	11	46
Pears	3.1	12	50
Pineapple, fresh	3.0	12	50
Plums	2.7	11	46
Prunes	11.4	46	193
Raisins and Currants	18.3	70	293
Raspberries	1.6	7	29
Rhubarb	0.2	1	4
Strawberries	1.8	7	29
Sultanas	18.4	71	297
Tangerines	2.3	10	42

Nuts

	Grams of carbohydrate per oz.	kcal	kJ
Almonds	1.2	170	711
Brazils	1.2	183	766
Cashews	7.0	178	745
Chestnuts	10.4	49	205
Coconut, desiccated	1.8	178	745
Peanuts	2.4	171	716
Walnuts	1.4	156	653

Vegetables

	Grams of carbohydrate per oz.	kcal	kJ
Artichokes	0.8	4	17
Asparagus	0.3	5	21
Aubergines	1.0	4	17
Avocado	1.0	25	105
Beans, broad	2.0	12	50
butter	4.9	26	109
French	0.3	2	8
haricot	4.7	25	105
runner	0.3	2	8
Bean sprouts, raw	0.0	8	34
Beetroot	2.8	13	54
Broccoli	0.1	4	17
Brussels sprouts	0.5	5	21

Vegetables (contd.)	Grams of carbohydrate per oz.	kcal	kJ
Cabbage, raw	1.1	7	29
cooked	0.2	2	8
Carrots, raw	1.5	6	25
cooked	1.2	5	21
Cauliflower	0.3	3	13
Celery, raw	0.4	3	13
cooked	0.2	1	4
Chicory	0.4	3	13
Courgettes	0.0	3	13
Cucumber	0.5	3	13
Leeks, raw	1.7	9	38
cooked	1.3	7	29
Lentils	5.2	27	113
Lettuce	0.5	3	13
Marrow	0.4	2	8
Mushrooms	0.0	2	8
Onions	0.8	4	17
Parsley	trace	6	25
Parsnips	3.8	16	67
Peas, raw	3.0	18	75
boiled	2.2	14	59
dried, cooked	5.4	28	117
Peppers, sweet	0.0	10	42
Potatoes, old	5.6	23	96
new	5.2	21	88
chips	10.6	68	285
crisps	14.0	159	666
Pumpkin	1.0	4	17
Radishes	0.8	4	17
Seakale	0.2	2	8
Spinach	0.4	7	29
Spring greens	0.3	3	13
Swedes	1.1	5	20
Sweetcorn	6.0	28	117
Tomatoes	0.8	4	17
Turnips	0.7	3	13
Watercress	0.2	4	17

Meat, Poultry (cooked)

	Grams of carbohydrate per oz.	kcal	kJ
Bacon, back, grilled	0.0	64	267
streaky, grilled	0.0	42	175
Beef (lean and fat)			
topside, roast	0.0	91	381
sirloin, roast	0.0	109	456
silverside	0.0	86	360
corned	0.0	66	276
Chicken, roast	0.0	54	226
Duck, roast	0.0	89	372
Goose, roast	0.0	92	386
Grouse, roast	0.0	48	203
Ham, boiled	0.0	123	515

Meat, Poultry (contd.)	Grams of carbo-hydrate per oz.	kcal	kJ
Heart	0.0	68	285
Kidney	0.0	45	189
Liver, ox, fried	1.1	81	339
Luncheon meat (canned)	1.4	95	398
Lamb, chop, grilled	0.0	110	454
leg, roast	0.0	80	334
Pheasant, roast	0.0	62	256
Pigeon, roast	0.0	66	276
Pork leg, roast	0.0	90	377
Rabbit, stewed	0.0	51	213
Sausages, pork, grilled	7.0	96	401
beef, grilled	6.0	78	326
Tongue, sheeps', stewed	0.0	84	352
Tripe	0.0	29	121
Turkey, roast	0.0	56	234
Veal, roast	0.0	66	276

Fish (prepared)

	Grams of carbo-hydrate per oz.	kcal	kJ
Cod (steamed)	0.0	23	96
Crab	0.0	36	151
Haddock	0.0	28	117
Hake	0.0	30	126
Halibut	0.0	37	155
Herring	0.0	54	226
Kippers	0.0	57	239
Lemon Sole	0.0	26	109
Lobster	0.0	34	142
Mackerel	0.0	53	222
Oysters	trace	14	59
Pilchards, canned	0.0	63	263
Plaice	0.0	26	109
Prawns	0.0	30	126
Salmon, canned	0.0	39	163
fresh	0.0	57	239
Sardines, canned	0.0	84	352
Shrimps	0.0	32	134
Sole	0.0	24	100
Tuna, canned,	0.0	80	334
drained of oil	0.0	60	250

Sugars, Preserves

Glacé cherries	15.8	137	573
Chocolate, milk	15.5	167	699
plain	14.9	155	649

Sugars, Preserves (contd.)	Grams of carbo-hydrate per oz.	kcal	kJ
Chutney, tomato	11.0	43	180
Honey	21.7	87	364
Ice cream	5.6	56	234
Jam	19.7	74	310
Jelly, packet	17.7	73	306
Lemon curd	12.0	86	360
Marmalade	19.8	74	310
Mars Bar	18.9	127	531
Sugar, Demerara	29.6	112	469
white	29.7	112	469
Syrup, golden	22.4	84	352
Treacle	19.1	73	305

Milk and Milk Products

Butter	trace	226	946
Cheese,			
Brie	0.0	95	397
Camembert	0.0	88	368
Cheddar	0.0	120	502
Cottage	0.6	33	138
Cream	0.0	232	971
Curd	0.0	40	168
Danish blue	0.0	103	431
Edam	0.0	88	368
Gruyère	0.0	132	552
Processed	0.0	105	439
Stilton	0.0	135	564
Cream, double	0.6	131	548
single	0.9	62	259
Milk, whole	1.4	19	80
skimmed	1.4	10	42
Yoghurt, low-fat			
plain	1.0	15	63
fruit-flavoured	4.0	25	104
Eggs	trace	46	193
Margarine	0.0	226	946
Lard	0.0	262	1096
Oil	0.0	264	1105

Cereals and Cereal Products

All-Bran	16.5	88	368
Arrowroot	26.7	101	423
Pearl barley, cooked	7.8	34	142
Bemax	12.7	105	439
Biscuits, plain	21.0	125	522
sweet	19.0	160	668

Note: 'Trace' indicates that traces of Carbohydrate are known to be present; an estimation may or may not have been carried out, but in any case the amount in question is of no quantitative dietetic significance.

231

Cereals and Cereal Products (contd.)	Grams of carbo-hydrate per oz.	kcal	kJ
Bread, brown or			
white	15.0	70	292
malt	14.0	71	297
Procea	14.0	72	301
Cornflakes	25.2	104	435
Cornflour	26.2	100	418
Energen rolls	13.0	111	464
Flour 100%	20.8	95	398
85%	22.5	98	410
80%	22.9	99	414
75%	23.2	99	414
Macaroni, boiled	7.2	32	134
Muesli	20.0	107	447
Oatmeal			
porridge	2.3	13	54
Pastry, shortcrust,			
baked	15.0	155	648
flaky	13.0	165	690
Puffed wheat	21.4	102	427
Rice, polished	8.4	35	146
Ryvita	21.9	98	410
Sago	26.7	101	423
Semolina	22.0	100	418
Shredded Wheat	22.4	103	431
Spaghetti	23.9	104	435
Tapioca	27.0	102	427
Weetabix	21.9	100	418

Miscellaneous

	Grams of carbo-hydrate per oz.	kcal	kJ
Mustard, made	0.0	17	71
Pepper	19.0	88	368
Salad cream	3.0	110	460
Salt	0.0	0	0
Tomato ketchup	7.0	30	125
Vinegar	0.0	1	4

Drinks	Grams of carbo-hydrate per oz.	kcal	kJ
Bournvita	19.2	105	439
Bovril	0.0	23	96
Cocoa	9.9	128	536
Coffee with			
chicory essence	16.1	63	264
Grapefruit juice,			
fresh	2.0	11	46
Lemonade	1.6	6	25
Lucozade	5.1	19	80
Marmite	0.0	2	8
Orange juice, fresh	3.0	12	50
Tea (Infusion)	0.0	1	4
Coffee (Infusion)	0.1	1	4
Tomato juice	1.0	5	21

Alcoholic Drinks

(*Note:* This gives calories, etc. per oz.; while the chart which follows gives the figures for an average serving)

	Grams of carbo-hydrate per oz.	kcal	kJ
Beer, bitter	0.64	9	38
mild	0.46	7	29
Stout	1.19	10	42
Strong ale	1.74	21	88
Cider, dry	0.75	10	42
sweet	1.21	12	50
vintage	2.07	28	117
Port	3.55	45	188
Sherry, dry	0.39	33	138
sweet	1.95	38	159
Champagne	0.40	21	88
Graves	0.95	21	88
Sauternes	1.67	26	109
Burgundy	0.11	20	84
Beaujolais	0.07	19	80
Chianti	0.05	18	75
Spirits,			
70% proof	trace	63	264

Alcohol is a food, producing seven calories (29 joules) per gram, and so the more alcohol your drink contains, the more fattening it will be. Volume for volume, spirits are almost twice as fattening as beer—but of course they are not drunk in equal volumes. Most people drink spirits in tiny, expensive measures and beer by the half-pint. So, in fact, a pub measure of whisky would be less fattening than a pub measure of wine (usually 4 oz.) or a half-pint of beer. Beer also contains carbohydrates, which increase its calorie content; there are none in spirits. If, however, your spirit is gin and you add tonic, you are adding more calories. Though many diets recommend cutting out all alcohol, you might find it less depressing to eat less than your diet allows and to make up the difference with a couple of glasses of wine—this would help to combat the greatest threat to the dieter's resolution, monotony.

Beers		kcal	kJ
Brown ale, bottled (½ pint)		80	335
Draught ale, bitter	,,	90	377
Draught ale, mild	,,	70	293
Pale ale, bottled	,,	90	377
Stout, bottled	,,	100	418
Stout, extra	,,	110	460
Strong ale	,,	210	879

Ciders	kcal	kJ
Cider, dry (½ pint)	100	418
Cider, sweet ,,	120	502
Cider, vintage ,,	280	1172

Table wines, white		kcal	kJ
Champagne (glass, 4 oz.)		84	352
Graves	,,	84	352
Sauternes	,,	104	435

Liqueurs		kcal	kJ
Bénédictine (liqueur glass, 2–3 oz.)		69	284
Crème de Menthe	,,	67	280
Anisette	,,	74	310
Apricot brandy	,,	64	268
Curaçao	,,	54	226

Table wines, red		kcal	kJ
Beaujolais (glass, 4 oz.)		76	318
Chianti	,,	72	301
Médoc	,,	72	301

Wines, heavy		kcal	kJ
Port, ruby (glass, 2 oz.)		86	360
Port, tawny	,,	90	377
Sherry, dry	,,	66	276
Sherry, sweet	,,	76	318

Spirits, 70° proof

	kcal	kJ
Whisky, Gin, Vodka, Rum 0.83 oz. (England: ⅙ gill)	53	222
Whisky, Gin, Vodka, Rum 1 oz. (Scotland: ⅕ gill)	63	264

(From The Composition of Foods, R. A. McCance and E. M. Widdowson. HMSO.)

Cognac

	kcal	kJ
Brandy (1 brandy pony, 1 oz.)	73	305

(From Modern Nutrition in Health and Disease. W. G. Wohl and R. S. Goodhart. Philadelphia.)

The 'kJ' figures given in these tables are approximate metric equivalents of the 'kcal' figures published in the original tables and cannot be attributed to the authorities quoted.

Index